THE GODSON

THE

GOD

A TRUE-LIFE
ACCOUNT OF
20 YEARS
INSIDE THE
◙ MOB ◙

BY WILLIE
FOPIANO

WITH JOHN
HARNEY

SON

ST. MARTIN'S
PRESS

NEW YORK

Design by Judith A. Stagnitto

Library of Congress Cataloging-in-Publication Data

Fopiano, Willie.
    The godson : a true-life account of 20 years inside
the mob / Willie Fopiano with John Harney.
        p.   cm.
    "A Thomas Dunne book."
    ISBN 0-312-09748-4
    1. Fopiano, Willie. 2. Criminals—Massachu-
setts—Boston— Biography. 3. mafia—Massachusetts—Boston—History—20th century.
I. Harney, John. II. Title.
HV6248.F569F66   1993
364.1'06'092—dc20
    [B]   93-27787

A Thomas Dunne Book

First Edition: November 1993

10   9   8   7   6   5   4   3   2   1

AT THE TIME of the events in this book, I was walking in darkness, and after these events I've had my ups and downs. But at the present, the light is in me, and I dedicate this book to the chapters and verses of John in the Holy Bible.

JOHN 3–16

For God so loveth the world,
that he gave his only Begotten Son,
that whosoever believeth in Him
should not perish but have everlasting life.

JOHN 8–12

Jesus speaks saying, I am the light of the world:
he that followeth me shall not walk in darkness,
but shall have the light of life.

JOHN 14–6

Jesus saith unto him, I am the Way, the Truth and the Life:
No man cometh unto the Father, but by me.

To MICHAEL J. HECHTMAN, one of the great American newspaper editors, and to Milton Goldstein, for his invaluable expertise and generosity.

ACKNOWLEDGEMENTS

THE AUTHORS WISH to thank Matt Belmonte and Myron Rush-etzky, of the *New York Post* library, the staff of the *Boston Herald* library, Tim Hays, literary agent and Paul Sleven, lawyer.

CHAPTER ONE

NOVEMBER 12, 1975:

I CAN'T SEE MY

KILLER'S FACE

I COULDN'T SHAKE the dream. Again and again I was walking down a narrow street in the rain and a figure comes rushing at me out of the greasy blackness. There is a gun, but before I can do anything he shoots me twice in the head. I collapse and roll into the wet gutter, bleeding and helpless.

The dream kept coming back, always clear and sharp and always the same. At first I tried to forget about it, tell myself it was nothing. Then it would jolt me awake that night, or the next night. For weeks this went on, and along with it came an eerie feeling, as if the shadow of death was hovering over me wherever I went. In my life there had been a lot of crazy, violent times, yet I got through them all with barely a scratch—and with no weird dreams. Finally, I saw that this time it was different. The dream was a message: Something bad was going to happen, something I had no power to stop.

The gunman in the dream had no face, and I think I know why. A lot of people had wanted to kill me at one time or another, and my subconscious probably rebelled at the idea of having to pick only one of them. Of all the faces who might have been behind the gun, one I never imagined was that of a dirty neighborhood junkie named Guy De Prizio. I hated junkies and drug dealers for all the lives they had destroyed and the pain they had brought. They had ruined the North End of Boston, where I grew up, and the one place I can honestly say that I love. It was a losing battle to keep them out, but I had made it my personal mission to make their lives as miserable as possible.

For example, I gave De Prizio regular beatings whenever I caught him selling dope or heard that he had been breaking into houses in the neighborhood. That had been going on for years, and I never thought of him as a threat. It would've been a joke. He was just somebody I roughed up now and then. Now though, De Prizio was terrified that I was going to kill him. Two local dope peddlers, Joey and Jackie DiFronzo, had put this bug into his head that I was after him. This they did because they knew that I was looking to kill them. Nearly a year earlier the DiFronzo brothers had murdered a friend of mine, Patsy Marcello, in cold blood.

Patsy was a young boxer, a North End kid. I had done a lot of boxing myself when I was younger and he wanted me to be his trainer. Patsy had known me for as long as he could remember, and I suppose he looked up to me. He may have thought I was doing him a huge favor when I said yes, but it was a great opportunity for me too. You see, from the time I was ten years old I had been leading what can truly be called a "life of crime". It had been a good and even a glamorous living since I was a teenager, but I was cruising into my early thirties now and I realized it was time to call it quits. Too many friends were in cemeteries or prisons and I'd had too many close calls that nearly landed me in both places. So I was finished with the heists, the scams, the feuds with the cops. The times had changed. It was a meaner, dirtier game.

Though I had tried moving to other places, I always wound up back on the same old streets. There wouldn't be many more chances. But training Patsy was a perfect opportunity for a fresh start, for something decent, and best of all it meant getting out of Boston for good. My plan was to take Patsy out to Las Vegas and spend a couple years working with him. He had talent and some real potential, yet there was no guarantee that he could break into the ranks of major contenders, let alone become champion, and it would take a lot of time and hard work just to find out. Still, it was the first time in years that I could look forward to something that didn't involve the risk of an indictment or a bullet in the back of the skull.

Then, while I was out West trying to get some money together, Joey and Jackie DiFronzo shot Patsy in some stupid street argument. He was unarmed—the DiFronzos were afraid to fight with fists.

The DiFronzos didn't just murder my friend—that was unforgivable by itself—they also destroyed whatever future Patsy and me might've had, all our hopes. Patsy didn't have to worry about it anymore. I did. I had to keep going somehow.

When I got back to Boston I hunted down Joey DiFronzo in one of his haunts and humiliated him in front of all his friends. If it were not for all the witnesses, he would've died on the spot. After that the brothers kept themselves well hidden whenever I was around. That wasn't good—if I couldn't see them, there was no way to tell what they were doing. And they knew they would eventually have to answer for Patsy.

In the meantime, I was more determined than ever to start a new life somewhere else. Only now I was low on cash. A North End pal suggested that we open a restaurant on the Freedom Trail to cash in the tourist trade from the Bicentennial of 1976. That seemed like a good idea. Once the Bicentennial was over, I'd sell out and move on.

By NOVEMBER 12, 1975, I had borrowed some money from a friend and renovations on the storefront where we were going to put the restaurant were well underway. That night I went down there and talked to the construction crew. Everything was pretty much on schedule. The tourists will like this place, I thought, and spend enough money so I can clear out.

After the crew went home, I headed over to a social club

across the street with three older men. There was Joe Semenza, a tough, standup guy who had been a close friend since I was a kid. There was Skinny Al—I had known him all my life, but I didn't know his real name. His first name wasn't even Al! The third man was another neighborhood guy whose name I am not going to mention.

We sat in the club for several hours playing poker. I tried to have a good time and enjoy the game, but the bad feeling was with me again, sticking like tar. There was no getting away from it. The day before I had even made a trip to the Arch Street Church. It had been a long time since I had been inside a church. I went over there in the afternoon, and the place was dark and empty. On the wall was a portrait of Michael the Archangel. I prayed to him, I prayed to God: Whatever happens, make me strong enough.

When it got late we decided to lock up the club and drop in at the Florentine Café, a neighborhood hangout at the corner of Hanover and Prince Streets. We walked up Prince Street, four abreast. In the distance, standing on the corner outside the café was Guy De Prizio. He was facing away from us. De Prizio had been acting very weird whenever he saw me, but I didn't think anything of it. Junkies always act weird.

I started to walk past him, and as I did a face peered around the corner of the building and ducked right back. An instant and he was gone, I barely saw him, but he looked familiar. That looks like Joey DiFronzo, I thought. The next second Guy De Prizio whirled around and shot me in the face. He was standing just a couple feet away and the shot came in an explosive flash. I threw myself down on my back. As I was going down De Prizio put the gun to my left temple and fired again. Another blast. My head felt like it had collided with a baseball bat, yet I was still conscious. I was looking right into the barrel of his gun. It was a .38. It moved closer and I could hear the crack, crack of Cuban heels on the cobblestones. De Prizio planted his feet by my right shoulder and aimed directly at my head. My mind was racing, sending out alarms. I threw my hands and forearms around my head. I even managed a small prayer: Lord Jesus, forgive me for all my sins, and get me through this.

Sparks came flying out of the barrel, and the roar of a gunshot rocketed off the silent brick buildings on both sides of us. But this time I didn't feel anything—De Prizio had somehow missed. Another shot and—another miracle—he missed again.

Then, the gun vanished and everything was quiet. De Prizio was gone. A sense of relief flooded over me. It was done—whatever was supposed to happen had happened and I was still alive. Yet even at that moment I couldn't help being amazed at who had done it. It didn't seem possible a punk like De Prizio could harm me. After all, when other kids were learning their multiplication tables I was shooting craps, playing numbers and working for some of the most feared mobsters in Boston. In my life I had robbed banks all up and down the east coast, more than I could count. I could write a manual on how to knock over an armored car. I had stolen millions and gambled it all away. I had been Meyer Lansky's bagman and smuggled fortunes overseas. I had tried to start my own family and nearly pulled it off. There wasn't a wiseguy in Miami, Las Vegas, or Los Angeles who didn't know me. In Boston I had survived one of the bloodiest gang wars the country had ever seen. Forty-eight men died and I nearly became the forty-ninth in a run-in with the man responsible for most of the bodies, a killing machine named Joe Barboza. Tough guys in prison had tried to take me apart and regretted it. Hoodlums had tried to kill me. Cops had tried to kill me. They were all gone and I was unscathed—until now.

It turned out that Joey DiFronzo actually had been hiding around that corner, egging De Prizio on. They both ran, but I was in no shape to fight back—my face was shattered and my jaw smashed. Blood, my blood, was running into the gutter. I tried to get up, but couldn't.

Half a minute had passed since I was about to walk into the Florentine. Joe Semenza and the other guys came running over as soon as De Prizio took off. Joe told me later that he felt bad that he couldn't do anything, but he was unarmed and as helpless as I was.

Shouts came from inside the Florentine. Windows were opening and lights snapping on in apartments above the street. People were trying to talk to me. Somebody called for an ambulance, and after a little bit there were sirens wailing from far off. I wondered if I would die before they could get me to a hospital.

Then it began to rain, just like in the dream.

CHAPTER TWO

SPRING 1955:

THE NICE WISEGUYS

HEY KID!" THE man had stepped out of the Florentine Café and was calling to me from across the street. "Hey, kid. You. Run down fast to the tailor's and get Canadian's suit."

That's how it all started—my life in crime, with a simple errand when I was ten years old.

The man put a dollar in my hand and I dashed off to Rocky the tailor as fast as I could go. The suit Rocky handed me was made of silk. It was big and dark and beautiful, clearly an important man's suit. As soon as I gave Rocky the money, I went charging back to the Florentine. The day was sunny and warm and I flew along like the breeze. It seemed like I had the greatest job in the world, and I was so excited that I nearly burst.

The suit belonged to Tony Sandrelli, who was called "the Canadian" because he was originally from Canada. Tony always looked like a million dollars. Me and the other kids used to watch him stepping out of his shiny new Cadillac in cashmere coats and two-hundred-dollar mohair suits with lapels sharper than our dads' razors. The man who had me go get Tony's suit was his friend, Henry Selvitella. Henry had been a boxer in the old days and, like most Italian fighters, had taken a very un-Italian name:

Noyes. It had been at least thirty years since he had climbed into a ring, but he was still known everywhere as Henry Noyes.

You could always find Henry and Tony at a table in the Florentine with a frail, quiet man with a thick Sicilian accent. His name was Frank Cucchiara, and he was known as "the Cheeseman" for a cheese importing business he owned a few blocks away on Endicott Street.

We all knew that these men were mobsters. We knew it from street talk and what we read in the papers, even if we were too young to have any idea exactly what they did or where their power came from. That was something we couldn't see. There were no machine guns or tough-guy bodyguards or bulletproof limousines around. All we knew was that they were better off than everybody else and people treated them as if they were important. They seemed to move in some exciting, secret world that was invisible to anyone who wasn't one of them.

The tourists come to the North End to see Old North Church, Paul Revere's house, and other relics of America's colonial days. They usually miss other landmarks, our landmarks, like the funeral parlor where Sacco and Vanzetti were laid out, or the grimy three-story building on Prince Street where the Brinks gang pulled off the biggest heist the world had ever seen. The gang's mastermind, Tony Pino, used to come around the neighborhood all the time and to us he was a bigger hero than Paul Revere.

For most of the nineteenth century the area had been Irish. It was the stronghold of Honey Fitz, the father of Rose Fitzgerald Kennedy, who lived on Salem Street. Then, in the 1890s, the Irish started moving out and Italian immigrants, mostly from the south of Italy—the Mezzogiorno—and Sicily, started moving in. By the first decade of this century they were coming by the tens of thousands, and by the time I was born, in 1944, the North End had long been solidly Italian. Italian and poor. Everybody worked, and worked hard. They just never got paid much. Sure, they were better off than our grandparents who got stuffed into disease-infested rat holes as soon as they stepped off the boat and were expected to be grateful for any dirty job. But any kind of prosperity and the things it could buy—a car, a house, college for the kids—that was still a long way off. Our fathers would take anything they could get. They were construction workers, factory workers, bricklayers, storekeepers, truck drivers, waiters, janitors, stevedores. A few of the really lucky ones had civil service jobs. No one had any real money, except, of course, the wiseguys.

In those days all the cops were still Irish. We were like fire and gasoline. To them, we were the wops and the guineas. They were the micks and the harps, although we couldn't call them that to their faces. I suppose in some ways it was like the old days in Sicily and the Mezzogiorno—we had always been at the mercy of invaders, and the Irish cops were just one more foreign army. Yet even the cops didn't dare mess around with the mob men. So in a way we kids saw them as protectors—people to admire. Every day after school we used to go over to a pool hall across from the Florentine Café, which had been a mob hangout since the 1920s. We liked to pretend we were close to something powerful and strange. But I wasn't content just to watch, I wanted to hang out with the wiseguys at the Florentine. So I would stand around outside the pool hall, hoping they would notice me. . . .

And one day Henry Noyes came out of the café and asked me to go get Canadian's suit.

THE RUN TO the tailor quickly led to other little jobs, and before long I was reporting to the Florentine nearly every day after school. The wiseguys sent me out for coffee or food, to take messages to this place or that place, to tell somebody that Henry or Frank wanted to see him. Now, other kids also tried to get in with the crowd at the Florentine—there were always plenty of wannabes around—but even in those early days I was singled out as an exception. The wiseguys seemed to think I had the right combination of finesse, nerve, and character: everything that was needed to one day become one of them. Flunkies they had to take care of their needs. Me, they wanted around because they liked and respected me.

At that time Frank, Henry, and Tony were all in their fifties, which seems ancient to a ten year old. They were good to me and acted like nice old men, very far removed from anything violent, or even illegal. Tony Canadian was genuinely loved by everyone who knew him. Even though he was an ex-boxer, Henry looked incapable of hurting anyone. Frank was very reserved and never raised his voice.

But these three men were actually very important in the history of organized crime in Boston. Long before I was born, they had helped overthrow an old order. And the overthrow began with a murder.

Up until the early 1930s, the rackets—like just about everything else in Boston—were dominated by the Irish. The Irish crews were ruled by the Gustin Gang, and Frank Wallace, of South Boston, ran the Gustin Gang.

But a new era was about to begin. In New York, Chicago, and other cities, Italian and Sicilian gangs had gotten rich and powerful off Prohibition. Between 1929 and 1931, a band of young mobsters seized control of the New York Mafia and reorganized the entire operation—a reorganization that began with the execution of a few old-time bosses. Once that was done they cast a greedy eye up the coast. Messengers from New York came to Frank Wallace "requesting" a share of a lucrative bootlegging operation that supplied booze to speakeasies all across New England. But Wallace angrily sent them away with curses and threats. He would not tolerate competitors, especially the Italians.

Finally, he agreed to a meeting with the leaders of the new North End mob, Filippo (Phil) Buccola and Joe Lombardo, at Lombardo's office. Both Buccola and Lombardo had strong ties to Charlie Luciano, the young chieftan of the New York Mafia. But rather than discuss partnerships and giving up slices of a very rich pie, Wallace was coming over to lay down the law to the upstarts: he was in charge.

On December 22, 1931, Wallace and two bodyguards

marched up three flights of stairs to Lombardo's C and F Importing Company in the Testa Building on Hanover Street. Wallace banged on the door and was answered by a blast of gunfire from inside the office. The gunmen threw open the door and raced down the corridor, still shooting. Barney Walsh, one of the bodyguards, was cut down on a stairwell landing. A mortally wounded Wallace staggered into a lawyer's office, collapsed into a chair, and toppled over. The other bodyguard, Timothy Coffey, survived by hiding in another office.

The assassins included Buccola, Lombardo and two young mafiosi, Frank Cucchiara and Henry Selvitella. Lombardo and Cucchiara were arrested, but no charges were ever filed—Coffey refused to testify before a grand jury.

Cucchiara had worked for Luciano in New York and with the Capone mob in Chicago. Selvitella was a local kid. Along with Tony Sandrelli, who had come down from Canada, they were the deadly instruments of Buccola's and Luciano's plot to dominate the Boston rackets. This was accomplished in short order. The Gustin Gang quickly handed over a big piece of their bootlegging and gambling enterprises. On January 6, 1932, just a year after the murder of Wallace, another rival, Charles (King) Solomon, a fight promoter, big-time bootlegger, and head of Boston's Jewish mob, was shot in a Boston speakeasy called the Cotton Club. When a nurse at the hospital asked who had done it, Solomon mumbled "a dirty rat." He died a few hours later. Solomon's killers were small-time Irish hoodlums, but they had been put up to the job by Frank Cucchiara, who had been advised by Luciano to use outsiders.

Frank Cucchiara and Charlie Luciano had been born just a few months apart in 1897, in neighboring villages in Sicily. They were always very close, even after Luciano was deported to Italy in 1946. Frank was Luciano's personal emissary at the Appalachian mob convention in 1957.

With Solomon and Wallace dead, the Italian mob's rule was uncontested. From then on, it held sway over Boston and much of New England, with the seat of its power in the North

End. Buccola became the boss of the new crime family, with Joe Lombardo as underboss and Frank Cucchiara as *consiglieri*. Henry Selvitella and Tony Sandrelli were appointed capos. This arrangement would last for the next twenty-five years.

BACK TO ME. When I started hanging out with the wiseguys I was in the fifth grade at St. Mary's School, and an altar boy. While I was not really a street kid, I had been getting into fights for as long as I could remember. My glasses were a big reason for that: I was almost always the only boy in my class who had to wear them. Other kids would start things with me, and I always let them have it. I could never back down, it just wasn't in my nature. After a few years of that I became a pretty good fighter.

My errands for the men in the Florentine took me to all kinds of places—bars, social clubs, gambling joints, and I quickly learned nothing brings respect faster than cash. If I was going to be like the wiseguys, I had to have my own roll. Gambling seemed like a good way to get my hands on some fast money. I had been watching the games long enough; there didn't seem to be anything to it. So I started seeking out a floating dice game that was run by a guy named Big Mike Magino. It was played right on the sidewalk, usually at North Bennett and Salem Streets. Sometimes they had to move it because of the cops, but I always found out where they were operating. Eventually, I started dropping by every day after school with a friend. He just hung around, but I always jumped right into the game.

One afternoon I noticed a big hard-looking guy who I'd never seen before. That's Joe Semenza, somebody said, he just finished fourteen years of hard time for killing a guy.

Joe noticed me right away too.

"Who's the kid?" he sneered to Big Mike.

"That's Willie," Big Mike said. "He's got money and he knows how to play. That's good enough for us."

Right at that moment I was shooting the dice, looking to get a nine.

Joe came up and called out, "Hey, I'll lay three to two, no nine."

"Bet," I said. It was worth five bucks if I won. Sure enough, four or five rolls later I had a nine.

When I asked Joe for the money, he laughed and waved me away. "We had no bet."

"You owe me five dollars," I said, making sure everybody heard me.

"There was no bet. Now, get outta here."

Then, I went right up to him, my chin practically on his chest, and demanded to get paid.

A cold, mean look came into Joe's eyes and he raised his arm, but Big Mike grabbed his hand.

"Joe, you laid three to two and you lost, so pay him."

Joe dug some bills out of his pocket and handed me a five spot. I took it, turned around, and went home.

Word of what happened at the dice game got back to Henry and he sent for Big Mike.

"I don't want anybody taking advantage of Willie, is that clear?" he said. Of course, it was already clear to Big Mike. Now it was clear to everybody else too.

Meanwhile, I started running into Joe around the neighborhood, and we became friendly. In fact, we would be good friends for the rest of his life. But we didn't hang out together a lot in those early days—after all, I wasn't even into my teens yet and Joe was nearly forty and an ex-con.

"We can't associate too much," he told me. "People will think I'm a fagin. I hope you understand."

Joe's best pal was Angie DeMarco. They had known each other since they were kids, but they were a lot tighter than most friends because they had shared some very rough times, including spending most of their youth in state prisons.

In the late 1930s, Joe and Angie joined a loose-knit crew that robbed bookies and crap games all over Boston. Their leader was a young gangster called Tony Pomo. They scooped up piles of cash in raids on betting parlors and backroom games—tens of thousands of dollars—and it was easy money because the victims couldn't tell the cops. It was a great racket for a couple of years. Then, in the fall of 1941, the wiseguys finally found out who was behind the stickups. That's the trouble with most great rackets—you can't bring yourself to quit until it's too late.

Some mobsters cornered Joe Semenza and brought him to Joe Lombardo, who was already a legendary figure in the New England mob—a wiseguy's wiseguy. Lombardo was well mannered, favored conservative business suits, and was known everywhere by his initials—J.L.—like some big corporate executive. With a combination of street toughness and old world gentility, he had successfully arbitrated dozens of squabbles over money and territory. His prestige alone probably prevented many a war, for no one questioned his authority or his honesty. He was stern and sometimes harsh, but above pettiness and prejudice, and he always kept his word. For Joe Semenza, going to meet Lombardo that day must have seemed like going before a judge, a hanging judge.

Lombardo had known Joe a long time and loved him, but the mob can never tolerate men who would steal so brazenly from them. Joe denied everything, but Lombardo wasted no time. Joe was offered a choice: His life would be spared in exchange for the lives of Angie, Pomo, and the other member of the gang, Phil Bellino.

Lombardo wanted an answer by the next morning. That was all. Joe stood up. He had barely said a word. Lombardo took his hand in a viselike grip and shot him a hard look. "Don't double-cross me, Joe," he said.

During the long and sleepless night that followed, Joe went over it all again and again, and whenever he thought of Pomo rage simmered up in him—this was his fault. They should have stopped the robberies long ago, but Pomo always insisted there was nothing to worry about: They wore masks, no one would ever figure out it was them. Then Pomo and Angie ripped off a very popular numbers operation known as the Italian lottery, and someone had recognized Pomo by his height. Joe had warned them against hitting the lottery, but Pomo told him to go to hell. Joe realized he had been stupid and careless, and could blame no one but himself. He would accept whatever penalty was waiting for him. But Angie and Phil, they were just kids, and Pomo had dragged them into this mess.

Jittery and exhausted, Joe arrived at Joe Lombardo's office at 9 A.M. the next morning. Lombardo kept him waiting until after three.

When Joe started to explain that he hadn't been involved in all the robberies, Lombardo cut him off. "I know all about your involvement," he said calmly, "and also know what happened wasn't personal or else right now you wouldn't be sitting here."

Joe pleaded for the lives of Angie and Phil. "They're two good guys," he said.

"They're sticking up crap games and bookmakers and they're good guys!" Lombardo shouted.

Yes, Joe said. They were young and didn't know what they were doing. Pomo had conned them into it.

"If they get away with this and no example is set, every hood in the city will be taking a crack at us," Lombardo said.

Finally, after a lot more pleading from Joe, he relented and a deal was struck: Pomo would be the sacrifice, and Joe and Angie had to do the job. Just in case they had any trouble, or a change of heart, Lombardo would send along his bodyguard, Joseph (Little Bozo) Cortese.

Joe got up to leave and again felt a vise crushing his hand and Lombardo's eyes studying his face. "Anything like this happens again, nobody gets saved. Understood?"

"Understood," Joe said quietly.

Pomo had learned there was trouble and gone into hiding, but Little Bozo tracked him down to a tenement apartment on Henchman Street in the North End. Pomo had to be taken by surprise and as quietly as possible. So Little Bozo, along with Angie and Joe, met a friend of Pomo's, Sal Venuti, in a café and had him bring them over to the apartment for a meeting. Venuti didn't suspect a thing. The apartment belonged to another friend of Pomo's, Alfonse Penta. They burst into the apartment and shoved Penta and Pomo against a table. Little Bozo pulled a revolver and without a word shot Pomo four times. "You got me!" Pomo screamed, and went down. Angie stabbed him several times to make sure he was dead. Venuti and Penta couldn't believe what had happened, but didn't dare say a word.

The killers wrapped the body in sheets and blankets, carried it down across Commercial Street and threw it in the harbor. Joe and Angie's debt to the mob had been paid, but the bad times were just beginning. A Coast Guard ensign and a sailor saw some men throwing something into the harbor and the cops found Pomo's body. Joe wasn't worried about that—until Penta told him that there were laundry marks on the blanket.

"You stupid bastard! When I was wrapping him in the blanket, why didn't you tell me then?"

"Joe, you know this isn't my kind of thing," Penta said. "I simply was stunned in all that happened."

The laundry marks eventually led the cops to the hitmen. Joe had killed Pomo to save Angie and Bellino; now he and Angie faced the chair for doing it. The charges got reduced from murder to manslaughter, yet Little Bozo Cortese, Sal Venuti, Joe, and Angie all drew stiff sentences. Alfonse Penta was luckier, and served only a few years. Joe and Angie both wound up doing almost fourteen years, and for most of that time they were in Charlestown State Prison, a big old stone place known as "the gray monster." There was no plumbing and their bathroom was a bucket in the corner of a cell.

Their friend Phil Bellino somehow got out of having to take part in the Pomo killing and stayed out of jail. Unfortunately, he didn't stay out of trouble, and a few years later formed a new crew with a local guy named Ed Gertson and an ex-Marine, Tex Williams. They held up gambling joints out in the sticks, far from Boston. Williams fingered a crap game he knew about in Newton, New Hampshire. The game was held in a garage next to a vacant building. The three robbers donned stocking masks, broke in through an office on the side and held up the game. There were about thirty men inside. As Williams was gathering up the money, one of the players went for a gun in his jacket and Bellino shot him.

The shooting spooked Tex Williams, who was only nineteen. Fearing that he might talk, his partners decided to get rid of him. What happened next was probably the stupidest act in the history of modern crime. It would be funny if three men hadn't died as a result. The day after the holdup, Gertson and Bellino split the take—nearly 60,000 dollars—then told Williams they had buried the money in the Lynn marshes and that he should go out there with them to get his share. For some reason they picked up Williams in a taxi and told the driver to bring them out to the marshes. When they got there Gertson told the driver they would be right back, and he and Bellino took Williams a few paces into the marshes and shot him. After that they walked casually back to the cab. The driver asked if their friend was coming.

"No," Bellino said and had him drive back to Boston.

The cabbie couldn't believe what was happening. Three men had gone into the marshes. There had been what sounded like a gunshot and only two men had come out. It didn't seem real. It must be a prank. As soon as his passengers were out of the cab, he went straight to the police. The cops too thought the whole thing was a joke and the cabbie had to repeat his story a dozen times before they reluctantly went out to the marshes with him and found Williams.

Bellino and Gertson were convicted of murder and sentenced to die in the electric chair at Charlestown, the same chair where Sacco and Vanzetti died. They appealed all the way to the Supreme Court and struck out every time. The governor refused to grant a reprieve and they went to the chair on May 9, 1947. Joe Semenza was at Charlestown, and used his influence with the guards to snag a visit to death row just moments before the executions. He grabbed Bellino's hand through the cell bars and said good-bye to both men.

Gertson and Bellino, by the way, were the last people to be executed in Massachusetts.

WHEN JOE FINALLY got out he got a job driving a truck and married his childhood sweetheart, who had waited for him faithfuly through all the long years. He started over, settled down and basically went straight. He and Angie were released on the same day, but Angie had a harder time of it. He couldn't find steady work and was always broke. He became angry and bitter and made no secret of his feelings. As he saw it, he had lost the best part of his life doing the mob's dirty work and now no one was lifting a finger to help him or offer him a job.

I was doing very well for myself. By the time I was thirteen, I had discovered all sorts of ways to make money—most of them illegal. It was small-time stuff at first, breaking into parking meters, peddling fireworks and bootleg cigarettes that had been smuggled up from the South. Then, some friends and I got together in a gang and burglarized a few stores. Much of the money was used to finance my gambling, and I enjoyed a lot of lucky streaks there too. (I should have quit while I was ahead. In my later years a lot of bookies were able to buy big houses and put their children through college, thanks to me!) So, I often had a roll of cash, and I used to help Joe and Angie out when they were short, palming them a twenty or a fifty. Young as I was, I realized they had been through a lot. Joe was very grateful, and there would be plenty of times when he could do something for me, one way or another. Angie, though, only felt shame and growing desperation. Here he was, in his late thirties, taking money from a kid.

Although Angie liked me, a lot of kids were afraid of him. He had a crazy brother who used to run in front of the marching bands during the Italian festivals pretending to be a conductor. He looked like a nutty Lawrence Welk. Whenever he did that some of the kids made fun of him and threw stuff at him. Angie saw this after he got out of prison and blew his top. He chased down two of the kids and cracked their heads together.

Angie looked pretty crazy himself, like a madman, really. He was balding on top with a roundish face and bugged-out eyes. He walked and moved in a very threatening way.

I didn't know it, but sometime in 1958 or 1959 he began shaking down bookmakers again. Joe guessed what was going on and begged him to stop. Joe Lombardo's old warning sounded like yesterday in his mind: *"Anything like this happens again, nobody gets saved."*

A lot of the bookmakers were afraid and kept their mouths shut, yet sooner or later somebody was going to complain to the wiseguys, and it wouldn't be hard to guess the robber's identity. Joe Lombardo was still going strong and had a very long memory.

Joe Semenza kept pleading with his friend: "Angie, remember 1941. There's no second chance. Please, do it for me." I felt something bad in the air. One night I stopped by a smoke shop at Prince and Hanover Streets run by a bookie named Fiore DeChristoforo. I asked Fiore if he had seen Angie. He hadn't, so I waited. A while later, I spotted Angie walking by and called to him.

"What's the matter, kid?" he said. "Everything all right?"

"Yeah, Ang, I was just going to ask you the same." From the way he looked I knew he was pressed for money, so I handed him 300 dollars.

He looked at the money, then at me. "Why are you doing this for me, kid?"

"I just don't want to see you get into any trouble," I said. "I thought you could use the extra cash."

"Well, I can," Angie said, looking like he was about to boil over. "But no matter how much money I have I still don't like looking at these mothers," meaning the wiseguys. Then he thanked me and quickly walked away.

Not long after that, on November 12, 1959, school broke for lunch and I went home. The news was coming over the television. What I saw made my blood freeze. First a photograph of Angie. Then the voice: *The police last night found the body of Joseph (Angie) DeMarco in an Everett dump. He had been shot six times in the back of the head.*

That night outside Fiore's was the last time I ever saw him.

CHAPTER THREE

A LIFE OF CRIME

ANGIE'S DEATH WAS a sad thing. Joe was devastated, of course—he and Angie had been through hell together—yet there was nothing we could do, except try to forget about it, and for good reason.

When a grand jury began investigating Angie's death Henry Noyes and Tony Canadian took the Fifth and the hitman disappeared until things cooled down. Nobody else said a word. Henry and Tony and Frank had almost certainly approved the hit. Nothing like that happened without them giving the word.

They were still the same nice old guys that I saw every day. They were also responsible for the death of my friend. Frank had even started calling me his "godson." But this was the same Frank Cucchiara who was tight with the notorious Lucky Luciano, the same Frank Cucchiara who had been at the Appalachian convention. It was all over the papers. Frank Cucchiara was a powerful man, a dangerous man, and so were Henry Noyes and Tony Canadian. While I was still too young for any kind of deep reflection, I knew you couldn't afford to think too much about stuff like that, you had to shove it over to a different side of your brain.

I suppose what happened to Angie should have made me

think about what kind of life I was getting sucked into. Instead, I figured that if you were cautious, didn't step out of line and didn't trust the wrong people you'd be all right. After all, Angie had broken the rules, not once but twice. If you played the game and didn't screw up you had nothing to worry about.

Not that I didn't feel a lot of guilt about what I was doing. My parents were religious people, and I believed in all the teachings of the Catholic Church. My father was a custodian and the most honest man you'd ever want to meet. My mother worked as a cleaning lady at the Statehouse downtown and kept a good home for her family. They had a daughter and three sons, and the only one to give them any trouble was their second child: me. I was the black sheep. I knew the crimes I committed were sins against God, and His church and my family. But the thrill of crime was just too much of a temptation.

For instance, one summer my friend Danny Puopolo admired a rifle that was hanging in the window of a shop on Hanover Street. It was a brand-new 30–30, a magnificent gun. Danny talked about the gun all the time, like it was a girl he had a crush on, so I decided he should get his wish. One night we took a five-pound sledgehammer and sent it flying through the store's plate-glass window, and Danny reached in and grabbed the rifle. Now, we could easily have paid somebody older to go buy the gun for us, but it was a lot more fun to steal it.

Every act like that, every crime, would send a jolt of adrenaline surging through me like crazy electricity. It was a terrific top-of-the-world feeling, a high, and like every high it became addictive. But no other addiction puts money in your pocket— and there were piles of it to be made on the streets. Instead of breaking my back at some dirty job for a week's pay, I could make a year's pay in one night and enjoy every minute of it. Crime paid—for me and for a lot of kids I knew, even those who had a lot more incentive to stay straight. One guy I grew up with went to the Boston Public Latin School, the oldest public school in the country and one of the finest, and graduated from Boston College, yet he got caught up in the street life and is doing a long prison sentence. Even if he had become a lawyer or a doctor, he couldn't have made as much as he did in the rackets. The lure of easy cash was just too powerful.

Everybody wanted to be a hoodlum. There were degrees— some guys got into it just a little, some more than a little. Me, I was in all the way. Before I was fifteen I was a veteran of holdups and heists. The gang I put together robbed payrolls and broke into stores, restaurants and businesses all over Boston. In those days no place had an alarm, so it was almost hard to get caught. In school, we did what we had to do to get by, and for most of us school was about to become a memory. But when it came to the ins and outs of stealing, no students were more enthusiastic or attentive. We learned how to break open safes that boasted six inches of maganese steel with just a sledgehammer, a two-pounder, and an awl. And when burglar alarms eventually did become a problem, we were soon well-versed on the latest technology and the best methods of getting around it.

In those years I hooked up with the kids who would form the core of my crew for years to come. There was Eddie Greco, a nice guy from the neighborhood. There was Danny Puopolo, a serious kid who played the piano and would later go to the University of Massachusetts after turning down a scholarship to Harvard. There was Peter Piso, Johnny Russo and Joe (Gorilla) Maioli, who were always up for anything.

Stealing was a lot of fun, even if we came back empty-handed or got chased by the cops. One night me, Joe Gorilla, and Peter Piso broke into a place near the North End. The safe was old and normally old safes were a snap. You'd flip them upside down and jimmy off a metal plate on the bottom. Under the plate was a layer of concrete and once you'd chipped through that you'd have the valuables. But this safe was embedded in the floor, so we knocked off the combination knob with a sledgehammer and punched an awl into the tumblers. That's always tricky and if you miss on your first shot, forget it. The door wouldn't budge, so we decided to peel off the front of the safe with sledgehammers and crowbars. That's the last resort, because it takes time and makes the most noise. We must've made quite a racket, because pretty soon the cops came roaring up to the front of the building. We took off out the back, jumped over several walls and hid in a playground, which had a terrible echo. We knew the neighborhood better than the law, but we could hear them looking for us.

"There's a bad echo. Don't make no noise," I whispered to Peter and Joe Gorilla when we stopped to get our breath. "Run on the balls of your feet."

"Yeah, you don't want 'em to hear the footprints!" Joe said. Peter started cracking up and fell on the ground. I hit him to make him shut up and nearly burst trying not to laugh myself.

Eddie Greco was a few years older and taught me how to drive when I was eleven. Even though a few years means a lot at that age, he was always good to me. He had a '47 Ford and I loved pushing the starter. Right after learning how to drive a car I learned how to steal one. That was easy. Nobody ever locked their car then, and you just slipped a piece of cellophane from a cigarette pack behind the ignition and pushed the starter. At first we stole cars just to ride around; later we used them in burglaries and robberies. You needed a car if you were going to lug out a safe or anything else that was big and looked good.

When driving I always wore a fedora pulled low on my head so I wouldn't give away my age. Then I piled pillows, telephone books, and anything else I could find under me. I looked older and taller, but I could barely reach the pedals.

My first court case was for an auto theft when I was thirteen, and, ironically, I had nothing to do with it. Some friends and I went joyriding several times in a black Oldsmobile coupe that belonged to a postal worker. We loved that car and took good care of it, as if it belonged to us. We always made sure to park in the same spot where we found it, and we even put gas in it.

One night we walked up to the Olds and there was a note on the windshield. "Whoever has been riding in my car had better stop it or I'm going to have to go to the police," it said. My friends wanted to take the car anyway. I said if this fellow was good enough to leave us a note we should leave it alone and steal another car. But my friends wanted the Olds, so I said forget it and went home. Well, that night the cops pulled them over and one of the kids said I had helped them steal it. He put the finger on me. The police came to my house and arrested me. I wound up getting a year's probation in juvenile court.

Naturally, my mother and father were horrified at the way I was turning out. They screamed at me for hours every time I got in trouble, and I just sat there and said nothing. They couldn't understand what was going on. At home, at church, at school, I was fine. Once I hit the streets, boom, I was carrying on like a little wiseguy, and no amount of punishment or Catholic guilt could hold me back.

I didn't understand the attraction of the streets, either, but they were a perfect fit with my real nature. To say I was wild in those days was putting it mildly. There was nothing I wouldn't do. What drove me was a deep, seething rage inside, and the streets were the only place I could let it out. You could always find a fight in those days. Kids from the North End were constantly battling the kids from the West End. They were Italian like us, but that didn't matter—we hated each other. Just across Boston Harbor, in Charlestown, you had the Irish Gangs. They were a tough breed—most of them grew up to be bank robbers. When I was thirteen we got into a big rumble with them on the Charlestown Bridge and I tossed a kid over the side. He made it back to shore and years later we laughed about it.

Where all the rage came from I don't know, I'll leave that to the psychologists. Sometimes I think I was possessed. Whatever it was, my wildness actually saved me many a time when fear would have been fatal.

ALL MY ACTIVITIES were keeping me out of school more and more. I was also developing a reputation as a young tough guy in the neighborhood, something that didn't escape the attention of the police. The arrest for the stolen car came after several minor scrapes with the law. Because I was under age there was not a lot the cops could do, and I knew it. They weren't allowed to lock me up in a cell, and the most they could do was hold me until my parents came to get me. Well, that's not quite right, because they never missed an opportunity to beat me up. It didn't matter what I was doing. A cop caught a bunch of us throwing firecrackers when I was eleven, and as soon as he saw my face he ran right over and grabbed me. I yelled at my friends to jump him, but they took off. I tried to get away but the cop's grip was too strong. He dragged me over to the squad car and hit me so hard with the back of his hand that my glasses snapped in two.

Concepts like police brutality didn't exist in those days. If the cops felt like smacking you, they smacked you. And since I was this smart-ass Italian kid who was always raising hell, they decided to make an example of me, usually in front of other kids. But the example fought back and didn't care about the odds. One time a cop started knocking me around in a back room of the police station. He was asking me all kinds of questions and didn't like it when I wouldn't tell him anything. I fought back and he had his hands full. So another cop came in, then another, and pretty soon I was fighting half a dozen of them. I didn't care. I backed into a corner and charged right into them.

They all hated me, especially this barrel-shaped cop I'll called Blackie. All the cops liked beating up the Italian kids, but he was the worst. I don't know if he was called Blackie for his hair, which was the color of coal, or for his temper. I was his favorite target. One day I was hanging out with some friends minding my own business and Blackie suddenly comes up from behind and grabs me in a chokehold. It jolted the wind out of me. "You're always a troublemaker, always making trouble," his voice blasted in my ear.

Another time the cops picked me up for something and threw me in the back of a squad car—right beside Blackie, who was wearing a giant smirk. I was barely in the car before I got a crack across the face with the back of his hand.

"Go ahead and hit me," he said, and smacked me again. "Just try it. Hit me."

If I had, the two cops in the front seat would have been all over me.

"Hit me," Blackie said again. "Go on."

Some day I will, I said to myself. Your day will come.

Another time, after I helped touch off a rumble in a movie theater, the cops threw me in the paddy wagon and drove straight to the Youth Services Board, a detention center in the suburb of Roslindale. The place was crammed with tough, rowdy kids from all over the state, and maybe the cops thought a couple days there would put the fear of God in me. It didn't, as the people who ran the place were soon to find out.

I had only been there a few hours when a black kid started shooting me a stare in the cafeteria. He was serving potatoes and I was in the line. As I got closer to him he kept it up, testing me, taunting me with his eyes. That's the silent language of places like that: Everybody eyes each other up, each trying to psych the other guy out or to have an excuse to be aggressive. And like I said before, a kid with glasses is always the first to be singled out. But I wasn't into looks, I was action. If you mess with me, I get you.

Finally, I was opposite the black kid. Still staring at me, he scoops up some mashed potatoes and slaps them down hard on my plate. Without a word, I threw the plate at him, and before he could recover I was over the counter and smashing his face with my fists. A friend of his ran over and I was fighting both of them when the employees pulled us apart. I told the kid if I saw him again I'd kill him and his friend. A while later I found myself back at the Youth Services Board for another couple days. Both kids were still there, but stayed out of sight.

THE 1950S ARE remembered now as a very conservative time when everybody tried to fit in, so it's funny when I think about how much nuttiness you could get away with in the North End—which, after all, is part of Boston, one of the most uptight cities on the planet. And I'm not just talking about myself. I'll never forget the night the cops raided our social club. I had started the place with Eddie Greco and Danny Puopolo. We were still kids and all we really did was shoot pool and hang out, but the police had the idea that we were gambling and took Danny back to the Division One police station on North Street.

After they left, Danny's cousin Nano shows up at the club.

"Where's Danny?" he says. When we told him what happened he went wild.

They can't do that, he kept saying. I'm going to get him out. Now, the whole North End knew that Nano wasn't playing with a full deck, but we'd never seen him this excited. There was no telling what he would do.

He went home and dug a tuxedo out of his closet. He put it on, along with a bow tie, but no shirt, and stuck an Abe Lincoln stovepipe hat on his head. Then he marched into the police station claiming that he was Danny's lawyer and demanding that they release him immediately. If they didn't, Nano warned, "higher authorities would hear about it." Now, his getup would have looked pretty weird at any time, but this was in the dead of winter. Here this guy comes in wearing a tuxedo and no shirt.

He kept carrying on until the desk sergeant finally got fed up and let Danny go just to get rid of Nano. Even Danny couldn't believe it.

Of course, we were used to Nano. Once when it was five below outside he came to school with a bow tie and no shirt, and during snowstorms he liked to wander around barefoot.

ABOUT THE TIME I turned fourteen Joe Semenza started taking me to boxing matches all over the Boston area. It was a lot of fun, and I knew some of the fighters from the North End. Since I was by now a veteran of many a street fight, I began to study the boxers closely, looking for a special style or technique. Gradually, I realized that a lot of them didn't have much technique, style, or talent. In fact, I knew I could beat most of the guys in the ring without even trying.

Before long I was right in there with them.

CHAPTER FOUR

THE RING

I WAS ONLY fifteen when I stepped into the ring, yet I felt right at home. My size was no problem, I was five-nine and weighed 160, which put me in the upper range of the middleweight division.

I did almost no training, and didn't have a trainer either. My workouts at the North End Union Gym on Parmenter Street consisted of hitting the punching bags and sometimes a little sparing with some other guys on a mat. That was about it. The place didn't have a ring. Luckily, I was blessed with natural strength and agility and there was no need for a lot of sweaty preparation or some would-be Cus D'Amato in my corner.

Once I felt confident enough for a real match, I entered some contests at the Rollaway Arena in Revere, a suburb of Boston. The winners of those fights would qualify for the Golden Gloves. Beyond that were the Olympics of 1964. Several people who watched me said I was good enough to make the team.

As I said before, most of the fighters were not very good, and all that stood between me and the Golden Gloves was a construction worker named Frank Brooks. He was twenty-four, built like a locomotive, and knew how to hit. Of all the boxers I would have to face he was the toughest.

The fight was on January 21, 1960. Brooks had tried to stare me down in the dressing room and before we climbed into the ring, but as soon as the bell rang I clipped his chin with my right. Brooks staggered a few steps before regaining his footing. He hadn't expected that. Picking up steam, he tried to force me against the ropes and into the corners. I charged at him with a barrage to the head and body and he went down on the canvas.

When he got up I kept hitting and dropped him again and again. I must have knocked him off his feet five times, but he never stayed down. My pals in the crowd were screaming for a knockout. Much as I would have liked to provide one, Brooks was just too solid. I knocked him around the ring until the end of the third round. I won by unanimous decision.

Losing made Brooks mad as hell. In the dressing room afterwards, he came over and demanded to know how old I was. Not wanting to embarrass him, I said that I was seventeen. Apparently that wasn't old enough to soothe his battered ego, so he started making wisecracks about how it was past my bedtime or something.

After a couple minutes of that I'd had enough.

"Look, pal, I just beat you in the ring," I said. "If you don't take a fast walk, I'll do it out of the ring."

Brooks gave me a sullen stare and walked away.

My next fight was a week away, and I knew I could beat any of the fighters who might be matched against me. Getting into the Golden Gloves would be a snap. Or so I thought. Unfortunately, my bad habits were about to catch up with me. I had become hooked on gambling, and the hook went very deep. Joe Semenza and I had been big losers in Fiore DeChristoforo's crap games. Joe was definitely the wrong man to have for a partner— he never won! Horses got lame as soon as he put money on them, his teams got shut out of every ball game he ever bet, and every throw of the dice was a loser. I blew all the money I had trying to get us out of the hole. Fiore gave us credit to try again, but the dice wouldn't cooperate, and by the time Fiore cut us off we owed him 2000 dollars. Joe was broke and I was broke, but like all gamblers we knew our luck had to turn around soon. As for the debt, well, we figured we could work something out. Fiore was a pretty good guy.

When I got out of school four days after the Brooks fight, Joe told me that Fiore wanted to see me in the room where he ran his crap game. Oddly enough, it was in the Testa Building on Hanover Street, where Frank Wallace had met his maker years and years before. I had no idea what Fiore wanted, only that he wasn't the type to put the squeeze on you for a debt.

Fiore got right to the point. "I've always been fair and never given you a hard time, right? I want you to do something for me."

"Sure, what is it?" I said.

Fiore moved closer, his voice friendly. "Now, listen closely," he said. "Paul Raymond from Somerville is fighting Thursday—he's the big drawing card and the place will be loaded with bettors. After the way you beat Frank Brooks you'll be a two- or three-to-one favorite no matter who you fight. Take a dive and we're even with the two thousand dollars."

The words hit me like a stone. It was the last thing I expected.

"Fiore," I said. "This is my chance for the Golden Gloves."

"Stop, Willie. With your ability you can win the Golden Gloves any time you want, but just not this time."

Fiore confided that he was owed more than 250,000 dollars and no one was paying him. "If my cash doesn't start flowing, I'll be in trouble," he said.

This was not a threat I was hearing. It wasn't throw the fight or else. It was a friend asking for a favor, a special favor. A friend who had done a lot of favors for me over the years.

The world seemed to have turned upside down.

At last I heard myself say: "This is gonna hurt, but I'll do it."

When I left the Testa Building that day I felt like I had left my soul inside.

*   *   *

JOE SEMENZA AND another friend, Big Ed Marino, drove me to the Rollaway that night.

"How do you feel?" Joe asked.

"Terrible. I'm sure I'm going to feel a lot worse later."

I was matched against William Hendricks, who was from Roxbury. Before the fight a bookie called Ben Gun came into the dressing room. Ben was a little bit of a guy who always walked real fast like he was looking to pick a fight. That night he was working for Fiore, taking all the bets. We didn't speak, but I saw him again just before the bell rang. He shot me a look and I gave a small nod. Yes.

I could have beaten Hendricks from a wheelchair, he was that bad. I decided to make the first round look good. It was almost too good—Hendricks nearly went down once when I jabbed him. After that he wouldn't come near me.

The bell rang for the second round. Hendricks still shied away from me, his gloves and arms hiding his face. We clinched in the middle of the ring. "Fight, you mother, throw some punches," I snarled.

Hendricks finally threw a soft punch and I dropped to the canvas. The referee counted to ten and when he was done I got up and went back to the dressing room. The entire arena was booing.

A North End pal came down while I was in the shower and asked what happened.

I told him I had gotten a sharp pain in my head that was so severe I couldn't get up.

He said he hoped I was all right.

"It was nothing," I said. I stayed in the shower a long time, as if I could wash off my shame.

There must have been an evil eye on me that night, because just before the fight I met a youthful, baby-faced hood from Somerville named Buddy McLean. He and his crew were there to see their pal Paul Raymond, who was at the top of the card. Big Ed introduced me to Buddy in the dressing room. It was funny how I met him on that night of all nights. The next year he would help touch off what became known as the McLean-McLaughlin War, a long, dirty feud that would change my life forever.

FIORE WAS WRONG. There'd be no more shots at the Golden Gloves. After that night something went out of me and I had no more desire to win. Over the next several years I tried to revive my boxing career many times, hoping for a fresh start. Nothing ever came of it.

But that didn't stop me from fighting outside the ring.

One night that August Eddie Greco and I drove out to the suburb of Wakefield in the 1956 Pontiac I had just bought—my second car. We had been tipped that a store out there had a lot of cash in its safe. We intended to break in and lug the safe out. But once we got there we couldn't get inside the place and after awhile figured we'd better forget it. We jumped in the car and hadn't gone more than a few hundred feet when the cops pulled us over. Apparently we'd made a lot of noise trying to break into the store.

They found burglary tools in the car, but the arrest didn't worry me. I was still a month shy of my seventeenth birthday. That meant my family could come and pick me up, or I'd be sent to the Youth Services Board for a day or so. There would be an appearance in juvenile court after that, which was always a joke. But I wasn't carrying any identification. The Wakefield cops didn't believe I was only sixteen and threw me in a cell. That made me very upset and I started yelling and banging on the bars. A cop walked by and I grabbed his jacket. At that, three officers yanked me out of the cell and brought me into a room. They said I now faced another charge.

"What?" I asked.

"Assault and battery," one of them shot back.

"Yeah? I'm going to sue you because you've got no right to keep me here. This is illegal. I'm only sixteen."

The hell you are, they said. I was going to be charged as an adult in criminal court.

"I know how old I am," I snapped. One of the cops didn't like that and started roughing me up. I picked him up and threw him on the floor. The other two came at me. There was a big commotion and more rushed in from outside. I dropped them one by one. It was like my fists were guns. Bang, bang, bang. Finally, a bunch of them piled on top of me and I heard something about a doctor. It felt like the entire Wakefield police force was weighing me down, but I kept thrashing around on the floor. Next thing I knew a man in civilian clothes was kneeling beside me with a syringe. After that everything went blank.

I WOKE UP TO the sound of voices. Whatever was in that injection had turned my blood to lead and it was a huge effort just to open my eyes. When I looked around I thought I had fallen into a horror movie. It was morning in a big room with a lot of beds. Along the sides of the room were cells—padded cells. Then I noticed the people—some of them wandering around talking to themselves, throwing their arms in the air, others were just hunched up and staring into space. They looked pale and dirty and all of them had strange, horrible expressions on their faces. It was unbelievable. At one end of the room a woman who looked like a nurse was sitting at a desk. I jumped out of bed and raced over to her. "Lady, where am I?" I said.

"Who are you?" she asked.

I was so groggy and disoriented it actually took me a couple seconds to remember. When I told her who I was she told me where I was—at the Mattapan state mental hospital!

This can't be real, I thought. I didn't remember anything after the Wakefield police station.

I pulled my brain back together and told the nurse I didn't belong there, that I was supposed to be in the Youth Services Board.

"Now, you just take it easy," she said calmly.

"No, I want to see the doctor in charge," I said, my voice rising.

"I can't do that."

I told her if she didn't do it I'd tear the place down. She must have pushed a button I couldn't see, because within seconds three doctors and three interns appeared. They formed a circle around me and one of them was holding a straitjacket that had my name on it.

"You'll never get that on me!" I said.

"Oh, no?" one of the doctors said sarcastically.

I picked up a lamp from a table near the desk. "If all the Wakefield cops couldn't handle me, you can't either."

Nobody moved.

"What do you want?" one of the doctors asked.

"He wants to see the doctor in charge," the nurse said. As she spoke, the doctor who ran the place walked in.

"What's all the commotion here?" he wanted to know.

The nurse told him. "This is William Fopiano and he wants to talk to you."

Still holding the lamp I told the guy that I didn't belong in a mental institution.

The head doctor took it all in stride. "You were brought here last night because the authorities couldn't control your actions. It looks like the same thing is happening now."

I explained that I only wanted to talk to him and his people tried to put me in a straitjacket.

The doctor told the others to put away the straitjacket and that he would handle me. He took me into his office and I told him the whole story.

"I'm not crazy and I'm willing to take a test to prove it."

"What happens if you don't pass the test?" the doctor asked.

"Then you can keep me," I said.

Well, I passed the test and a day later I found myself back at the Youth Services Board. After Wakefield and Mattapan I wanted to kiss the ground.

It was a hot day and the staff was passing out popsicles on the lawn. I couldn't believe the kids. Some of them seemed like babies—only nine or ten years old. I felt a lot older and looked even older than that. My nose was broken from boxing and I had a goatee. At first the kids thought I worked there.

"No, no, I'm in the same boat as you," I said. I took a popsicle and sat down on the lawn with them. They asked me all kinds of questions about the stuff I had done.

This was the last the Youth Services Board would see of me. It was the last time I'd get off so easy, and I knew it. In a month I would be seventeen, and from then on every crime would carry a much bigger risk. The cops could throw me in a jail cell and a judge could send me to prison. But those were the risks of the game.

THERE WAS ANOTHER sanity test I had to pass when I was released from the Youth Services Board—this time with Frank and Henry.

They had heard I was in Mattapan and wondered what the hell was going on. "Is Willie cracking up on us?" Henry asked Joe Semenza. He said it as if he were joking, but Joe could tell that Henry wanted an answer to his question. As soon as I got bailed out of the Youth Services Board I went straight over to the Florentine and assured them that everything was all right.

ANOTHER KIND OF insanity began about this time. One night I was driving up Prince Street and saw crazy Nano walking with two other guys I didn't know. Nano asked for a ride even though they were only going a couple of blocks over to Hanover Street.

"What are you doing tonight?" Nano asked after they all piled in.

"Why?" I said.

"Come with us. We're going over to my house."

"Yeah? What am I supposed to do at your house?" I said. I didn't like the looks of the guys he was with.

"We're going to get high," Nano said. They had hypodermic

needles and some paragoric—in those days the poor man's heroin.

Drugs were virtually unheard of then, yet the thought of sticking poison in my arm turned my stomach.

Instantly, I slammed on the brakes and smacked Nano in the face. He and his friends jumped out of the car and took off.

I didn't realize it then, but I had just witnessed the first symptom of a plague.

CHAPTER FIVE

THE PRICES WE PAY

THE WAKEFIELD JOB didn't bring me a cent, and it proved very costly—six months in jail, my first sentence.

Me and Eddie Greco beat the breaking and entering charge, and the fight with the cops came to nothing. Then, the grand jury hit us with possession of burglary tools. For some reason my case had been transferred from juvenile to criminal court. We went to trial, and quickly saw that the prosecutor had us. Eddie's lawyer, a guy named Leavitt, came to me with a proposition. If we got convicted Eddie was facing at least a nickle—five years. He was twenty-one and had a long record. But if we stopped the trial and plead guilty, Leavitt could make a deal: probation for Eddie and six months in jail and three years probation for me. Because of what happened in the police station, the prosecutor and the Wakefield cops really wanted to put me behind bars, even if only for a short time. Eddie they didn't care about. So, Leavitt wanted me to be the fall guy.

Eddie swore by Leavitt and thought he was great. Personally, I didn't think he was very good at all. I also didn't like him and the feeling was mutual. He was sarcastic and often wised off to the wrong people—like me. When me and Eddie walked into his office one time, Leavitt said to Eddie: "Oh, you're in good company again." When we left I told Eddie to warn Leavitt not to press his luck. But when he came to me with the deal I put all that aside for Eddie's sake. "Get me the six months," I told Leavitt, and that's what I got—along with the probation. I arrived at the Billerica House of Correction on October 4, 1961, a little more than a month after my seventeenth birthday.

The place was minimum security; all the inmates were serving short sentences. Yet a prison is a prison, and I had thoroughly prepared myself mentally. I was ready for anything. On my second or third day I was walking across the yard and a young guy who thought he was tough laughed at me. I immediately walked over and whacked him against a wall. Bang—down he went, then the guards grabbed me. The fight meant three days in the hole—locked up in total darkness with only half a meal a day. But it was worth it because after that most of the prisoners knew they couldn't mess with me. When I got out of the hole one of them came over and shook my hand. He was big and good-looking and told me he admired the way I fought. He had been a boxer himself in the navy, he said. His name was Albert DeSalvo. A few years later he would confess to being the Boston Strangler.

We became friendly, and I asked what he was doing there.

"I got two years on simple assault," he said.

"What's that?"

"They couldn't convict me on burglary or a sex offense."

"Are you a sex offender?" I asked.

Albert laughed. "No, I touched a woman's hand when I was inside a house. That's why I'm here. I'm a professional house burglar."

He said he wanted somebody who could handle safes and I told him I was his man. Die Bolt, York, Mosler, you name it, I could crack open the best.

"A lot of these are wall safes," he said.

"No problem," I said. "Five minutes or less."

Robbery and sex were Albert's main interests, and in the latter department he was a freak of nature. That I realized one day when we were in the shower. His joint was the size of a baby's arm. I couldn't help noticing.

"What the hell is that?" I said.

He laughed and tugged proudly at himself. "Don't you know that when I got to court, I was there for assault with a deadly weapon!"

Albert boasted about mixing business and pleasure. He cased homes he wanted to rob by posing as a salesman or an agent for a modeling agency, and going around during the day when only housewives were likely to be home. Albert was one of the great charmers of all time, and once he'd conned his way in the door, he was often tempted to go further. He had a rap like you wouldn't believe, and during the course of these seductions he'd get very excited and the women got turned on when they saw the small mountain swelling in his pants.

By the time he was through talking he'd have their clothes off. Later he would come back and rip the house off. I asked how many times this had happened. Albert winked. "Hundreds, hundreds."

He certainly had a way about him, and he could talk you into just about anything. At Billerica he was making jewelry boxes, carved wood with velvet linings. They were good boxes and very well made, but Albert was such a good talker I would have bought one no matter what it looked like. I had another prisoner inscribe the box he sold me with the name of a girl I liked: Rita. By the time I got out of jail Rita was dating somebody else, so I held onto the box. In the 1970s I started dating another woman named Rita, a cocktail waitress in Las Vegas. *That* Rita got the jewelry box. Only I told her I made it, and not because I wanted to impress her. If I told her that Albert DeSalvo—*the Boston Strangler*—had made it she would've flipped!

DeSalvo took my phone number and said we'd hook up once we were back out on the street. He never called, which is just as well because he also liked to invade houses—storm in with guns while people were at home. I steered away from stuff like that because you might have to hurt innocent people.

*   *   *

I SAID THAT most of the prison inmates didn't try to mess with me after that first fight, but one of them didn't like the way I carried myself. He and DeSalvo were sort of running things and he thought I ought to be showing him more respect. I had a job making brushes in one of the shops and he worked next door in the laundry. I caught him glaring at me a few times, but I stayed cool.

One night one of his punks delivered a message to my cell: He was planning to knock the shit out of me and would do so at the first opportunity. I told the punk to give his man a message back: "Tell that asshole when I get my hands on him I'll mop the floor with him." The punk couldn't believe he was hearing this from the mouth of a seventeen-year-old kid.

"Just tell him," I said.

The next morning I left my glasses in my cell and didn't even stop in the brush shop where I was supposed to be. Instead, I went straight into the laundry and walked up to the tough guy.

"You want to threaten me?" I said. He dropped whatever he was doing and came flying at me. I backed up a couple steps and caught him with a few quick pops to the head. He was a lot bigger than me, but the fight was no contest. I dropped him again and again, till finally he didn't get up. The fight lasted for fifteen minutes or more. A friend of mine, Pebbles Doe, had sneaked away from his job in another part of the prison to be with me, but I didn't need him. Among the other spectators were a couple guards who saw the whole thing and didn't make any move to stop it. They just hung out and enjoyed themselves. It was free entertainment.

A FEW DAYS after I arrived in Billerica, I borrowed a Sunday newspaper. HUB GAMBLER BLASTED IN GANG-STYLE AMBUSH was the headline. Underneath the big letters was a photograph of Fiore DeChristoforo. He had been shot and badly wounded when he came out the Coliseum restaurant on Hanover Street in the North End. Fiore had gotten on the wrong side of the wiseguys for being too independent and outspoken. The crap game had become very lucrative and popular. Too popular: Twice that year Fiore got raided, and one of those times he slugged a detective. There were warnings. He was carrying too much heat. He shot his mouth off too much and certain people were offended by his conduct. But Fiore was having none of it. He didn't want to hear about silent partners or protection, he would run his business his way and if someone didn't like it, too bad.

Before I went to Billerica he had it out with Henry Noyes outside the Florentine. Henry liked Fiore and had tried to protect him, but he said the game was no good for the neighborhood. When Fiore talked back Henry slapped him right in front of everybody. Most guys would've cleared out after something like that happened. Most guys would've backed down the moment the wiseguys began turning the screws. Not Fiore. It wasn't in his nature to give in or be afraid.

Now, this may sound strange, but I always liked him. Sure, he got me to throw that fight, but that was my decision and I was mad at myself for having gone along. He was a good, decent guy. I remembered the times he let me hang around his place when I was just a little kid and let me feel like one of the guys. He loaned me money when I needed it and always treated me with respect.

Fiore DeChristoforo never hurt anybody. Once he caught a man who worked for him taking money, but let it go. He had a way with animals, too. Bring him the most vicious dog and in an hour he'd turn it into a pet. All the kids in the neighborhood loved Fiore. He sponsored a softball team and paid for all the uniforms and equipment. The sidewalk outside his smoke shop was called Christy's Corner and hundreds of kids used to hang around on warm nights, just to be near him. When he got shot they lined up to donate blood. The detectives came to the hospital wanting to know who shot him. "I'll take care of it myself," was all Fiore would say. He hated cops and never gave them a nickle.

That's why they were always bothering him. He kept getting frisked all the time, so he couldn't carry a piece. The men who were waiting for him outside the Coliseum that night knew he'd be unarmed.

Fiore was very strong and started getting better, and that threw a scare into the people who tried to kill him. He almost certainly would've walked out of the hospital if it hadn't been for the pneumonia. A couple weeks after the shooting I flipped on a transistor radio in my cell after doing some push-ups. Fiore had died.

His father was as tough as Fiore and wanted blood. He went right up to Tony Canadian and shoved a gun in his belly. Tony turned white, but for some reason old man DeChristoforo didn't pull the trigger.

After Fiore died you never saw kids on Christy's Corner.

The Coliseum was the place where Angie DeMarco had eaten his last meal. It might as well have been the lion's den, because it was Tony Canadian's hangout. Why Angie and Fiore went up to a place like that when they were in trouble with the wiseguys is beyond me. They both had more balls than brains. After that the Coliseum became known as "the Last Supper."

In a way, Fiore had the last laugh. The wiseguys probably figured they'd take over his operations and help themselves to whatever money was around. But they didn't count on Fiore's right-hand, a tall, fat fellow called Buffy. When his boss was shot, Buffy skipped town. The wiseguys might have expected that. But he ran off with all the money—I heard it was around 200,000 dollars. *That* the wiseguys didn't expect, and when they found out they were fit to be tied. They sent people after Buffy but never caught up with him. Buffy was in the wind.

About twenty years later, in the early 1980s, I noticed a big man at the Tropicana casino in Las Vegas. Something about him was familiar and I moved closer. Sure enough, it was Buffy, older, balder, still heavy, and still alive. I wondered if he was gambling with what was left of Fiore's loot.

Besides DeSalvo, I made friends with several guys at Billerica: Pebbles Doe and a guy I'll call Mike Tooher, who were from
Charlestown, and a guy I'll call Tommy Dennehy from Roxbury.
Mike and a couple of other guys were looking to get transferred
to another jail, the Concord Reformatory. It was supposed to be
a better place. The authorities had rejected their requests for a
transfer. But there was another way to get one, a surefire way—
start a strike or a riot. Mike proposed instigating something after
work in the day room, the recreation area where we watched
television and played games.

"Sure," I said. "I'll get Tommy and Pebbles to spread the
word and get as many guys as we can."

Now, a disturbance always carries the risk of a longer sentence, or worse. Situations like that can easily get out of control.
But I didn't care. I was sick of Billerica and wanted out just as
much as Mike. One of the guards claimed—falsely—that I
cursed at him, and that landed me back in the hole. He was
constantly on my ass, trying to provoke me. I mentioned the fights
I had at Billerica, yet aside from that I was a model prisoner and
played by the rules. It didn't matter. I was always locked in my
cell after dinner, while other inmates were allowed to hang out
in the day room and watch television and play cards until lights
out.

After a few months I asked to be transferred to the Charles
Street Jail in Boston and finish my sentence there. It was only a
short walk from my house and my mother wouldn't have to travel
twenty-five miles every week. The authorities turned me down
flat, so when Mike suggested causing some trouble I was up for
anything.

What happened was this: After work a couple hundred inmates gathered in the day room and refused to leave. It didn't
take long to get the whole place going. Everyone had a complaint:
about the awful food, about the guards, about too few privileges.
We started yelling and screaming and banged on the doors and
windows. The guards were spooked and didn't dare enter the

room. They huddled outside and ordered us to come out. I looked out the window for the guard who sent me to the hole, hoping I'd have a chance to get back at him.

A few of us hunted around for weapons, things to throw, but everything in the room, all the chairs and tables, was bolted to the floor. That probably prevented a full-scale riot.

After repeated warnings the guards lobbed tear gas into the day room, and all the troublemakers, including me, were locked in our cells for several days. Yet the strategy worked. Not long after that Mike and his pals were sent to Concord. And after they left I got transferred to the Charles Street Jail.

CHAPTER SIX

WARNINGS AND FIXES

As soon as I got out of jail in May of 1962 Henry Noyes asked to see me. One look at him and I could see he was worried about something. It turned out he was worried about me, and for good reason. I had been inside a little more than six months, but in that time the Boston underworld had changed and become dangerously unstable. The old ways, the old alliances, were being shattered one by one, and I was coming out to a game that had suddenly turned rotten and mean.

A war was about to explode, and Henry could see it coming the way an old fisherman who has been putting out to sea for fifty years can feel in his bones the approach of a storm.

The McLean-McLaughlin War would last for years and kill dozens of men. It was bloodier than the gang wars in New York in the early 1930s, and probably right up there with Chicago in the 1920s. More than once I nearly became one of the victims. I know what outsiders always say: that gangsters only kill other gangsters, so what. But I knew several of the men murdered in the McLean-McLaughlin War, and I can tell you that some of them were not violent people and not bad people. Some of them never hurt anybody. Sure, they were criminals, and in the eyes of their law-abiding fellow citizens they belonged in jail. Fair enough. But they didn't deserve to die, especially like that.

LIKE MOST WARS, the McLean-McLaughlin War began over a minor incident. In this case, it was a fight over a girl at the resort town of Salisbury Beach in the late summer of 1961. Two young Irish gangsters who were associated with Buddy McLean's Somerville crowd had taken a house at the beach. They were with two girls. Sharing the house with them was George McLaughlin and a girl he had brought. George's older brother, Bernie McLaughlin, ran a gang in Charlestown.

George McLaughlin couldn't take his eyes off one of the girls with the Somerville boys. She was gorgeous and had very big breasts, or so the story goes. George got very drunk—that's when he was most dangerous—and made all kinds of crude remarks to the girl. The Somerville boys told him to knock it off, and when George tried to paw her they gave him a bad beating that put him in the hospital for a couple of weeks.

I don't know what story George told his brother, but Bernie McLaughlin was greatly offended by the beating. He quickly arranged a meeting with Buddy McLean and demanded that the two Somerville boys be whacked.

Up until this point the Charlestown and Somerville gangs had always gotten along pretty well. They were neighbors; Charlestown is part of Boston and right next to it, just to the north, is Somerville, an old suburb. Both groups were mostly Irish, but they also included Italians, Greeks, Jews, Yankees, and others. Both had their own rackets and there were very few disputes. Buddy McLean was a man's man, a stand-up guy who called it the way he saw it. He had a lot of common sense. To him, it was a simple matter: George had gotten out of line. He got drunk, tried to pick up another guy's girl and whatever he got he deserved. End of story. Now, let's forget it.

Bernie McLaughlin didn't see it that way at all. For some reason the incident had blown up into a matter of honor. He wanted blood. Buddy told Bernie to forget about it, he wasn't going to get involved. But it was already too late to not get involved. By trying to stay out of it, Buddy became Bernie's enemy.

A FEW WEEKS after that, Buddy was home one night and noticed that the family dogs seemed very nervous. They were barking and whimpering. Something was outside. Buddy grabbed a gun and peered out. Three men were near his car. Buddy threw open the door and the men scattered, but he recognized one of them as Bernie McLaughlin. Buddy went over to check on the car. Five sticks of dynamite were underneath, wired to the engine. The bomb was meant for Buddy, of course, but he wasn't planning to drive the car. His wife was going to use it to take their children to school the next morning.

Two days later was Halloween. It was also Bernie McLaughlin's last day on earth. A gunman blew him away as he walked along City Square in Charlestown. Bernie was hit in broad daylight, near the Bunker Hill Monument and a stone's throw from the City Square police station.

Buddy and another man were arrested after the sole witness to come forward, a woman, fingered Buddy as the triggerman and the second guy as the getaway driver.

The woman then had second thoughts, maybe because she realized what kind of people she would be testifying against. Whatever her reasons, she changed her story and said that Mc-Lean only "resembled" the killer. The cops had to let Buddy and the other man go, but Bernie McLaughlin's brothers, George and Edward, who was called "Punchy," were already plotting their revenge. The entire New England underworld would eventually be dragged into the feud, forced to take sides and all because of a man who couldn't keep his hands off another guy's girl.

THE WAR MIGHT not have been as long or as violent if the character of the Italian mob had not been changing at the same time.

In the mid-1950s Phil Buccola, the head of the Boston family, retired to his native Sicily. Some said he saw the handwriting on the wall at the time of the Kefauver Committee hearings—that the full power of the federal government was about to be unleashed on the mob, and the days of the wiseguy were numbered. Others thought he was simply burned out and not up to the job anymore. He left abruptly, so abruptly that some of the bosses in New York who had always maintained an interest in the Boston mob didn't even know about it until he was already out of the country.

Buccola returned to America for a short visit in 1957. Henry told me that Charlie Luciano made Buccola go back and apologize to Frank Costello and other mobsters who had their noses out of joint, and say good-bye properly. When Buccola went to New York, Costello said: "Now you did it right. Now you can go. And don't come back." And that was the end of the meeting.

Buccola's departure left a vacuum at the top that was eventually filled by a family from Providence, Rhode Island. They operated out of an office there and the New England mob became known as "the Office." The Providence people picked a Boston crew to help them run things in Massachusetts. The upshot of all that was that Frank, Henry, and Tony Canadian were gradually pushed aside. Young blood was coming up, and the important decisions were now being made in Providence. Frank dismissed the new Boston crew as "a bunch of bookies." He wasn't afraid of them and they still had to defer to him and his friends. Even in the 1960s no one dared to slight a friend of Charlie Luciano. Yet Frank's era was fading. These men who had loved and protected me since I was a child were now the old guard and wouldn't be around much longer.

All that was probably on Henry's mind when I came to see him that day. It's a good thing he was concerned, because I wasn't worried about anything. By this time I had quit school and was raring to hit the streets again. The world was a giant cash register and I couldn't wait to get my hands in the till.

Henry embraced me and got right to the point. "Will, I'm concerned about you. Times have changed. Things aren't like before. There are people around here younger than myself with different philosophies. They're going to destroy whatever good is left. I don't want to see you get caught up in a bad situation. Frank and I already talked about your future. We haven't much time left. When we're gone, it's going to be a mess. We're worried about how you're going to handle it."

"How would you handle it?" I asked.

"Good question," Henry almost smiled. "I know you're smart and growing fast. But you're seventeen—you're young enough to be cut down and molded."

"You mean making me the way they want me to be?" I said.

"Yes," Henry said, probably knowing that could never happen. I wasn't about to be bossed around and I had no desire to become a made man of the Office.

"Can anyone make a cat out of a dog?" I said. "A dog out of a lion? People will have to take me the way I am."

I told Henry not to worry, that I could take care of myself. But I was in hot water again almost immediately.

First it was a breaking and entering charge involving the burglary of a construction company. It was dismissed for lack of evidence.

That case was still pending when I pulled into a gas station with two friends one night that summer. Four sailors and a couple of girls were standing around. While we were getting gas the sailors made a couple of remarks that I didn't catch. I got out of the car and asked if they were talking to me. They all laughed. A sudden white rage blazed up inside me. In my waistband was a loaded .45 that I planned to use in a stickup later. The gun flew out from under my shirt and I shoved the barrel under the chin of the sailor with the biggest mouth. Everybody froze.

"What's so funny?" I said.

Little beads of sweat decorated the sailor's face and he didn't think anything was funny now. I told him that unless he apologized a bullet was about to make a trip from his chin through the top of his skull. He was speechless; his mouth moved but no words came out. After several tries, he managed to stammer out an "I'm sorry" and the others assured me they were very sorry too. Naturally, they took down the number of our license plate and phoned the police as soon as we drove away. Even if they hadn't gotten the plate number, we were driving a red Corvair—not exactly the kind of car that blends into a crowd. It took about twenty minutes for a cruiser to spot us. When they came after our car we roared off, zigzagging through the narrow, winding streets of the North End, bouncing over the cobblestones. They were pretty far behind when we reached Prince Street. One of my pals was driving and I had him make a sharp right on to Thatcher. I jumped out while the car was still moving, dashed into a nearby building and stashed the gun on a roof. Then I ran the three rooftops over to my house.

The cops picked up my friends in the Corvair and showed up at my house later that night. The sailors identified me, but the gun was nowhere to be found. The court let me out on 5000 dollars' bail.

I WAS CHARGED with weapons possession and went before Judge Elijah Adlow in Municipal Court. The cops and the district attorney's office were pressing hard for Adlow to find probable cause and turn the case over to a grand jury. They wanted me bad. But Adlow had an embarrassing question for the prosecutor: "Where's the weapon?"

They put cops on the stand who said no weapon had been found, but that nylon stockings with eye holes cut into them were on the front seat of the Corvair. That showed I intended to commit a crime.

Adlow asked me who owned the stockings.

"My friend's wife who owns the car," I said.

The judge picked up one of the the stockings. "In this heat all they look like to me is air-conditioned stockings."

That got a good laugh, from everybody except the prosecutor and the cops. And when Adlow let me go they were seething.

EDDIE GRECO AND two other friends, Joe (Gorilla) Maioli and Joe D'Minico, congratulated me and helped celebrate my victory.

Joe Maioli wasn't bad looking or anything, but he had a lot of hair and his build sort of resembled that of an ape, so he was always Joe Gorilla. He was also pretty violent and constantly in trouble. His first pinch came at age eight, and by the time he was seventeen he'd been arrested so many times that he made the paper. A judge nearly had a stroke when he took a look at Joe's juvenile record and announced from the bench that it was the worst he had seen in his entire career.

Joe D'Minico was notorious around the North End for something that happened a few years earlier. He broke into a store called Johnnie Walkers that sold saddles and riding accessories. His accomplices were Eddie Greco and another neighborhood character we called George Macaroni. They grabbed a few thousand dollars, and Joe helped himself to some of the goods. Well, the next day he appears on the street in broad daylight decked out like Roy Rogers—in a ten-gallon hat, cowboy shirt, boots, spurs, neckerchief and even a holster. The cop who arrested him thought he was seeing things!

That was bad enough, the whole neighborhood was laughing, but as soon as he made bail Joe goes storming over to the corner hangout, looks at everybody and says: "All right, who ratted on me?"

People acted like he was the village idiot, but Joe was far from stupid. In fact, he was a specialist at opening safes, even the sophisticated models. I had watched him smack the combination knob off a manganese steel safe with a sledgehammer, then penetrate the tumblers with an awl, moving them just so until the door swung right open. With safes he had the finesse and skill of a great lover seducing an icy virgin. Other times, though, he just didn't think. Those of us who knew him and liked him tried to laugh with him, not at him, but it was impossible to keep a straight face.

ABOUT THE TIME Judge Adlow let me off, a bunch of us were lounging around in front of Bova's bakery at Prince and Salem Streets (that was the corner hangout I just mentioned. It's known as Bova's Corner.) and Joe pulled up in a car that happened to be stolen. He asked if anyone wanted to come with him on a score. He intended to burglarize a supermarket. It was eight o'clock on a summer night and still light out, so we said no thanks. Joe got mad and drove off. Screw us, he would do the job himself.

This is what happened next: Joe went to the back of the building and took a big hook attached to a rope and hurled it up to the roof, catching it on the parapet. After scaling the wall and lifting himself onto the roof, he slipped over to the skylight and carefully removed the putty around the glass. Then he took the glass out of the frame, buried the hook in the roof tar and dropped the rope to the floor below. Slowly, he went down, hand over hand. He was arrested as soon as he touched the floor.

The supermarket was still open.

JOE D'MINICO'S OLDER brother, Carmine, was another piece of work. He was a real funny guy, but kind of slow. One night a bunch of us were walking along and all of a sudden Carmine disappears. Nobody knew where he went. Then somebody spotted something moving inside a darkened candy store. It was Carmine. He had sneaked around the back and broken into the place. We ran around and dragged him out, hoping nobody else had seen him. "Hey, come on, there's at least twenty-six dollars in here," he said.

He was always doing stuff like that. Another time he got arrested for breaking into a jukebox when you could still get two songs for five cents. Carmine left his prints all over the jukebox and a newspaper headline called him "the twenty-eight-year-old nickel snatcher."

Carmine was harmless, but you had to understand him. He sang Frank Sinatra songs all the time, even late at night when he was walking back to his house on Prince Street. He got complaints from neighbors about making too much noise, and I don't know what he said or did, but he got two brothers mad enough to go after him. They came up to him on Bova's Corner and smashed him in the head with a sledgehammer, full force. Carmine went down like a dead man. Me and Joe Gorilla saw it happen from down the street and immediately rushed over and beat up the two brothers. I thought I was too late; Carmine's head was a bloody sponge. We checked him, he was still breathing. It's amazing he wasn't killed on the spot. We had more trouble when the cops came. It turned out one of the brothers was a fireman. How he ever passed the fireman's test I don't know, his eyes were bugged-out and he looked even nuttier than Carmine. Anyway, guess who got arrested: Me, Joe Gorilla and *Carmine*.

We spent three weeks at the Charles Street Jail in Boston. My lawyer, Max Glazer, told us to stay there. That way, it would look good for Judge Adlow, who had a soft spot for the North End crowd. Glazer could do a deal with him, and if we served some time nobody would ask any questions. But if we made bail and got into more trouble, Adlow might get mad and refuse to help us. It was a good move, because Joe Gorilla was determined to kill the two brothers for what they did to Carmine. "They're lucky I'm in here," he kept saying.

I shared a cell with a man who had just gotten twenty-five years for a bank robbery and was waiting to be shipped to a federal prison. It was the first time he had been in trouble—before that he had been straight. The guy had a *Playboy* magazine, which in those days was not considered contraband, and Carmine asked to borrow it. The bank robber knew about Carmine and felt sorry for him. He was wearing a bandage around his head and the wounds were still oozing. It's a miracle Carmine was still able to function. He was crazy enough *before* getting hit by the sledgehammer. Anyhow, a couple of days went by and Carmine didn't return the *Playboy*. The bank robber didn't say anything, but I was a little embarrassed and went up to Carmine at dinner.

"You gotta give it back, Carmine. You can't keep it," I said.

"I'm still reading it, I'm almost done," he said, so I told him to bring it back as soon as he was finished. But a couple more days passed and the *Playboy* didn't appear.

"How long does it take you to read this thing?" I said to him.

"Two more pages, two more pages," Carmine insisted. I wasn't sure he was able to read at all.

"All right, throw it on the bed at supper time," I said. "Make sure now, Carmine."

It wasn't until after breakfast the next morning that I found the magazine on one of the beds. It looked very, very thin. No, he couldn't have, I thought. But, sure enough, every photograph in the magazine had been cut out. I couldn't believe it. The bank robber just laughed, and thought it was funny. "I know that sledgehammer did a number on him," he said.

At Charles Street you were locked down twenty-three hours a day except for meals, and it wasn't until that night that I was able to slip over to Carmine's cell. All the pictures from the *Playboy* were pasted on his wall.

"Carmine, how could you do that?" I said.

Carmine pointed to the centerfold. "Oh, I had to take her out. Then, the little pictures, they were nice too."

"But Carmine, the magazine didn't belong to you."

He looked at me as if I was the one who was crazy. "But those guys just want to read the stories. They don't want to see the pictures." What could you do with somebody like that? I had one of my visitors bring another *Playboy* for the bank robber.

After two weeks we went before Judge Adlow. On the stand the fireman made out like we were a threat to him and his brother.

Then Carmine unwrapped his bandages and showed his head to the judge.

Adlow was stunned. "How could this happen?" he said sharply, and asked us who hit Carmine. We said we didn't know.

Adlow grinned. "That's what I like about you North End guys. You never rat on anybody." The cops couldn't believe their ears. Adlow fined us 150 dollars and we walked.

Joe Gorilla wanted to kill the brothers the minute we hit the street, but I told him to wait—and to warn me in advance so I'd have an alibi.

The fireman's brother lived on Prince Street, and after we got out I spoke to a friend of his on Bova's Corner. "Look," I said, "tell him we're willing to forget everything, even if his brother ratted on us. But if anything happens to Carmine, they're going to be the losers."

I made that move on Frank's advice, so I'd be in the clear. "If the hit comes off you ain't gonna get any heat for it," he said.

As it turned out, Joe Gorilla wound up back in Walpole before he could put the hit on anybody. Carmine was never bothered again.

THAT ALL HAPPENED in September and October. In January 1963 I got caught robbing a supermarket. Danny Puopolo and me had been looking for a good score, and someone introduced us to a guy named Joseph (Jack Ass) Francione who had information. There was a supermarket on Bennington Street in East Boston that had at least 25,000 dollars lying in the safes every Saturday night.

We took a ride over to the place. The supermarket was on a busy thoroughfare, but there was nothing right next to it and it looked pretty easy to get in and out.

What about the alarm? I wanted to know.

"That's the good thing about it, there is no alarm," Jack Ass said. It seemed too good to be true. If there was so much cash, why no alarm? But Jack Ass kept assuring us that there was no alarm and nothing to worry about.

Jack Ass was a lot older than us, thirty-three. He was also a suspect in the 1.5 million-dollar robbery of a mail truck in Plymouth, Massachusetts, in August 1962. (That knocked the Brinks job into second place on the list of biggest cash heists in U.S. history.) Because of the heat that was on him for the mail robbery and because of his age he was reluctant to risk a long sentence. So we'd do the score and he'd be the getaway driver.

There were two safes. We didn't have time to fool with them ourselves, so the supermarket manager was crucial—he had to open them for us. Lying in wait for him outside the place was too dangerous, so we planned to grab him at his home after he locked up and make him take us back to the store and open the safes. Jack Ass followed the manager for a few days and got his routine down.

On January 5, 1963 we were ready. It was a cold night. Before the robbery Danny Puopolo and I visited a shrine, an enormous statue of the Blessed Virgin that looks down from Orient Heights in East Boston. I said a prayer that things would go all right, then we went to meet Jack Ass.

We knew exactly what time the manager closed the store and how long it took him to get home. Jack Ass dropped us about a half a block from the man's house.

"Look, he's usually alone," Jack Ass told us. "But sometimes he's with his kid."

"Wait a minute," I said. "How old's the kid?"

"He's about twelve."

"Jeez, I don't want to do it if there's a kid there."

"What are you talking about? Everything's set. You gotta do it. Now come on!"

We got out of the car and ran over to the manager's house. I was praying he would be alone. But a couple of minutes later the car pulled up and I saw a small figure on the passenger side. Danny and I pulled ski masks over our faces and went up to the car. We were both in black. I had a snub-nosed .38 caliber special, and told the manager and his son to move over. Danny got behind the wheel and I jumped in the backseat. "Put your heads between your knees," I said.

The boy was scared and I felt bad. He was only a few years younger than me. After a few minutes I let him sit up and patted his head. There was a candy bar in my jacket and I gave it to him.

When we got back to the supermarket Jack Ass was already in place, parked across the street at a funeral parlor. He was driving a big black Cadillac. It fit right in.

We parked in front of the store. If the cops went by they would think the manager had forgotten something and come back. The manager unlocked the door. We took him to the cashier's office and made him open up the safes. Jack Ass had been right about the money—there was a pile of it. We tied up the manager and his son with clothesline and threw the cash into an airline traveling bag.

When we were done, Danny and I raced to the back of the store. We would leave that way. As we were unlocking the door I heard a tremendous crash and turned around. The manager had freed himself and in a panic dove through a plate-glass window. He got cut up pretty bad.

We threw open the door, went outside—and practically bumped into a cop. We started running, and stopped when he fired a warning shot. More cops were pulling up. Handcuffs snapped onto my wrists. It was like the sky had just caved in. It was supposed to have been an easy score, and now here I was facing enough beefs to put me away until my hair turned gray.

When Jack Ass saw the police he drove off. He had been dead wrong about the alarm: There was a silent one inside the safes that was triggered automatically when they were opened at an unusual hour.

A MONTH LATER we were out on bail. I was on probation for the Wakefield job and expected to be shipped off to a prison any day for violation. But that was the least of my worries. Now, I was looking at a lot of hard time for the supermarket score. Jack Ass felt very bad about what happened and helped Danny and me get a well-connected lawyer, Dan O'Connell, a former state supreme court justice. O'Connell made it known that he could arrange a fairly light sentence—the price was 15,000 dollars. That was for the fix. On top of that there were other fees and costs that came to about 10,000 dollars. Now, we had to put some more scores together to pay for it all.

A payroll heist at a South Shore shopping center gave us— Danny, Eddie Greco and me—15,000 dollars, but we had been told the take would be twice that much. Eddie threw in his share to help pay the lawyer.

It was now March and we were still short 10,000 dollars. Eddie called my house one night and told me where we could get it: at the Peppermint Lounge, a popular joint downtown. He had heard they kept at least that much in the safe.

Danny was sick with the flu, so we brought another guy with us, Joe Guarino. We broke into the Peppermint Lounge and by the time we got through with the safe it looked like an empty sardine can. We took the money and went out the back. There was no alarm this time, but for some reason we were having bad luck with cops and back doors—a cop happened to be just outside. He grabbed Eddie, who was carrying a box with all the cash. Joe and I got away and went back to Bova's to figure out how we could get Eddie out.

As we left two detectives arrested us and a few hours later we were sharing a cell with Eddie at the South End police station. That was about the last place I wanted to get pinched. A bunch of South End cops had jumped me one time when I came out of a nightclub. They took me back to the station and gave me a bad beating. There were too many of them to fight. They had so much fun they didn't even bother to charge me with anything serious.

Me and Joe and Eddie were brought down there early on a Sunday morning. The cops wanted all of us bad, especially me. Over the next day they grilled me again and again and kept the pressure on. I didn't know why the process was taking so long, until I realized that the cop who arrested Eddie probably couldn't identify Joe or me. That made the cops burn even more. This time I had really gotten under their skins and they had all they could take from me. On Monday morning a sergeant yanked me out of my cell and paraded me in front of a bunch of officers lined up for the morning roll call. Then he made a little announcement:

"This man is William Fopiano. He's out on bail for armed robbery and kidnaping. He has an extensive arrest record and is the prime suspect in robberies, break-ins, and assaults in the Boston area."

After going on some more about what a menace I was to society, the sergeant told his men: "If you see him running from a crime, or even near a doorway, shoot him."

It was open season on me.

I didn't have much time to worry about any of that, because that same morning Eddie, Joe, and me were taken to police headquarters for a lineup and put in a big room with a lot of other men who had been arrested over the weekend.

I was wearing a new black felt hat that cost me 25 dollars. I loved the hat, yet I didn't want to have it on in the lineup; it made me look too sinister. But if I left it in the room one of the sleazebags would swipe it. So I made a deal with Joe and Eddie, whoever got called for the lineup last would wear the hat. Eddie was called first. Then me. "Don't leave the hat behind," I told Joe.

I was ushered through a door and found myself on a stage with a single microphone. I was facing a blaze of bright white lights. Behind the lights were a roomful of cops who I could barely see. They told me to step up to the microphone and asked me several questions. Then I was told to join Eddie on the side of the stage.

After that Joe came out, and when he did I couldn't believe my eyes. Apparently, Joe was also concerned about looking sinister—you see, he had the sort of face that would make the softest jury in the world think "guilty" the moment they set eyes on him. So he walked into the room with the hat flattened out and at a crazy angle on his head, and he's doing this wild walk as if he were drunk. He looked like Crazy Guggenheim.

A cop behind the lights asked him his name.

Joe walked up to the microphone and said, "Joe."

"Joe what?"

"Joe Guarino."

There was a pause and the cop asks: "Mr. Guarino . . . have you ever been in a mental institution?"

Everybody broke up at that, even the cops. I almost fell on the floor I was laughing so hard. Here I was under arrest for one beef and about to go to prison for another, but I couldn't stop laughing.

The cop asked Joe what he had been doing before the arrest, and Joe said he had been with me.

"What were you doing in such good company?" the cop asked, and everybody started laughing again.

"He's my friend," Joe said. "Sometimes I go over to his house and steal a meal."

"You stole a lot more than a meal, Mr. Guarino," the cop said.

It went on like that for a while. Joe and that cop could have played the Catskills.

THE LINEUP CAME to nothing. I was right—the cop who arrested Eddie couldn't identify Joe or me. He had never seen our faces. That meant we would probably be back on the streets soon. But something very weird happened on our way out of police headquarters. They were taking us back to the South End station and we were loaded into a big van with about twenty-five other men. I looked around and noticed that I was the only prisoner not wearing handcuffs. The van suddenly stalled in the middle of the street as it pulled out of police headquarters. The door to the van was opened, and right after that two officers who were nearby suddenly disappeared. Then it all became clear—they were hoping I'd make a run for it so they would have an excuse to kill me.

Joe, Eddie, and me just looked at each other. Finally, another van pulled up about fifty feet away and they told us to get into it. I was the last one out of the stalled van. Cops lined both sides of the street and they were all looking at me. I sprinted to the other van.

The cops back on the South End knew they had to let us go, but they dragged their feet until Dan O'Connell came up with a payoff—1000 dollars apiece for Joe and me. Most of the cops in those days were just as crooked as us.

A FEW DAYS later Danny Puopolo and me were steered to a jeweler who was known to carry around a lot of cash. We got 8000 dollars and a handful of good-size rocks. All this we turned over to Jack Ass who paid O'Connell.

The DA's people wanted to put us away for twenty years on the supermarket beef, but O'Connell made a deal with a judge he knew, Lewis Goldberg. In exchange for a payoff to the judge, we would plead guilty, draw a five-year sentence, and be out in less than two.

O'Connell told me all this beforehand, and warned me to keep my mouth shut. I couldn't even tell Danny, who assumed we were going to serve at least five years. Meanwhile, O'Connell was afraid I'd blow the deal with all my activities.

There was one other hitch and it had nothing to do with me. Just a few months before my case came up, Suzanne Clift, a debutante and niece of the actor Montgomery Clift, killed her boyfriend in her grandmother's Beacon Hill mansion. She shot the poor bastard in the head and left him sprawled naked on her bed. I always heard that she also cut off his joint, although it was never mentioned in the papers. Anyway, she took off to Brazil and the boyfriend was found by the grandmother three days later. Suzanne came back to Boston and was hit with a second-degree murder charge. But by the time she went to court her family had supplied her with a squad of expensive lawyers and psychiatrists and a flock of prominent character witnesses. The judge was none other than Lewis Goldberg. Not only did he allow her to plead guilty to manslaughter, he sentenced her to ten years *probation*—as long as she voluntarily checked into a mental institution.

All that went down in February, and there had been a bit of an outcry. Goldberg was getting some heat, and Dan O'Connell wanted to bring me before him in the fall, when things had cooled off. But he was so afraid I'd wreck everything with one arrest too many that he rushed me into court in March. He said it was a good thing I was getting off the streets; something bad was bound to happen if I didn't, and he was probably right.

O'Connell also worried that somebody might decide to investigate Goldberg before I saw him, and that his superiors would transfer me to a tough judge. Luckily, we went to court as scheduled on March 21, and before the session started O'Connell went into Goldberg's chambers. When he came out he sat down next to me and whispered, "I got you five years at the Concord Reformatory."

I whispered back: "I don't want to go to Concord. I want to go to Walpole. All my friends are there."

O'Connell made a face and sighed. "All right, I'll be back in a minute."

A little while later, O'Connell was whispering to me again: "Okay, three-to-six at Walpole. You'll still be out in less than two." That was fine with me, but why three-to-six, I wanted to know. It was an unusual sentence. Normally it's three-to-five.

O'Connell explained the extra year: "That's for the judge, to make him look good."

Judge Goldberg came out after that and called the court to order. It was a little like watching a movie after somebody has told you the ending.

Danny, who was in the dark about the fix, couldn't believe the light sentence.

Almost immediately we found ourselves on a van bound for the prison. On the way we stopped at the county jail to pick up men who had been sentenced the previous day. A group of them came toward us and I spotted a familiar face. It was Eddie Greco, who had just gotten a three-to-seven sentence for the Peppermint Lounge beef.

It was good seeing him, and made the thoughts of my immediate future a little more pleasant.

CHAPTER SEVEN

THE JOINT

THE DAY BEFORE we went up to Walpole, Henry Noyes sent for Joe Semenza and asked him to send word to his friends there so we wouldn't have any problems. Joe had already taken care of it. One of his closest friends from the old days was Tony Pino, the man behind the Brinks robbery back in 1950. Another inmate who was asked to look out for me was Joe D'Urbano. I had known Joe when I was a kid. Everybody liked him. He was colorful and funny and had a lot of spirit. Whenever he saw me he'd yell "catch" and two bits would fly into my hand. One day when I was ten, I stopped at a candy store to buy bubble gum on my way to school and glanced at the newspapers. Pictures of Joe and two of his friends were on the front page. They had killed the owner of a gas station during a stickup.

All three guys got life and were sentenced to Charlestown State Prison. Joe was only sixteen when this happened. Joe Semenza was in Charlestown at the time and took care of them. He showed them how to adjust, how to do their time. Now, Joe Semenza was asking Joe D'Urbano to do the same for me.

*   *   *

WALPOLE WAS A new prison, an enormous modern-looking place. We were put in Block 8, where all the new arrivals went for the first two weeks. While a guard was explaining the rules of the institution I noticed three black inmates staring at us. They were obviously veterans of the place and the guard didn't explain why they were there. He didn't have to—as soon as he left they wasted no time in making introductions.

Their leader was a big lifer named Henry Hunt. He was a stool pigeon and had been given the run of the new men's section as a reward. He and his pals were on the prowl for fresh new boys to turn into punks. A punk was an inmate who served other inmates. That meant things like washing underwear and satisfying a lot of sexual hunger. Hunt and his pals were like starving wolves let loose in a meat locker. And what could have looked more tempting than an eighteen-year-old white boy.

"Hey you!" Hunt yelled.

"What do you want?" I said.

He pointed to the corner. "I want you to get that bucket and clean every bar on the flats [the cells on the block]."

"Gee, there's a lot of bars there," I said.

"That's right, boy," Hunt snapped. "There's the sink, fill it with water. There's the soap and sponge, now get to work."

"If you want me to do all that work, you fill the bucket and get the soap and sponge."

Hunt looked at me. "All right," he said, and to my surprise he went to the sink and filled the pail. After that he handed it to me along with the soap and sponge.

Calmly, I wet the sponge. Then I stuck my arm out and raced up the cell block, touching the top bar of every cell with the sponge. On my way back I let the sponge brush against every bottom bar. This took less than a minute. Then I dumped the sponge in the bucket, picked up the bucket and slammed it into the sink.

I whirled around to face Hunt, who was at a loss for words. Before he could say anything a burly dark-skinned man with a big head and thick black hair came up and immediately started yelling at Hunt and the other two with a finger in their faces. The three blacks melted away and the burly inmate walked over to introduce himself. His name was Joe Barboza and he said that Tony Pino and Joe D'Urbano had sent him. They were in the minimum security section of the prison, and would see us in the gym that night.

I thanked Barboza but said he didn't have to intervene, we could have handled Hunt and the others ourselves.

"It's better this way," Barboza said. "Now, nobody will bother you." Then he left.

THAT NIGHT I met Joe D'Urbano for the first time in eight years. He greeted me warmly and introduced me to Tony Pino, who I had been hearing about for most of my life. Tony was round and stubby and in his late fifties. I could see right away that he was very witty and a good guy.

They told us—Danny, Eddie, and me—to put in for Block 7. Two of my friends were already there, Joe Gorilla and Joe D'Minico. Their beef was pure bad luck. They had been driving to a score in Revere and there was an accident along the way. A cop became suspicious when he noticed that the two Joes stared straight ahead, and didn't even glance at the wreck or the flashing lights. He pulled them over and found guns and burglary tools in the car. Those guys were in prison so much that it was like their home.

Barboza was in Block 7 too, and when our two weeks of "orientation" were over, that's where Danny and me wound up. Eddie was put in a different block.

Barboza seemed to want to be my pal. I had heard a little bit about him before I got to Walpole. He was Portuguese and originally from New Bedford, Massachusetts, the old whaling town. Most of his life had been spent in institutions. At Concord he had led a riot and beat up several guards. He was in Walpole now on a parole violation. His nickname was "the Animal," and in the years ahead newspaper and magazine stories almost always referred to him as Joe "the Animal" Barboza. When it came to killing, I always thought he was more of a device than an animal. Yet, Joe "the Device" Barboza didn't have the same ring. Barboza himself preferred to be called "the Baron." He even had his last name legally changed to Baron when he got out of Walpole. We didn't have much in common, but like many men who crossed my path he was a former boxer.

He treated Danny and me well and gave us steak sandwiches from the kitchen every night. Barboza had a sense of humor too. Danny was determined to use the time to get his GED, so our first day in Block 7 he went to the library and came back weighed down with all these books. They were thick too; one looked about two feet wide. Danny could barely carry them all. Barboza did a double take and said: "What's he gonna do? Jump over the wall?"

One night Barboza came over to my cell and after some small talk said, "That supermarket you got busted on, wasn't there a third party?"

"Yes there was," I replied. "And nobody knows who it is."

"I think I know," Barboza said.

"Let's talk about something else."

"It was Jack Ass, wasn't it?"

I didn't like the way the conversation had turned. "Joe, it doesn't matter who it is," I said. "It's not good to talk about these things."

"That's okay, but I know it's Jack Ass," Barboza said.

The next night Barboza came over again and told me he was going to do me a favor.

Whatever the favor was I didn't want to know about it and changed the subject.

I HAD OTHER worries: I was barely settled in at Walpole when a warrant came ordering me to appear at a probation hearing. They were trying to slap another three years on to my sentence for violating the probation on that Wakefield burglary.

They threw me into a van and I was on my way to the Middlesex County Court in Cambridge before I had a chance to call anybody. Eddie Greco was going back for the same beef and we rode together. His lawyer was waiting for him when we got to court. It was Leavitt, the wiseass.

When we sat down he leaned over and whispered: "You want me to represent you?"

"You! No way!" I said, so everybody could hear. "With you, I'll get another three years."

But I had to have help, because on the bench sat a man who had to be the toughest judge in Massachusetts. Felix Forte had handed out life sentences to the Brinks gang. You couldn't make deals with this judge. He'd slap three years on you in a blink if he felt like it. The probation officer began making noises about how bad I was and wanted to get started right away, but I stood up and said I didn't have a lawyer, and hadn't been allowed to call one. When I told Forte that my lawyer was Dan O'Connell. He softened a little and agreed to put off the hearing till the next morning. He and O'Connell had been on the bench together. I called my mother and told her to get hold of O'Connell right away. But the next morning the court officer started calling the cases and O'Connell wasn't around. He finally walked in just as my case came up.

"Hold everything," he boomed from the back of the courtroom. Then he strode right up to the bench.

"I know this boy," O'Connell pointed at me. "He's being reformed right now in Walpole." He said I was taking up a trade, carpentry, and that would make me a good citizen when I got out. It was hard not to laugh: Walpole didn't have a carpentry program.

When O'Connell was done, the probation officer got up and waved a stack of papers at the judge.

"Look at this, your honor! Look at this record! All these arrests! Assault, robbery, burglary. He's running wild in the streets!" He demanded that Forte keep me off the streets an additional three years.

Forte studied the record for a few minutes and looked up angrily at the probation officer. "Why are you so persistent now? This man has been arrested for burglary, he's been arrested for assault. If you had violated him before, he wouldn't be in Walpole for armed robbery now," he said. "Why didn't you violate him then?"

Of course, the probation officer couldn't very well tell Forte that the authorities were looking to send me away for a long time on something big and let some of the minor stuff slide.

Whatever excuse the probation officer gave, Forte didn't buy it: "I sentence this man to let the three years run concurrently." The probation officer packed up my records and stalked out of the courtroom.

IN THE JOINT you live in a space a little bigger than your average closet. And you sleep just a few feet from your toilet. After lights out, a guard beams a flashlight on you every hour. If he doesn't see some flesh in the bed, he opens the cell and shakes you awake. If that happens too many times they haul you off to solitary. Every day you're ordered around, by shouts of guards or squawks of loudspeakers. It takes a long time to adjust to all that. I also had a hard time adjusting to the other inmates. Again and again, I got into trouble for fighting. Finally, I got moved to Norfolk prison, which is about a mile from Walpole. Barboza somehow learned about the transfer before anybody else, and was the first to give me the news.

He told me something else: "Buddy McLean is at Norfolk. He would like to see you."

"Sure, I'd like to see Buddy," I said. "The last time we talked was at the amateur fights. He was with Paul Raymond."

Barboza nodded. "Good. When you get to Norfolk, look for Buddy. Don't let him look for you."

I said nothing.

*   *   *

BUDDY HAD BEEN convicted on a concealed weapon charge the year before and had become friendly with Barboza at Walpole. I spotted Buddy just after I arrived at Norfolk. He saw me coming and stuck out his hand. We chatted a while, and he brought up Big Ed Marino, who had been killed in a stupid barroom argument in 1960. We both had liked him and we both missed him.

"Joe's going to do the favor you asked," Buddy said.

I just looked at him and didn't say anything.

"I'll be leaving here soon," he said. "Rico Sacramone is being transferred here. Stay with Rico. He's nice people."

I said I already knew Rico, we had boxed together. He was a good man.

There was no more talk about the favor and not long after that Buddy was out on parole.

At Norfolk there were more fights and that cost me a shot at parole in May of 1964. By September of that year I was back at Walpole. I didn't have to deal with Barboza—he had been freed in April.

Despite my reputation as a troublemaker, Tony Pino was able to get me into the minimum security section, and that's where I served the remainder of my sentence. There were windows in minimum security, which meant natural light and a little fresh air, and that makes all the difference in the world when you're doing time.

In the movie *The Brinks Job*, Tony was played by Peter Falk. It was a good performance, yet there was a lot more to Pino than the lovable, wisecracking slob of a thief you see on the screen. He was an expert at disguise and the best of actors—he could pretend to be anybody and pull it off as well as an Olivier. Using those gifts, he could blend like a chameleon into any place he wanted to rip off. When it came to conceiving and executing robberies, he had the imagination and precision of a composer writing and conducting a symphony. Pino is best known for the Brinks heist on January 17, 1950. But for years before that his crew had been stealing piles of money from Brinks trucks and Brinks customers and nobody ever caught on.

Pino was fifty when he was sentenced to life in prison, yet he did his time like a man and never complained. Although he had no education he was highly intelligent, and one of the funniest people I've ever known. He was always clowning around and could make you laugh all day.

Joe Semenza loved him and used to talk about him all the time when I was growing up. When Joe got out of prison in the summer of 1955, the FBI and the cops were on Pino's tail constantly. The heat was full blast and it must have taken its toll, but that never stopped Tony from helping out a friend. He had Joe meet him at a coffee shop on Prince Street, just a stone's throw from the Brinks building. Tony couldn't stay in one place very long because he was being followed all the time.

"Joe, take care of yourself," Tony said and shoved five one-hundred dollar bills into his pocket. Joe couldn't thank him enough, but Tony had to run. Joe split the money with Angie DeMarco and used the rest to marry his girlfriend.

The following year Tony and seven of the Brinks crew were hit with an indictment only four days before the statute of limitations expired. They had been betrayed by one of their own, Specs O'Keefe.

Not long after the heist, Specs and another Brinks bandit, Stanley Gusciora, were arrested in Pennsylvania on relatively minor charges. Sensing they might have found a weak link, the federal government made sure Specs and Gus got the toughest sentences possible. Joe Semenza told me that both men were repeatedly beaten in prison to get them to talk. Gusciora ultimately died from all the abuse, yet he never cracked.

Specs was released on parole in 1954 and came back to Boston a loose cannon. He accused the others of holding out on him, and even claimed that they had set him up to be arrested. An ailing sister had wound up as a charity case, and he blamed his partners for not taking care of her while he was away. They had all agreed not to divide the money until the statute of limitations expired, on January 18, 1956, but Specs wanted his share now. He began sticking up crap games and bookie joints where the other Brinks guys hung out. At one point he even kidnapped Tony Pino's brother-in-law, Vinnie Costa, who lived on Hanover Avenue in the North End. Worst of all, Specs was suspected of shooting off his mouth about the heist to anybody who would listen. He was clearly unstable, and a guy who is unstable cannot be trusted.

A notorious hit man from New York, Elmer (Trigger) Burke, was imported to take care of him. Specs was climbing out of his car in a Dorchester parking lot on June 16, 1954, when another car roared to a stop alongside and somebody inside opened up with a machine gun. Specs, who was on his way to see a girl-friend, was not seriously wounded, even though the gunman blasted forty slugs at him point-blank. The story I always heard was that Trigger liked Specs and didn't want to hurt him.

A couple days after the shooting Trigger was arrested in a Boston rooming house and the cops found an arsenal, including the machine gun. He was already wanted for murdering a friend during an argument on Manhattan's Upper West Side and the cops may have hoped his capture would be the big break in the Brink's case.

But two months later gunmen broke into an old carriage entrance to the Charles Street Jail. They went straight to the yard and, as a shocked and helpless guard watched, walked out with a very grateful Trigger Burke. They got away in a car that was driven by a hood dressed as a woman. It was a spectacular jail-break, and it happened on August 29, 1954—my tenth birthday.

The law finally caught up with Trigger down south the next year and he eventually went to the electric chair at Sing Sing prison in New York State. By the time he was arrested the Brinks investigators didn't need him, since Specs had finally caved.

After recovering from his wounds Specs was jailed again on a parole violation. By mid-January 1956 the federal statute of limitations had already run out, and there were only days to go on the state statute. That's when Specs sent for the authorities and told them everything they wanted to know. He squealed and sent Pino and the eight other surviving robbers to prison. In spite of the convictions and in spite of spending more than 20 million dollars on the case, the FBI found only a fraction of the 1.2 million dollars in cash stolen from the Brinks building.

B EING WITH TONY Pino was good for me and thanks to him I finally settled into prison life. He got me a job in the kitchen for awhile, then in the warehouse. You were supposed to unload trucks in the warehouse, but usually only one truck a day would come in, and it would be carrying one box. I just hung around all day. It was beautiful. Pino had a lot of clout at Walpole, and sometimes it seemed like he ran the place. Within the prison kitchen he had his own private kitchen, and every day I ate Italian food that was as good as anything you could find on the outside: linguini with clam or marinara sauce, tomato sauce made from fresh tomatoes, sausages. Once in awhile we even had lobsters. Where they came from and how Pino got them I don't know. The other men in our section were all solid and reliable. There was mutual respect and no rivalries or craziness. Nobody had anything to prove. Most of the other Brinks robbers were there and I became friendly with all of them, especially Adolph (Jazz) Maffie and Vinnie Costa.

The section was a who's who of New England crime. Just across from my cell was Croce (Charlie) Centofanti, a famous bank robber. Us younger guys thought Charlie was cool because he owned two Thompson submachine guns equipped with silencers. When he was only fifteen the papers nicknamed him "Houdini" for his escape from an East Boston courthouse. After the cops brought him back he told the judge: "I intend to be a good boy from now on," and the judge let him go. That was back in the thirties and Charlie had been in and out of the can ever since. He tried to break out of Walpole too, through the ventilation system, but got stuck—he was too thick. Charlie was as mean looking as they came, but he passed the time playing jazz or rhythm and blues on his guitar. He even wrote some of his own songs.

Next door to Charlie was a man I'll call Gerry O'Brien, an Irish-Italian guy from the West End of Boston. Gerry and his partner, Lefty Gilday, had stuck up a Greek bookmaker, who then did a very unusual thing for a bookmaker—he reported the robbery to the cops. Gerry and Lefty got fifteen years on that beef. Maybe because he was half-Irish and half-Italian, Gerry was always able to strike a balance and stay friendly with everybody. For instance, he was probably the only man who socialized with *both* sides in the McLean-McLaughlin War and lived to tell about it.

Lefty had played a little professional baseball before turning to crime full time—that's how he got his name. After getting out on the bookie robbery beef, he got mixed up with a crew of young radicals. They killed a cop and Lefty wound up back in Walpole. Today, he's considered one of the best jailhouse lawyers in the country. He's gotten a lot of guys off, though he's still doing time.

A few cells from them was Rocco Balliro, who had twice busted out of the Charles Street Jail and once from the New Bedford House of Correction. During one of his escapes, he sought out Joe Semenza, who had met one of Rocco's brothers while he was doing time. Everybody was looking for Rocco, but Joe successfully smuggled him out of Boston and sent him to a friend in Connecticut. Rocco was supposed to lie low there until things cooled off. But a few days later Joe got a frantic call from his friend.

"Joe, what kind of guy did you give me? He sneaked out and I found him casing a supermarket down the street! This guy's crazy! Where'd you find him?"

Rocco was in Walpole for a double murder. He and his twin brother, Salvatore (Rudy) Balliro, got into a nasty shoot-out with the cops in February 1963. Rocco's girlfriend, Toby Wagner, and her two-year-old son, Mark, were killed in the cross fire—she had smuggled him hacksaw blades when he was in New Bedford. Rocco was charged with their murders, though he always said they were shot by the cops. Nevertheless, he pled guilty so Rudy could get off on a lesser charge.

JOE D'URBANO'S LIFE sentence was cut and he was paroled in December 1964, after serving ten years. I was very happy for him. Joe Semenza told me that Joe was just a boy when he went to Charlestown, but prison life didn't bother him and he did his time like a man. Joe D'Urbano has been straight ever since. By the end of 1964 I knew I had a good shot at parole the following May. The new year seemed to hold a lot of promise. Then, on January 26, 1965, I picked up a newspaper. Screaming from the front page was this: 18th GANG VICTIM SLAIN IN REVERE. When I flipped the page the dead man's photograph was staring up at me. It was Jack Ass. A lot of memories and thoughts snapped together in my mind to form the only possible conclusion—this was the "favor" Joe Barboza and Buddy McLean had been talking about. Now, they could claim that I owed them, and as soon as I was back on the street they would be coming to me for a favor in return.

Like it or not, I was mixed up in the McLean-McLaughlin War.

CHAPTER EIGHT

WAR TIME

WHILE I WAS in Walpole, the war got hotter and meaner and gradually took on a life of its own. Like a bonfire that gets out of control and ignites an entire forest, it soon became too big and too savage for anyone to contain. It would consume the men who started it, and many more after them.

Of the original participants, only George McLaughlin is alive today, and that's probably because he got convicted of murder just as the whole thing was about to boil over in 1964. He got drunk at a christening party and killed a young bank clerk. Not only did it have nothing to do with the war, he shot the wrong man. He thought the clerk was someone he had been arguing with at the party. George was sentenced to die in the electric chair, but lucked out again when capital punishment was abolished. His brother Bernie was killed by Buddy McLean, his brother Punchy by Joe Barboza.

Even by underworld standards, the war was an ugly, gruesome business, so much so that the most depraved and monstrous acts became routine. This is only one example:

Frank Benjamin was a guy I knew slightly at Walpole. He and Barboza had been friends since they were teenagers. Within two weeks of his release in April 1964, Frank stopped off to meet some friends at a Boston bar run by Wimpy Bennett, a hood who had some minor role in the Brinks heist. Frank got loaded and bragged that he was going to take out the whole McLaughlin crew. He picked the wrong place to mouth off. Wimpy went to a phone and called Ed Punchy McLaughlin, who said he would be right over and to keep Frank there. But Frank tried to leave, and Wimpy shot him at the bar—in front of more than a dozen people. The customers ran and he dragged the body into a back room. When Wimpy returned to the bar, McLaughlin still hadn't arrived. After a few minutes he went back to where he left the body and found Frank crawling around on the floor. Wimpy quickly shot him in the head. When Punchy finally showed up they agreed that since there were so many witnesses and so much blood the only thing to do was to burn down the bar and dump the body someplace.

But Punchy wanted to do one more thing first—cut off Frank's head and leave it on the doorstep of someone on the McLean side. He got a saw and went to work, and only when he was finished did he notice that Frank had been shot in the head. He asked Wimpy if the gun could be traced. Wimpy wasn't sure—he got it from a cop.

Punchy said in that case the head had to disappear. After setting fire to the bar and leaving the body in the trunk of a car, they drove out to the country, intending to bury the head in the woods. But when they got there they had a falling-out: Punchy, who was unarmed, refused to venture into the woods as long as Wimpy was carrying the gun. Several times he asked Wimpy to hand it over, and the more he insisted the more nervous Wimpy became. Finally, Wimpy took Punchy back to his car and drove off with the head.

That story is told in *Barboza*, the book Barboza did with journalist Hank Messick.

IN EVERY WAR, it is the young, strong, unattached guys who make the best soldiers, and I was a prime recruit. I had to do something, and fast. The parole board let me go on May 21, 1965. That morning I kissed Tony Pino and said good-bye to the rest of the gang. Home was my first stop. It was great seeing my family again. I had missed them. My two brothers were almost nine and almost four. The younger one was still a baby when I went up to Walpole.

Then it was time for some urgent business. I called Joe Semenza and we got together on a corner, the same corner where we had first met shooting dice all those years before. I told him about Barboza and Buddy McLean, how they were trying to draw me in. There had been no one at Walpole I could talk to about it, and Joe was the first to hear the story. We decided it was best to go see Frank Cucchiara and Henry Noyes right away. They were together, standing on Hanover Street, and had been expecting me to come around. Both looked a little older, but they seemed to be in good shape. I was hugged with great affection.

"There seems to be something on your mind," Frank said after a bit. "Is there?"

I said there was.

"Would you like to talk about it?" Frank asked.

"Yes, but not here. Can we go in the Florentine?" All four of us were soon settled in a corner booth and I laid out the whole thing for Frank and Henry.

When I was through Frank said, "Do you have any idea how to handle it?"

"Yes," I said. "I just wanted to let you know what was going on."

"Tell us what your move is going to be," Frank said.

My plan was not to look for Barboza or Buddy. "As far as I'm concerned, nobody told me what the favor is and I still don't know what the favor is. I do know that if I run into them they're going to tell me their good deed and put me under obligation."

"And what will you say?" Frank asked.

"I'll tell them I had no idea what the favor was, that I had no animosity against Jack Ass and wouldn't approve of it. Also,

Frank, if it's all right with you and Henry, I would like to also say I would have to check with you before it goes any further."

Frank said that was perfect, and Henry told me to "do it exactly like that and as soon as something happens, let us know."

BARBOZA'S CAREER AS a hit man began almost the moment he left Walpole in April 1964. He was thirty-two and a free man for only the second time in his adult life. He converted to Judaism to marry a woman he met before he went into prison. (His first wife, who was sixteen years his senior, had divorced him when he went up on another beef). If he found religion, it couldn't have been for more than a couple hours, because he came roaring back to the streets right after the honeymoon. In prison he had gotten tight with Buddy McLean, who knew that he had a very valuable soldier on his side, for there was nothing that Barboza wouldn't do. He was perfect for a war. Never before had anyone come across a guy with so much enthusiasm for the kill. He operated with a speed and precision that was almost mechanical, yet he was so charming and magnetic that his victims usually never even knew they were in danger. He never refused a request that involved the taking of life, and volunteered for a lot of jobs. Word got around and he was soon free-lancing for other outfits.

In his book, he babbles on and on about the crimes of others, but is downright coy when it comes to discussing some of his own deeds, especially murders. In some cases he tells you why this guy or that guy deserved to get whacked, and his part in setting up the hit, but it's always "a gunman" or "some people" with Buddy McLean who pull the trigger. Only once does he come out and admit to killing somebody, and he claims that was in self-defense. In other cases he blames murders that I know he committed on other men.

Some of the people involved in the Plymouth mail robbery were being shaken down by Bobby Rasmussen, who I had known at Norfolk. He did my laundry for two packs of cigarettes a week.

He was a friendly, funny guy and didn't seem the type to put the squeeze on anyone, especially the Plymouth crew.

Anyway, the Plymouth gang offered Barboza 15,000 dollars to take care of the problem, so he had some mutual friends invite Rasmussen to take part in a house score that was supposed to yield 10,000 dollars. The robbers had a key to the side entrance to the house and a combination to the safe. Before they got there, Barboza and Nicky Femia, a member of his crew, covered the floor and furniture with plastic. Then they waited.

The guys who were with Rasmussen arrived and got him to go in first. When he walked through the door Barboza came up from behind and hit him with a baseball bat. Rasmussen went down and Barboza swung the bat again and again. Within minutes, Femia had gathered up all the plastic sheets and he and Barboza had loaded Rasmussen into a car. They drove to Watertown, Massachusetts, and dumped the body. Before they left, Barboza put a bullet in Rasmussen's head. In his book, Barboza describes the slaying in great detail, yet claims "an ex-baseball player" wielded the bat and that he wasn't even there. Barboza was called "the biggest killer." He was also the biggest liar.

For Barboza, violence was always the solution. He would kill without hesitation, and swiftly as a cobra. Jack Ass, for instance, had invited Barboza over to his place for a drink. As he was reaching for a bottle in the kitchen, Barboza shot him in the head. To this day I don't know why Barboza killed Jack Ass. As I said before, Jack Ass was a suspect in the Plymouth job. He never mentioned the robbery to me, and personally, I don't think he had much to do with it. But who knows, maybe Barboza was taking care of another problem for the Plymouth crew. Then again, maybe he really did do it to put me in his debt.

Another time, two men from Providence turned up in Boston with a load of hot television sets. Barboza didn't like one of the men, but pretended to be interested in buying their goods. As soon as the coast was clear, he shot them both in the back of the head and stuffed their bodies in the trunk of a car.

Inflicting pain was his sport, his entertainment. He loved

to slice and slash and beat men bloody with a club. After all, once you're dead you can't feel anything. One of his rackets was a shylock business and he couldn't wait for customers to fall behind on their payments because that gave him an excuse to hurt them. I think he deliberately made loans to bad risks. There was a skinny North End kid about my age, Wacky Jackie Civetti, who was a real bug, but a nice, funny bug. He borrowed money from Barboza, and ducked when it came time to pay. Wacky Jackie knew how dangerous Barboza could be, and didn't care. "To hell with him, let him come after me," he said. He was always game for crazy stunts like that. That's how he got the name Wacky. Barboza went crazy looking for him, but couldn't find him. This went on for weeks. Finally, Barboza spotted Wacky Jackie on Fleet Street, jumped out of his car and just slashed him until there was blood all over the pavement. Wacky Jackie came out of it with a lot of scars on his chest, arms, and neck, but at least he lived.

I KEPT CLEAR OF Buddy and Barboza until July 1965, when Barboza's closest friend, Romeo Martin, was found shot to death in his car, the twenty-third victim of the war. The night he was killed he had told his twenty-year-old bride that he had an appointment. Martin drove a short distance from their apartment in Revere and stopped to pick up a passenger—who immediately pumped five bullets into his chest.

Word quickly got around that the killer was Barboza himself. Martin had had a long-running feud with a hard-nosed police detective named Walsh, and blamed him for the death of a friend at the hands of police a couple of years earlier. Because of all the murders, Walsh had been turning up the heat, and Barboza thought if he made a "gift" of Martin to the cops there would be less pressure on him. He had a deadly logic. It probably made perfect sense to him. Yet there may have been an additional motive: Barboza knew that Martin had more balls than he could have on his best day, and for that reason feared him.

Romeo Martin's funeral was at St. Leonard's Church on Hanover Street, across from the Florentine. I stood in front of the Florentine and watched the six pallbearers bring out the coffin. As they came closer I saw that Barboza was one of them. He spotted me in an instant and as soon as Martin's casket had been loaded into the hearse he came bounding over and shook my hand.

"You've been out two months and didn't come to see me." He sounded like someone who's been ignored by an old friend.

"I've been very busy straightening out things," I said.

Barboza said he could understand that, but he expected to see me, and soon. "I'm at the Ebbtide Lounge. I'm there almost every night and never miss weekends. I can't really talk now because of the funeral."

"I'll see you there this weekend," I said.

"Good," Barboza said, and went back to comfort the mourners. A big flowery wreath was carried out of the church. That was a gift from Barboza. The family had asked him to be a pallbearer because he was Romeo's friend. And to think he was the one that had put him in the ground.

THE EBBTIDE WAS in Revere, and that weekend I went over there. The best thing is to take care of business like that right away. If you let it linger, it only gets worse. Joe Barboza was at the bar with Rico Sacramone, who I had not seen since Norfolk. We all shook hands and Barboza offered to buy me a drink. The bartender was putting the glass in my hand when Barboza said, "I took care of that favor."

I turned to face him. "Salute," I said, and we all raised glasses. I had intended to tell him that there was no favor, and no obligation, but this was Barboza's turf, and a real bad place to disagree with him. There was no telling what was on his mind. Many of his victims died after having drinks and schmoozing with him like this. A gun or a knife could appear in the next instant.

He looked at me, as if sizing me up. "Buddy wants to see you," he said.

I told him I was planning to go down to Cape Cod for a month or two. After two years in Walpole I needed some time at the beach.

"If it's all right with you, I'll see him when I get back," I said.

Barboza tried to pin me to a date, and persisted when I told him I wasn't sure when I'd be back in town. At last we agreed on the middle of September. Then we all shook hands again and I left.

When I told Frank and Henry about the meeting they were worried, but there was little they could do. People like McLean and Barboza seldom come right out and ask you to do this or that. It's never like: We want you with us in the war, or we'd like you to put the hit on somebody we don't like. No, they get you in more subtle ways, and in stages. First you meet this one, then he tells you that one wants to talk to you, and that guy says you ought to see someone else. So you make the rounds, always in public places, and before long this is noticed. Rumors spread: Hey, I think he's with Barboza. He's hanging around with the McLean gang. He's with them. And when that's what everybody thinks, it might as well be true. Then you realize that you have to be on their side because there's nowhere else to go. You're all alone. Now, you need them for protection, and they can make you do whatever they want.

I hoped my strategy would keep me out of that kind of trap. I knew I'd have to go see Buddy McLean alone. Because of the violence, a jittery paranoia had spread like a disease through both factions in the war. If I showed up with someone else, Buddy's suspicions would be set off like a fuse and there was no telling what would happen.

Buddy's hangout—his bunker—was another bar, in Somerville. I drove over there one afternoon in the middle of September. As I was looking for a place to park a big man walked right in front of my car. I slammed on the brakes and he motioned for me to roll down the window.

"What's your name?" he asked.

"Willie."

He told me that Buddy would be out in a minute and to pull the car over to the curb.

When I did he said, "You have to step out of the car, so I can frisk you. If you don't want to be frisked, you can leave."

"You can frisk me," I said and got out of the car.

Buddy McLean popped out a side door of the bar as soon as the frisking was over and put out his hand. He had changed a lot since I first met him at the fights in the Revere Rollaway. The war had made him anxious, hard, and brutal. In the years since he shot Bernie McLaughlin he had killed other men, some in horrible ways. One time he and and some other guys (Barboza was one of them) trapped a member of the McLaughlin gang, a man named Hannon, in an apartment and got him to talk by holding a blowtorch to his genitals. When they had heard enough they killed him. A friend of Hannon, Willie Delaney, had the misfortune to be there with him. Buddy really had nothing against him, but a witness couldn't be allowed to live. They were a little more humane with Delaney—he was handed a fifth of whiskey and some Seconals. After he passed out, he was strangled and thrown in a river along with Hannon. When he wasn't acting as an executioner, Buddy was ordering others to do it for him. But his enemies were not amateurs and killed back. Friends and associates had been slaughtered, and he was afraid to trust the loyalty of others who he had known for years. Betrayal was his greatest nightmare, and for good reason: Again and again he had been the target of the McLaughlin gang.

On the surface he was as outgoing and cheerful as always, but he was quick to anger, as I was about to find out.

"Wasn't that nice of Joe to do that favor you asked for?" Buddy said after we had shot the breeze for a few minutes.

It was time to lay my cards on the table: "Buddy, I'd like

to explain a few things before we go any further. Joe insisted he was going to do me a favor. He never told me what the favor was. If Joe told you otherwise, he's lying."

Buddy was no longer smiling.

"If you didn't know what the favor was why didn't you let me know that in Norfolk?" he snapped.

"I didn't want to create any waves," I said. "And I wouldn't approve of his actions against Jack Ass. And if I did, I would have to consult with Frank Cucchiara."

Buddy flew into a fury. What was going on, why the fuck hadn't I said something before. I didn't budge, and he ended the meeting with this: "Well, now I know where you stand. This will be between you and Joe."

Frank and Henry were very relieved to see me come back from Somerville alive.

"Buddy is not the guy we have to worry about, he bowed out gracefully," Frank said after I told him how it went. "But, when he tells Joe you called him a liar, he'll be looking to clip you. I know you can handle these situations. Just be careful."

SIX WEEKS LATER, Buddy McLean was dead. On the night before Halloween he and Rico Sacramone and another man were cut down by five shotgun blasts in front of a crumbling, abandoned theater in Somerville. When the medics lifted Buddy onto a stretcher they found a pistol in his waistband. Rico told me later that they had been "looking for a couple of guys." Instead, they were the ones who walked right into an ambush. The killer, in a stocking mask and black topcoat, was hiding in a darkened doorway of the old theater.

Buddy was shot in the head and chest and lingered on for a day or two. Rico and the other man pulled through. The hit was a double revenge for the two dead McLaughlin brothers. Bernie McLaughlin had been whacked almost exactly four years before. And eleven days earlier, on October 20, Barboza, Nick

Femia, and Tommy DePrisco had killed Punchy McLaughlin while he was waiting for a bus to go to the murder trial of his younger brother, Georgie. Punchy had a gun in a paper bag, but couldn't get it out in time because he had only one hand—he had lost the other one when Buddy shot him with an automatic rifle. Barboza shot Punchy five times, putting one bullet in his groin.

In his book, Barboza claims that he and his crew had first tried to take out George McLaughlin right in the exercise yard of the Charles Street Jail before his trial. Windows in the Massachusetts General Hospital next door and several apartments on Cambridge Street looked right down on the yard, excellent perches for a rifleman. Barboza said he was able to get into these places easily, but George refused to come out of his cell, probably guessing what his enemies had in store for him.

It was two members of the McLaughlin crew, Connie Hughes and his brother, Steve, who whacked Buddy McLean. Steve Hughes, the most feared of the McLaughlins, was the triggerman. His strategy was to clip McLean first, then Barboza.

"What good are a tribe of Indians without a chief," he once cracked to a friend.

Barboza struck back two weeks later. Frank and Henry had warned me that he had been spotted in the North End. On November 15, they sent for me, and Frank asked how friendly I was with a guy named Bobby Palladino.

"I met him in Norfolk, not that friendly," I said.

"Good. Were you with him recently?" Frank wanted to know.

"No."

Frank finally got to the point: "Palladino's dead. Barboza killed him early this morning not far from your house."

Palladino had tried to stay neutral in the war, but Barboza suspected him of siding with the Hughes brothers. Femia and Barboza invited Palladino out for drinks at the Iron Horse bar in the North Station. They stayed there for several hours. When the

three of them got into a car to leave, Barboza shot Palladino in
the back of the head. In his book, Barboza said the slaying was
so bloody that the killers had to take off all their clothes and
toss them down a sewer, and torch the car.

Palladino was the twenty-eighth victim of the war.

CHAPTER NINE

BARBOZA

BY EARLY 1966 Barboza had temporarily forgotten about me and moved on to bigger things. He became an executioner for the Italian mob bosses. The war had nearly wiped out the Irish gangs who had once acted as enforcers for the wiseguys. The Italian mob in Boston had always been smaller than in other large cities, and much of the work was handled by others. That structure had been battered by the conflict, and some of the more independent racketeers began to think they could operate on their own, that maybe the wiseguys had gotten soft. The mob bosses in Providence realized that order had to be restored, and defiance stamped out. Like most rulers, their authority was built on prestige—on the *idea* that they held power—and they couldn't afford to have anyone scoffing at them. The chaotic situation also presented an opportunity—to take advantage of the disarray and simply seize control of all the rackets. Anyone who didn't want to go along was to become another victim. Here, greed was the primary motive. The bosses couldn't resist a chance to make some more money.

Barboza was their instrument. They used him to wipe out anyone who was independent or even looked independent. Now,

I should note something here—although Barboza worked with and for Italians, he harbored a special animosity toward wiseguys and their friends. He saw the mob as a vast conspiracy to shut him out of the big time. At the same time he had an insane hope—to one day be the first non-Italian inducted into the mob, the first Portuguese made man. Maybe he thought he could make that happen by wiping us out. Barboza hoped that working for the bosses would be his entrée into the mob. It was a foolish wish.

His work for the mob didn't prevent him from settling a few scores on the side. First there was Connie Hughes in May, and Steve in September. Both died the same way, riddled with bullets while driving on a highway. In both cases, gunmen in other cars opened fire on them with M-1 automatic rifles. Connie Hughes's car crashed and caught fire. One bullet smashed through a car a block away and embedded itself in a house.

Steve Hughes was killed with an old bookie, Sam Lindenbaum, who was driving the car. Apparently, they spotted the two cars tailing them and tried to get away. But the killers caught up and blasted away in a murderous cross fire. The slugs tore Lindenbaum's fingers off as he was holding the steering wheel. Steve Hughes, who had a loaded pistol on the seat beside him, had been shot twice before in previous assassination attempts. That March he had been hit five times in an ambush.

The only survivors this time were two Chihuahua dogs in the backseat.

BARBOZA'S CREW WAS almost as dangerous as him. His best friend, Nicky Femia, who was from East Boston, used to come around the North End by himself once in awhile and I got to know him, though with somebody like that you can't afford to turn your back. He was tall and dark with short wavy hair and always had a thin moustache. Though he looked about forty, he was only in his mid-twenties.

My parole required that I have a legitimate job, and I

worked as a manager at a North End restaurant that was run by a man friendly with a lot of wiseguys. Wednesday nights the place always served something special; we'd roast a pig or boil lobsters. By the winter of 1966 these cookouts had really caught on. The restaurant was jammed every Wednesday, and the crowd always included several mobsters. Even wiseguys from New York had heard about the place and would drop by when they were in town.

Barboza knew about these feasts and who went to them, and got the idea that he could settle a lot of scores all at once by going in and taking out the whole joint. How many he planned to kill I don't know—I'm sure he would have loved to blast the St. Valentine's Day Massacre right out of the record books. Barboza was so taken with this bloody scheme that he couldn't resist sharing it, and word got out. So on the Wednesday night it was supposed to go down, the restaurant was empty. We didn't have a single customer. You'd think we had been serving rat poison. It was a cold, bitter night outside, and with nothing to do I took a seat at the bar. I had been there for awhile when five rough-looking guys came trooping into the dining room, and I recognized three of them: Chico Amico, Tommy DePrisco, and Tashi Bratsos. Barboza's men. I didn't know what the hell to expect. If they wanted to wipe us out they could do it. No problem. I had a gun on me, but it did no good; they were five-handed. Behind me, the bartender was shaking so much I thought he was going to break something.

The owner went over and spoke to them, and after awhile they turned around and left. They probably figured if that they were going to make a move, why kill just one or two when they were looking to whack eight or ten. As it turned out, Femia was waiting in a car outside.

Barboza, the man who dreamed up the whole thing, was temporarily off the streets, serving six months at Deer Island for disturbing the peace. But like I said, his crew was almost as dangerous as Barboza himself.

*   *   *

MY OLD CREW was slowly but steadily coming back together. Eddie Greco and Danny Puopolo were back on the streets, and we hit the big time with bank jobs and armored car robberies.

Every score was timed down to the last second, and executed like a commando raid. Nothing was left to chance. When a tip on a good score came, I would get all the guys I needed together in an empty social club and bolt the door. First I would say that anybody who wasn't willing to risk doing fifteen years could leave right now and there'd be no hard feelings. They'd still be our friends, they'd just get the lesser jobs. No one ever left. Then, I reminded them there was always the remote chance that we might have to kill someone, even a cop. And if we got caught, that was life, maybe even the chair. Again, no one left.

"All right, who wants to do it?" I'd say, and everybody screamed and howled at the top of their lungs. Once a couple guys got carried away and fired pistols right into the ceiling. Luckily, nobody was home upstairs.

We were all friends on a secret mission, and the camaraderie pumped us up, so that when it came time to do the job we were all on adrenaline. The police, prison, even dying didn't scare us. We literally fought each other in the rush to be first inside the places we hit. The guy in front would be shoved aside by someone else. Then somebody would grab him by the hair and cut ahead of him. No one ever held back.

The excitement was all natural too, because I didn't allow booze and drugs. If I saw a guy take even a nip before a job, he was out. Every man was expected to stayed in shape. I jogged all the time and could run ten miles in the heat. I did push-ups by the hundred so I'd have no trouble picking up sacks of money.

After a score we occasionally put on suits and went out to a nightclub or fancy restaurant, though we were careful not to be flashes and attract too many eyes. Those celebrations were always kind of "so what" affairs. After all, what could we do that was more exciting than the heist we had just pulled off. It was much more fun to plot even bigger and better scores.

In those days kids didn't usually leave home until they got

married or moved out of town, and me and my crew were no exception. Everybody lived with his family, it was the routine thing to do. We kept side apartments for girls and parties and stashed weapons, cash, and cars in various places. One night I came home very late and found my mother waiting up for me. She was worried and upset and that bothered me.

"Look, I'm twenty-one. I'm grown-up now," I said. "I don't want to see you bothered. I'm better off going back and doing my parole. Then, I'll come back and get my own apartment."

She never bothered me about my activities after that. I couldn't change and she accepted it.

LATER THAT SPRING Frank called my house and asked to see me. When I met him he had bad news: Tony Canadian had cancer, and the doctors had found it too late to save him. It was sudden and shocking. Tony had always been so strong and lively. Young as I was, I had known plenty of people who weren't around anymore, and I had to live with the threat of death every day. In spite of that, Tony, Frank, and Henry had always seemed indestructible, a law onto themselves. They had been around forever, like the cobblestones, like the old brick buildings. It was as if Old North Church had suddenly collapsed.

"He hasn't much time," Frank was saying. I don't think he could believe it either. Tony was home and I went to see him the same day. He looked terrible, yet he was more concerned about me than his own pain.

"Willie, listen to Frank and Henry and you will be all right," he said.

I told him to forget about me, I wanted to help him in any way I could.

"We all have to die," Tony said. "I don't want yours to be premature. Listen to Frank and Henry for me. Listen to them and you'll be all right."

I promised him that I would, and spent the rest of the afternoon with him.

*   *   *

THE OLD MEN were always telling me to control myself, but they had their own rages. A few weeks after I learned about Tony, I got a message from Joe Semenza to go see Henry Noyes at the Florentine right away. When I got there he looked like he was going to explode.

The first thing out of his mouth was this: "Willie, do you have a gun close by?"

"I have one on me," I said.

Henry got up. "Give it to me and come with me over to John's candy store."

Although Henry had been known to blow his top now and then, I had never seen him like this and didn't know what to do. His voice was normal, low and steady, but he had the look of a crazy man. I thought maybe if I talked to him he'd cool off a little. "Tell me what happened first," I said.

"I just had an argument with John. He tried to make me look foolish in public."

"That jerk? He ain't nothing, Henry."

"He thinks he's something when he's drinking," Henry snapped and held out his hand for my .38. There was nothing I could do. Henry was determined to get even with John and I had to back him up.

We drove over and I double-parked outside. John was an old Italian guy about the same age as Henry. He was waiting on a few customers, but as soon as we walked in he began screaming at Henry from behind the counter. I could tell right away that he was drunk as a skunk. He spotted my pistol in Henry's belt, reached under the counter, and took out a shotgun. The barrel was pointed right at my face and I lunged for it just as the thing discharged. A loud roar went off in my ear and something brushed the top of my shoulder. Henry pulled the .38, but John was too quick for him and banged it out of his hand with the barrel of the shotgun. Then he picked it up and started shooting at me and Henry as we dashed out of the store and down the street.

A couple of shotgun pellets had grazed my shoulder and there was blood. Now, I wanted to get back at John. I raced home and got two more guns. As I was about to leave my friend Joe Bono pulled up in my car—I hadn't been able to get to it when John chased us out of the store. Joe was heads up to get the car out of there before the cops had time to start asking questions. While we were talking, Joe Semenza showed up with another message, this time from Frank: He already knew what had happened and I was to put away the guns and go see him.

"I'll handle this from now on, is that clear?" Frank said when I got to the Florentine. Henry was sitting meekly beside him, looking very embarrassed. All the fury was out of him.

"Willie, you don't know how sorry I am for what happened. I almost got you killed." Henry's voice cracked and he had to stop. "If you got killed I would have died."

I smiled at him and tried to make him feel better. "Henry, you don't owe me anything. It's all part of the game. I'm just glad you're all right."

"No," Henry said. "I'm going to make it up to you in a big way. I'm going to do something for you."

Frank and Joe Lombardo were pretty upset with Henry for awhile because he had handled the thing badly. A war was on and the last thing they needed was to have a legitimate guy whacked in broad daylight by a known mobster. John was to be left alone. Nothing ever happened to him and he finally died of natural causes. A couple of days later I got my .38 back. Lombardo had sent one of his men to pick it up from John.

IN MY CALMER moments I knew that getting into trouble was bad for business, and since Walpole I had tried to lay low as much as possible. But sometimes trouble found me, like on that foggy night not long after I heard about Tony Canadian. I had parked my car about a block from my house, and as I was walking home something whacked me hard in the back of the head. Before I could react, a set of brass knuckles slammed into my face. Another blow set off bursts of cartoonish colors in my eyes. I was reeling, and it was all I could do to stay on my feet. There were two of them, one with the knuckles and the other guy had some kind of club. Battered as I was, I fought like it meant my life. I got in close to them and stayed there so they couldn't use their weapons. When it was over they were both on the pavement, knocked out, and I was bleeding like a faucet. Something had fallen on the ground during the fight. It was a pair of handcuffs. My attackers were police detectives. I called Frank and he took me to a doctor who could be trusted not to report certain injuries to the cops. I had taken a bad beating. For the next few weeks my face was covered with patches, and I had no thought except how to get even.

After I healed I bought two boxes of cherry bombs, 144 in all, and laid them out on my parents' kitchen table. Carefully, I sliced open 143 of the firecrackers and dumped the gunpowder in a pile. Then I packed it into one of the cardboard boxes the cherry bombs had come in. I put the last cherry bomb on top of the powder and cut a small hole in the top of the box for the fuse. Finally, I sealed the box tight with tape. It had taken me a couple hours for the whole job. The cops had been bullying and threatening me ever since Blackie and his cronies had fun knocking me around when I was just a kid. Now they had ambushed me right on the street and probably would have killed me if I hadn't been able to fight back. They thought they were tough, but now I was going to cut their balls off.

Of course, a spark could easily have set my homemade bomb off right there in my family's kitchen and blown up me and most of the house, but I wasn't thinking about stuff like that. I was all action. I called a couple friends and we piled into a convertible. Then we headed for the Division 1 police station a few blocks away on North Street—a place I had been in more times than I could count. The fuse was short. I lit it just before we reached the building and heaved the bomb at the front of the station house as we were rolling past. We sped away into the night with a heavy blast thudding behind us. The explosion blew out most of the windows on one side of the station house, and shattered windows at the city printing department building two doors away. One newspaper said it was the first attack on a police station ever heard of—that kind of stuff is only supposed to happen in banana republics. The city wound up with a nice repair bill, but they got off easy—I had been aiming for the gas pumps in the garage. A cop who had been filling up at the time got knocked down by the blast.

I think the cops knew I did it, and—as usual—they had nothing on me, although that didn't stop them from getting a little revenge. This time they used psychology instead of brass knuckles. Rather than come after me, they put the heat on Joe Lombardo, the family's elder statesman. He conducted his business in a restaurant he owned called Giro's on Hanover and Commercial Streets. All of a sudden the cops began slapping tickets on all the cars in front of the place and threatened to tow anybody who was double-parked. And they made sure it got back to Lombardo that they were leaning on him because of the bombing. Their strategy had the desired effect: It made Lombardo furious at me, and you don't want to be on the wrong side of somebody like that. It was a little like being in hot water with the local nobleman back in Italy. Luckily, I had another local nobleman in my corner—Frank Cucchiaria. He told Lombardo that I had been jumped by the cops and blew my top. That smoothed things over, but Frank made it very clear he expected me to keep in line.

Still, I couldn't resist rubbing it in the faces of the cops one more time. A guy my age who I'll call Jimmy Sforza came to me with an idea for a pretty good score at a coin shop. At the end of his spiel Jimmy said there was one big catch: the store was right across from police headquarters. Did I want to do it? he asked. Did I want to do it! I almost kissed him for asking me.

Along with my friend Peter Piso we staked out the store for a couple days. Two men worked there, and there was a back room. The job turned out as smooth as glass. We went in and Sforza and Piso quickly hustled the two guys into the back room and grabbed the coins while I kept an eye on the door. While everybody else was in back, two middle-aged men walked in. One of them was carrying a cardboard box and apparently had an appointment. When they saw what was happening they turned white. With my gun I motioned them over to the counter.

"Take whatever they got," a voice said from the back. I looked in the box. It was filled with old coins.

The man who had been holding it whispered softly: "It's my life savings. Please don't take it."

The guy was scared to death. Sforza and Piso came out with coins from the safe. "What's in there?" one of them said, pointing at the box.

"Nothing," I said. "Let's go." I don't mean to suggest that I was some sort of Robin Hood. My only interest was in getting even with the cops. It didn't make sense to rip off some poor guy who wandered into my revenge. The take was fair, about 20,000 dollars. I didn't care about the money, the thrill was pulling off a heist right under the nose of the Boston police department.

Tony CANADIAN SENT for me again. He was in bed most of the time, and looked worse each time I came around. He told me that he and Frank and Henry were going to do something for me, but didn't say what.

"Will you make a promise to me before I die?" he asked.

Of course, I said.

"Promise me whatever instructions Henry and Frank give you, you will do them for me? It concerns your future. That's my only wish for you."

"I promise."

He smiled. "Good boy. Now, I can rest."

He died on August 28, 1966.

The next day I turned 22, a good age to quit messing around and consider the future. I was not a made man, a member of the family, and that was because I didn't want to be involved with anyone else. I didn't ever want to owe anyone. Being part of somebody else's organization wasn't my nature, and from early on my goal had been to run an organization of my own. I had started with a crew; it was the best around. A crew that good can be the foundation of a family. And for the first time I began to think about starting my own family. Henry and Frank were with me all the way. As I said before, Frank had no love for the crew that was running the Office in Boston. Even when I was in my teens he'd tell me: "Don't let them try to captivate you. Don't bother with anybody except us. We'll take care of you."

If Boston had been a larger city there might've been room for expansion, but Boston has always been a one-family town. So if I was going to establish a new family, it would have to be someplace else.

IN THE MEANTIME, I had more pressing matters. After the murder of Steve Hughes in September, Frank warned me to be very careful: Barboza was looking for me again. My friends stayed with me wherever I went, and I was careful never to be alone. I never left the house unarmed, yet, I couldn't help looking over my shoulder and imagining the winding cramped streets of the North End as death traps. Fortunately, Barboza's luck was about to run out. On November 5, 1966, he was pulled over with Femia, Tashi Bratsos, and Patsy Fabiano, and the cops discovered an M-1 and a .45 in their car. Barboza's bail was set at 100,000 dollars, and he assumed his wiseguy friends would have him back on the street in no time. But the bosses had no more use for their killing machine. The dirty work was done and now Barboza could rot in jail for all they cared.

Bratsos, who had made bail, and Tommy DePrisco were dispatched to collect the money to spring Barboza. They had raised about 70,000 dollars, mostly from shakedowns, when they got to a North End bar, the Nite Lite Lounge on Commercial Street, around midnight on November 17, 1966. They were told to hang out till the place closed at 1:00 A.M., then there would be a meeting and a contribution. After the customers left, Bratsos and DePrisco joined four or five other men at one end of the bar. They discussed the bail money and other subjects, but the talk was just bait. An order had come down—Barboza's men were not to leave the place alive. Bratsos and DePrisco probably didn't realize what was going on until they saw the guns. They were both shot in the head right at the bar. The bodies were found one on top of the other in Tashi's Cadillac in South Boston. The 70,000 dollars disappeared. The Nite Lite was a hangout of some old-time Sicilians, and I always suspected that Frank might have had a hand in the hits. Naturally, he never mentioned it.

When Barboza learned what had happened to DePrisco and Bratsos he went beserk, and ordered Chico Amico and Patsy Fabiano to kill whoever was responsible. This time Barboza's enemies acted first. Amico's car was shattered by automatic-rifle fire as he was pulling away from a bar in Revere on December 7. One of the slugs split his skull. Hours later the Boston district attorney threw Fabiano in jail just to get him off the street.

That virtually demolished Joe Barboza's crew. All his dreams, his ambitions, had suddenly turned to ashes. Because he was a repeat offender, he faced a very long time behind bars and, worse, he was now in great danger in or out of the joint.

It wasn't long before he received a visit from two FBI men who sensed an opportunity. The agents did a great job playing with his head. They played secret tape recordings of a boss belittling Barboza, calling him "a bum" and "expendable." Far from making him one of their own, the wiseguys had cut him loose like garbage. They're wiping out your crew, the FBI men told him. They killed your pals and you're next. On April 11, 1967, Barboza was indicted as a repeat offender. A week later, yet another of his associates, Joseph Lanzi, was murdered in Medford, the forty-fifth victim of the war. Barboza had one chance to stay alive, and that was by helping the Justice Department destroy his former associates. Otherwise, he'd be nailed as a repeat offender and be on his own in the joint.

So Barboza began a new career—as a squealer, and over the next few years he became the FBI's star informant, a key

witness at big mob trials and even before a congressional committee. The government was very grateful, at least for awhile. All
charges were dropped and Barboza was given a new identity in
the federal witness protection program—he was one of the first
to get in on that racket.

For the wiseguys, using Barboza turned out to be a very
big mistake. He put many of them in prison, and it took years
for the mob to recover.

Efforts were made to get to Barboza before he could take
the stand, but it was too late. Without firing another shot he
nearly brought down the organization that had spurned him.

ESCAPES

ON FEBRUARY 24, 1967, the phone rang. It was Albert DeSalvo. I couldn't believe it. He had busted out of the Bridgewater state mental hospital with two other inmates early that day and there had been bulletins all over the radio and television. The news papers that afternoon told people to shut themselves up and lock their doors. One headline even warned: WOMEN BEWARE! HE'S A SMOOTHIE.

Albert was calling from a pay phone in Haymarket Square, just a few blocks from my house, and wanted me to help him. Every cop in the universe was hunting this guy, and he calls me.

Albert had been arrested for several burglaries and sex assaults in 1964. While locked up he confessed to the murders of thirteen women in the Boston area between 1962 and 1964. Most of the victims, who ranged in age from twenty to eighty, had been strangled with stockings and attacked sexually. He supplied stunned investigators with extensive details of the killings, which had terrorized the city. Although some experts didn't believe him and maintained that only five of the murders could have been the work of the same man, Albert convinced enough detectives, psychiatrists, and reporters that he became the Boston Strangler in the public imagination.

Despite the confessions and all the hoopla stirred up in the press, Albert was never tried for any of the Boston Strangler slayings. Instead, he got a life sentence for the robbery and sex charges because he was a repeat offender. His trial had ended just a month before the escape.

AFTER TELLING ALBERT I'd be there in five minutes, I got hold of Johnny Russo, who lived just around the corner. We shot over to Haymarket Square in my car and Albert jumped in the back as soon as he spotted us. He was wearing a thin pea coat and shivering in the cold. We started driving around. I didn't dare stay in one place.

He looked tired and nervous. One minute he'd be the same old Albert, cheerful and always with the wisecracks, the next he'd be jumpy and talking real fast. Now, I had never believed that he was the Boston Strangler. Sure, he was a sex maniac, but I had known plenty of killers in my time and that just wasn't Albert's M.O.

"So what is all this shit I keep reading?" I said, glancing at Albert in the rearview.

"I didn't kill anybody," he said. "Do you think I'd kill an old woman? I'm not that desperate."

"Albert, you're no killer. Don't worry, the word is out. But what the hell happened?"

"Do you remember that guy who killed the gas station attendant after he got out on parole, George Nassar?"

"Sure, I remember him," I said. "What's Nassar got to do with you?"

"He's the one that did the murders. He's the Boston Strangler."

Then Albert told me his story. George Nassar was the first convicted murderer to kill again after being paroled from a life sentence. It was a notorious case. He robbed a gas station in Andover and shot the attendant while the man was on his knees begging for his life. He got pinched and met up with Albert back

in the can. Now, Nassar was a psycho. He never talked to anybody, but Albert the charmer somehow got him to open up, and
admit that he had strangled several women.

That gave Albert a bizarre idea. He was looking at a life
sentence on his beef, but, ironically, the Nassar murders just
might be his ticket out. He would get Nassar to tell him everything, then confess to the murders himself. Nassar's lawyer was
F. Lee Bailey, the young hotshot who had represented Barboza
and cleared Sam Sheppard, the doctor convicted of killing his
wife.

Albert's plan was to plead insanity in the Boston Strangler
case, eventually get off, then clean up with a book and movie
deal. In exchange for that, Nassar would get Bailey to represent
for Albert. The whole thing sounds nutty, I know, but Albert had
great faith in his ability to talk his way out of any mess.

Up to a point his strategy worked like a charm—he got a
lot of people to believe he was the Strangler, and the case generated enormous publicity. But Albert's insanity defense was
thrown out at his trial on the original charges, and he got life. If
he was indicted for the murders and ruled sane, that meant the
electric chair. Yet the state seemed to be in no hurry to try him
again. Meanwhile, everybody else was cashing in on the Boston
Strangler story, his story, and he was stuck in Bridgewater and
his family didn't have a cent. The whole thing had backfired, so
he busted out.

I handed Albert some codes that we used for guys who had
to go on the lam—messages that could be sent over Western
Union whenever money or a place to hide was needed. I also
gave him a couple pay-phone numbers to call in case he needed
to get a message to me. Finally, I gave him a thousand bucks,
and advised him to get very far away real fast. I suggested Canada, he talked about going to Mexico.

We talked and rode around on the expressway for maybe
twenty minutes, and I was anxious to get him out of the car. The
cops would have a field day if they nabbed me with DeSalvo. I
asked Albert where he wanted to be dropped and he said back

in Haymarket Square. He would probably get a bus, he said. He thanked me and got out.

Albert was actually on the verge of giving himself up, which is what he did the next day. The cops said they found no money on him and I don't know what he did with that thousand bucks. It's always bad to have a lot of cash on you when you're arrested, so he probably gave it to somebody or dumped it somewhere.

While we were riding around Albert had told me something interesting: that Nassar lived on Charter Street in the North End while he was out on parole. That made something click. Charter Street is right near Bova's Corner, and I remembered seeing a strange-looking guy walking by there every day. Nassar was not from the North End and any outsider sticks out. You always notice them, especially a weird guy like that.*

I never saw Albert DeSalvo again. He went back in the joint and stayed there. In November 1973 he was found dead in his bed at Walpole. He had been stabbed 24 times.

ABOUT THAT TIME I heard about what had to be one of the most outrageous and ingenious escape attempts ever tried anywhere.

At Norfolk there was a guy from Dorchester named Richie Arquilla, who was a few years older than me. When we got out, he used to come around the North End and we'd get together. Joe Sememza had been tight with Richie's older brother, Louie, at the old Charlestown prison, and he liked Richie too. One time after Richie left, Joe said to me, "You know why those brothers turned out that way? Their father killed their mother right in front of the kids, then killed himself." Joe shook his head, and the conversation somehow got on Louie, and that's when Joe told me about the incredible escape they very nearly pulled off.

Louie first met Joe after being sentenced to Charlestown on a bank robbery beef around the time of the Brinks score. When

*Nassar has denied ever committing the Boston Strangler murders. He has never been charged with any of them.

Louie was paroled in 1956, Joe introduced him to me. I was twelve years old, and Louie thought Joe must be off his rocker to let a boy hang around with him like that. But Joe assured him: "Someday soon he'll fill both our shoes."

Louie's freedom didn't last long enough for him to find out. Only six months after getting out of Charlestown, the feds got him on another bank robbery, and he wound up in Atlanta with a twenty-five-year sentence. There were eight men to a cell in Atlanta. There is a way, a method, to doing hard time, but his only thoughts were of escape. After months of planning, he tried to break out and got caught scaling the big wall. They threw him into isolation, and he soon learned through the grapevine that he was going to be transferred—to Alcatraz. Men went to Alcatraz to be broken. In his cell Louie began doing push-ups and jumping jacks, thousands of them, for hours on end. When he wasn't working out he was pacing his tiny space. He never seemed to stop. The authorities began wondering if he was losing his mind, but Louie's brain and body were fully occupied devising another way out. He knew he would be put on a plane to California, and taken over to Alcatraz by boat. Because he was a known escape risk, there would be armed agents all over him like a cheap suit. Through other inmates he got messages to two friends on the outside, a man I'll call Bobby, and Joe Semenza. They sent word back to him and more messages were exchanged. He let them in on his scheme, and asked for their assistance. There wasn't much time, the transfer was coming up.

Joe loved Louie like a brother and was willing to do anything for him, but his plan was very complicated and sophisticated, and required the aid of a powerful man with big connections. Joe knew of only one man with that kind of influence. He went to see Joe Lombardo, the wiseguy's wiseguy. I don't know if Arquilla and Lombardo were friends, I'm not sure if they even knew each other, but Lombardo went all out to help and really put on a show. I know that he always loved Joe Semenza, and admired him for doing all that time on the Pomo killing without complaint. Maybe that's how he returned the favor.

Whatever his reasons, Lombardo immediately reached out to some friendly politicians and federal judges to learn exactly when and how Arquilla was going to be moved. Once he possessed all the information, he got to somebody who was handling the paperwork and stalled the transfer until everything was set up.

"Everything was working perfectly in our favor," Joe Semenza told me all those years later. "We found out what type of plane was going to be used and the flight pattern to San Francisco. The only thing we didn't know was the exact plane they planned on using. The authorities in both institutions, Atlanta and Alcatraz, were causing some static and questioning why it was taking so long. It was six weeks' overdue until the break came that we needed—from an FBI agent who used to be with the Boston bureau. We thanked J.L. for that one."

The agent took care of everything and assured J.L. that there would be a parachute under the second seat in the second-to-last row, eight feet from the rear exit. A gun and a bobby pin would be hidden in a compartment under the sink. Precisely one hour and five minutes after takeoff, Louie would free himself and order the pilot to lower the altitude to 3000 feet and reduce the speed from 200 to 150 MPH. Then he would parachute from the plane, his friend Tony waiting on the ground to pick him up.

The day finally came, and Louie knew every detail of the operation, thanks to two friends in the prison who had regularly relayed information from the outside.

When he left lockup, he was frisked and taken to the airfield in shackles and handcuffs. Aside from the two agents guarding him, there were no other passengers on the plane.

He acted nervous and told the agents he was afraid of flying. He asked for a cigarette to calm his nerves. All through the flight he complained of air sickness. Exactly fifty-five minutes after takeoff, he said he was having bad stomach pains and asked to go to the lavatory. The agents pulled him out of his seat and hauled him over to the bathroom. There were chains around his waist that were attached to the handcuffs, and his ankles were bound by shackles. One of the agents frisked Louie again, turned him around, unbuttoned his pants and dropped them to his hips. Then the agent closed the lavatory door and told him to knock when he was through.

Louie sat on the toilet and opened the compartment under the sink. Taped to a drainage pipe was a .32 automatic and a bobby pin. Louie quietly freed himself and grabbed the automatic, but it had no ammunition, which made him furious.

He burst out of the bathroom, and the agent who was standing near the door couldn't believe his eyes. Now, it was his turn to be frisked, and Louie discovered that the man was unarmed. He told the agent to call his partner, who was sitting in the front. That agent didn't have a gun either. Louie checked under the seat in the second-to-last row. Sure enough, the parachute was there. Then he went up to the cockpit and told the pilot to bring the plane closer to the ground. He turned away for a second and one of the crew jumped him. Hearing the struggle, the agents rushed up from the rear, wrestled Louie to the floor and slapped the cuffs back on.

Tony was watching the plane from the ground with a high-powered telescope. He was carrying plane tickets, money, and a new passport for Louie. The plane swooped overhead at the right altitude, but no one jumped out.

So Louie wound up on Alcatraz, but not for too long. After the spectacular escape of Frank Morris and the Anglin brothers in 1962, the government shut the place down the following year and moved all the inmates to other prisons. Louie did his time well, and used it to get an education. When I ran into him after his release in 1971 he sounded like a college graduate. His escape attempt was hushed up by federal authorities who feared a public outcry, since he obviously had help from dirty people inside supposedly incorruptible law enforcement agencies, including the FBI. As far as I know it has never been made public until now.

* * *

IT WAS THE mid-sixties. The times were a-changin', as the song went, but in the North End we made sure they didn't change too much, as a bunch of hippies who took an apartment in the neighborhood quickly found out. Actually, we called them beatniks in those days. I didn't mind hippies or beatniks in general, as long as they kept to themselves, but these people were pigs. They were dirty and arrogant, and wandered around their apartment in the nude at all hours with no drapes or shades on the windows. They showed no respect for anybody. Families with little children lived right across from them and were very upset.

All this I learned when an old Italian named Pasquale came and asked for my help.

At first I thought he was kidding around, but I went over to his place and saw them with my own eyes. There was a girl and four or five guys and none of them was wearing anything.

"Don't worry about it. I'll take care of it," I said.

I got hold of a few guys and we went up to the hippie pad a couple days later and knocked on the door. When one of them opened up we rushed in and clubbed them pretty good and broke the place up. The girl we left alone, but she just sat there glassy-eyed like nothing was happening. Anyway, by the next day they had all cleared out.

MUCH MORE SERIOUS trouble came to the North End in the spring of 1967: an arsonist started torching apartment buildings. He usually struck at night when everybody was asleep, and people woke up to find themselves trapped in an inferno. Five people died, two of them kids. I'll never forget the newspaper photograph of a young mother being carried from the funeral of her two children. The family lived just a block from my house. The entire neighborhood was terrorized. For weeks our crew patrolled the streets round the clock and had everybody we knew keep their eyes open. Any outsiders we came across were challenged immediately. Some of them took offense at being given the third degree by a bunch of tough Italian kids and lost their tempers, so we roughed them up. After a while the fires just stopped and the firebug was never caught.

The fires made the neighborhood very edgy, and so did an even more devilish menace that was creeping in—drugs. You may not think of a working-class Italian area as a likely spot to find a serious drug problem, but it was very bad, and still is today. A lot of kids I grew up with became addicts and would think nothing of stealing from neighbors, friends, and even their own families to feed their habits. When I was a boy nobody locked their doors, even when they went out. You could walk right into a friend's apartment and wait for them to come home. But the firebug and the junkies made everyone scared and suspicious. After that, it was locks, bolts, and bars.

Still, there was something to be grateful for: the McLean-McLaughlin War seemed to be over at last, and my friends and I tried to go on as before. When the warm weather came we gathered on Bova's Corner, just as we had for most of our lives.

One day our friend George Macaroni rolled up in his car. His real name was Macalone, but we called him Macaroni. It sounded better.

"Hey Georgie, your tires are bald," Eddie Greco called out. Georgie was always afraid of being taken, and hated to buy anything. But now it was clear he had to get new tires.

Eddie had a friend who sold tires and went to call him up. When Eddie came back he said, "Look, he'll give you a deal on new whitewalls. I just talked to him and he said he'd take care of a friend." So George went over to the garage and came back a couple of hours later with a set of brand new tires, looking like everything was wonderful. That expression only lasted until he got out of the car. His face suddenly turned white, as if he was going to have a stroke or something. Without a word, he jumped back in the car and roared off. Nobody knew what was going on. After a little while it dawned on Eddie that it might have something to do with the tires, and he called his friend. But there was no answer, and the reason there was no answer was because the tire man was sprawled out on the floor, unconscious. George had gone back to the place and punched him out.

When George finally got back to Bova's Corner he shook a finger at the new tires: "That guy tried to fuck me! He said he'd give me whitewalls. These are blue walls. What kind of shit is this?"

We tried to explain to Georgie that the tires were supposed to be blue and that the blue would come off, and that in fact he had whitewall tires. We tried to explain, but we were all laughing too hard to talk.

THE PAPERS WERE full of Barboza singing arias about his former friends. But he had nothing on me, he was in the past. For me, there were bright new opportunities ahead. That spring Frank and Henry asked me to go down to Florida to meet Meyer Lansky.

CHAPTER ELEVEN

MEYER

WHEN IT COMES to gangsters, the name Meyer Lansky is certainly as well known as those of Al Capone, Bugsy Siegel, or John Gotti, yet unlike the last three guys, Meyer never wanted to become a household word, and hated the attention. Like Frank Cucchiara, like Henry Selvitella, like Phil Buccola, Meyer had learned early on that flashiness is dangerous because it brings publicity. And publicity is always very bad for business.

By the mid-1960s, Meyer no longer had the luxury of being unknown. It was bad enough that he had been named by the Kefauver Committee in 1951 as one of the top racketeers on the East Coast, and that Hank Messick in a 1965 *Miami Herald* article had called him "the biggest man in organized crime today" with a fortune of 300 million dollars. But in 1967 his system for transporting money in and out of the country had been exposed and badly shaken. Meyer was in charge of keeping track of the cash skimmed from several casinos in Nevada and the Bahamas. His partners in this operation were wiseguys, who were constantly looking over his shoulder. Couriers, bagmen, took the money in suitcases from Las Vegas and the Bahamas to Miami. From there it went to banks in Switzerland. This system worked very well, until one of the couriers, a Swiss named Sylvain Ferdmann, dropped a piece of paper at the Miami airport listing a mob deposit at the International Credit Bank in Geneva. The paper found its way into the hands of the authorities. FBI bugs had also identified two other couriers, Benny Siegelbaum, an old friend of Meyer, and Ida Devine, the wife of Irving "Niggy" Devine, who had ties to mob men in Las Vegas. Ida Devine hated to fly and carried skim money cross-country by train. She wasn't hard to spot either, for she often wore a mink coat, and came to be known by FBI agents as "the lady in mink."

Some major blunders had been made, yet because the FBI bugs turned out to be illegal, Meyer managed to escape prosecution. In his biography of Meyer, *The Little Man*, Robert Lacey contends that in 1967 Meyer sold out his interests in Las Vegas and pretty much got out of the skimming business.

I can tell you that that is not true. He simply devised a new money-running operation. I know, because I was the courier.

IN MARCH 1967, Frank and Henry told me to go down to Miami "to meet some people." Meyer Lansky's name came up. So did that of Santo Trafficante, the boss of the Florida mob who had a finger or a hand in just about everything. I had heard something about the trouble Meyer was having, yet Frank and Henry were deliberately vague about what was supposed to happen when I got down there. The day before I left I sat down with Frank, and, for once, he did most of the talking. "You've got a good education now," he said. "Put it to work. The impression you give at the beginning is the one you will live by. Be yourself and let your natural instincts be your guide. The important thing is not to be used. What you want to do is your part and no more. If you become used, you will be disrespected. Only you can balance the pendulum. I won't be there to help you. I'll know how things are going from the report I get from Lansky. It's imperative to have a good relationship with Santo Trafficante. He's a good man and a fair man."

Then there were basic rules, rules that Frank himself had

always lived by. "Don't talk to too many people, limit your conversation. Don't socialize, and don't ever drink even a drop of booze."

I wanted to go to the Fountainbleau Hotel in Miami Beach, the swankest mob hangout there was, but Frank told me to check in at the Castaways further up the beach. My instructions were very brief: Go to the Dream Bar on Collins Avenue and the Seventy-ninth Street Causeway and ask for a man called Patty.

A few minutes after I got there we got into a car and drove to a house in North Hollywood. Patty introduced me to the man who answered the door—"this is Santo Trafficante." Santo brought me inside, and said Meyer was waiting for us in the living room. Patty disappeared and I didn't see him again until the meeting was over. I don't know who owned the house, maybe it belonged to Trafficante, but there was no one else around, no hangers-on, no bodyguards.

Meyer Lansky was a small, dapper man in a blue sport jacket and blue shirt open at the collar. Blue was his favorite color and he wore it often. He had a classy manner, and there was nothing showy or phony about him. As soon as he spoke, I could tell that he was intelligent and had a good sense of humor too. In fact, he did most of the talking. I didn't open my mouth unless I was asked a question. Santo was Sicilian and reminded me a little of Frank Cucchira. He joked a little, but mostly watched and listened.

Frankly, Meyer made me feel very comfortable. It was all small talk at first. He was very nonchalant. Then all of a sudden it was right down to business, and he zeroed in on what I had been doing back in Boston. I told him some stuff, though not everything. I didn't want to scare the guy.

"You have to be available at all times," he said. "And you can't have any heat. If it's serious enough, they'll follow you, listen in on you. That we don't need."

I told him I wasn't carrying any heat. Of course, I *was* carrying heat, but from the Boston cops, not from the FBI, which is what he meant.

He said if everything worked out, I'd be his next courier. This time the money-running operation was going to be run differently, and only five people would know about it. "There is us three," Meyer flicked a hand at Santo and me, "Frank, and Phil Buccola. Whoever else comes in the picture with you knows nothing about the others."

Another thing, he said, "we're not going to gather in social places. I will see you, but just when I think it's right."

Meyer stopped for a moment. He had a quick sharp gaze that never left me when I answered a question. "Do you know Jimmy Blue Eyes?" he asked.

I said I didn't, although I certainly knew the name: Vincent "Jimmy Blue Eyes" Alo. He'd been around almost as long as Meyer.

"Well, you're going to see him," Meyer said matter-of-factly. "He knows nothing of what's going on with this."

That was hint enough: don't hang around with Jimmy Blue Eyes. Jimmy was reporting back to New York about Meyer's transactions. They had been friends and associates for decades, but Meyer was concerned because Jimmy was carrying enough heat to set a house on fire.

For me there were three "principal stops", as Meyer called them: the Bahamas, London, and Switzerland, and two "meaningful," Rome and Paris.

They were going to start me off by bringing money back from the casinos in the Bahamas. If those assignments went well, Europe would be next.

Meyer handed me a slip of paper. "Tomorrow you will have your picture taken at this address." The photo would be put on an identification card—which in those days was all you needed to go back and forth to the Bahamas.

The meeting went on for two hours. At the end of it, Meyer asked: "Is everything understood?"

"Perfectly," I said.

Meyer sat back in his chair. "Frank thinks very highly of you. Everyone thinks very highly of you. And so do I."

*   *   *

ORIGINALLY, I WAS supposed to stay in Florida for awhile. Frank and Henry had given me a list of people to look up. But while I was down there a Boston wiseguy, Johnny Beale, was whacked and left in a Miami Beach parking lot. I had nothing to do with it, yet Henry told me to come home. There was too much heat over the killing.

If I was going to have my own organization, it would have to be set up someplace besides Boston, which was getting too crowded and too dangerous. Frank thought South Florida was a good place. He wanted to make contact with the top men in Miami, and after that around the country. That way I wouldn't owe my place to any organization, and I wouldn't have to deal with middlemen.

"You will fit like a glove," Frank said. "Once that happens, this thing of ours grows up and spreads out. You won't have to fight for survival on the streets and rob to make a living." Gradually, Frank was leading me into his world of secrets, an invisible world I had been longing to enter since I was a boy watching the wiseguys in the Florentine. He became my guide to the hidden ways of the mob man, to the mysterious ways that he held power.

Learning who to trust was one of the keys to survival. Frank said he trusted Italians more than Americans, Sicilians more than Italians, his *paisani* more than other Sicilians. Most of all he trusted his family, his kin. Blood was the most sacred and lasting tie, stronger than friendship or even marriage. It is no accident that in our initiation ceremonies, the new man sheds a few drops of blood when he takes his vows.

"The most important gift we are born with is trust," Frank told me. "That is the foundation of a family."

The other keys to survival were secrecy and silence, and there Frank was the master. He was very, very low-key, and so quiet you never knew he was around. He never wasted words, and told me only what I needed to know, so much of what I learned came in snatches, things said here or there when he was in the mood. That was especially true of the past.

For instance, when I came back from Florida he asked me a funny question: "Meyer don't drink no more, does he?" It was a crazy thing to ask. Meyer was the steadiest, calmest, and soberest guy around. Nothing ever fazed him. But Frank said there was one time when Meyer lost control, and he had been there when it happened. Meyer's first child, Bernard (who was always called Buddy), was born crippled, and his wife, Anne, went crazy and blamed the boy's condition on Meyer's sins. Meyer couldn't handle it. He walked out on Anne and Buddy, called up his friend King Solomon in Boston and arranged to stay at the Essex Hotel, where Solomon lived. Meyer drove up to Boston with Jimmy Blue Eyes, and Frank met them when they arrived. Frank said Meyer spent the next several days drinking himself into oblivion. No one could believe it. He had never acted like that before. Then Meyer pulled himself together as quickly as he had fallen apart and went quietly back to his family. His single drinking bout must have really spooked the wiseguys, because here it was more than thirty-five years later and Frank was asking: "Meyer don't drink no more, does he?"

In the old days, back in the 1920s and 1930s, Frank had seen plenty of wars. He said he had "been there" when the New York mob boss Giussepe Masseria was assassinated at a Coney Island restaurant in 1931. Charlie Luciano engineered that hit and the hit on Masseria's successor, Salvatore Maranzano, the same year. Those killings brought Luciano to power, and Frank was one of his key men. When the war in New York was over, he picked Frank to go after the Gustin gang in Boston. As the New England mob became strong, Frank's career prospered. Luciano got shipped off to prison in the mid-1930s, and shipped out of the country in the mid-1940s. When I was a kid Frank visited Luciano in Italy, and he remained loyal to his old friend down through the years. Others did not. In 1957 Vito Genovese and other younger New York mobsters ordered the execution of Luciano's friend Albert Anastasia, who was slaughtered in a bar-

left: Willie Fopiano.
September, 1969 —
California

lower left: This is when it
first started — Age 10.

lower right: Willie
Fopiano, 1966.

WANTED FOR MURDER

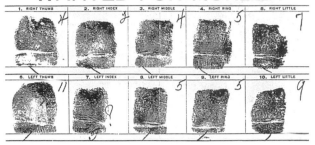

| 1. RIGHT THUMB | 2. RIGHT INDEX | 3. RIGHT MIDDLE | 4. RIGHT RING | 5. RIGHT LITTLE |
| 6. LEFT THUMB | 7. LEFT INDEX | 8. LEFT MIDDLE | 9. LEFT RING | 10. LEFT LITTLE |

FRANK CARUSO, alias FRANCO CUCCHIARA
(Photograph taken in 1925)

DESCRIPTION: Italian; age 35 years; height 5 feet 4½ inches; weight 164 pounds; stout build; complexion dark; eyes dark chestnut; hair dark chestnut; occupation grocer.

We hold warrants charging Frank Caruso, alias Franco Cucchiara with murder by shooting, December 22, 1931, Frank Wallace and Bernard Walsh.

Arrest, hold and wire at my expense.

MICHAEL E. CROWLEY,
Superintendent.

December 30, 1931.

Frank (the Chessman) Cucchiara was a boss by himself and took orders from no one.

Prince Street in Boston's North End. The site of the January 17, 1950 Brink's robbery.

Brink's Bandits: second left, Vincent Costa; third left, Tony Pino; entering the Suffolk County Courthouse for the trial in 1956.

below: Henry (Noyes) Selvitella and Tony (Canadian) Sandrelli going into a grand jury hearing (1959) for the murder of Joseph (Angie) DeMarco.

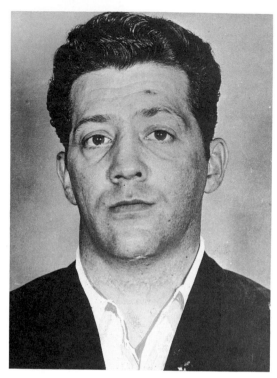

Bobby Palladino became the 28th victim of the McLean-McLaughlin War at the hands of Joe Barboza.

below: Tommy DePrisco and Arthur Bratsos, two henchman of Joe Barboza. Both were killed while raising money to free Barboza — imported Sicilians poured lead into their heads.

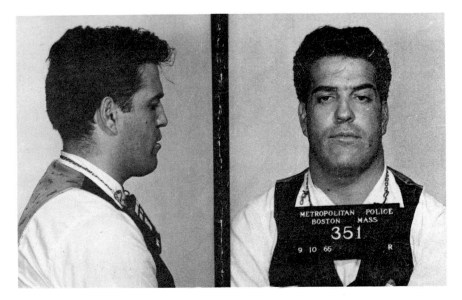

above: Joe Barboza. Known as "the Killing Machine."

lower left: Jack (Jack Ass) Francione. Another Barboza victim.

lower right: James (Buddy) McLean. He made the first hit killing Bernard McLaughlin and intensifying a war that left over 50 dead.

The body of Connie Hughes — covered with blanket. Killed for the murder of James (Buddy) McLean.

My days with Meyer Lansky; February, 1968. Together with my girlfriend Joanne.

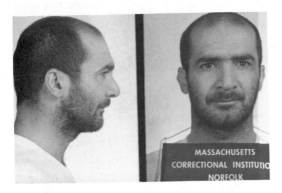

Peter Piso — consistent and dependable.

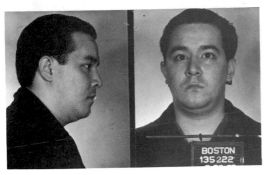

Butch Capone —nerves of steel.

Joe D'Minico — Burglar/safecracker. Incarcerated for 30 years for various crimes.

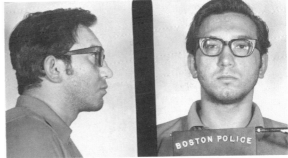

Eddie Greco — solid and always ready for anything.

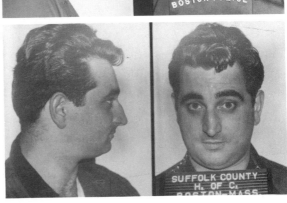

The Godson

ber chair. The same year they took a crack at Charlie's successor, Frank Costello, right in the lobby of his apartment house on Central Park West. Other men loyal to Luciano also got knocked off. Seeing the handwriting on the wall, Costello had tried to bow out gracefully, which a lot of people thought was very funny after the way he treated Phil Buccola when Buccola tried to do the same thing.

The hit on Anastasia, the attempted hit on Costello, and the other killings had a single motive—to rip down what was left of Luciano's old order. Genovese and his allies even got Meyer Lansky to cut back on Luciano's share of the profits from rackets that Luciano himself had created. Frank said Charlie was getting only about 500 dollars a week at the end. It would have been less of an insult to have given him nothing. But Meyer had to play ball with whoever had the juice—Vito Genovese was running the family in New York, while Meyer's old friend and partner Charlie Luciano was in Italy, washed up. The old don could only watch helplessly from his exile, and Frank said he died of a broken heart.

Genovese's betrayal was galling to Frank. "If I was there in New York I woulda made the rounds," he told me. "I'd do it alone. Always do it alone, nobody can squeal on you except yourself." Genovese was Neapolitan and his power play caused great concern among Sicilian mobsters like Frank and Santo Trafficante. Frank said the Appalachian mob convention in 1957 was meant as a peace conference. Instead, the cops came and arrested just about everybody.

Frank knew everybody at the convention, many of them from way back. In the 1920s he had worked for Al Capone in Chicago, and whenever that name came up in a conversation, he'd say "Al was a good man, one of us," like remembering a long-lost friend.

THE NAME KENNEDY provoked a very different reaction. "They're just a lucky family," Frank would snap when somebody on the radio or the television started gushing about how great they were. He told he had first met old Joe Kennedy during Prohibition when they were both involved in bootlegging. During the war they made a lot of money importing olive oil—when nobody else could get their hands on it. Frank and Joe Kennedy also did business together in an immigration racket. The wiseguys made a lot of money peddling papers to Italian immigrants who wanted to stay in the country. Over the years they sold thousands of visas, passports, and even citizenship documents. The operation began after the federal government cut back on immigration in the early 1920s and lasted well into the 1950s. Citizenship cost about 500 dollars a head in the 1930s, and had risen to as much as 1500 dollars when I was a kid. It was Joe Kennedy who supplied all the offical paperwork to the mob.

Frank sometimes grumbled that Kennedy was "*pidocchioso*" (which means "full of bugs") because he hadn't always delivered on his promises. "They shoulda shot him thirty years ago," he said another time. Yet Frank actually didn't mind old Joe; he could do business with him. It was the boys he despised. In fact, the few times I ever saw Frank really angry was when the Kennedy brothers came up. Jack Kennedy, he said, had been elected to the Senate with the mob's help. Not only did he turn his back on the wiseguys once he was in office, he betrayed them by launching all kinds of investigations into organized crime. He made his name at the expense of the very men who helped put him in power. Jack did a few favors for the wiseguys, but they had to go through his old man every time. Frank and others said Jack could never forget that mob men had helped make the Kennedy fortune and hated them for it—and for what they knew about his family.

Joe Kennedy was friendly with Frank Costello, and when Kennedy asked Costello to help him put Jack in the White House, Frank Cucchiara made a special trip to New York to warn Costello not to do it. "I tell him they had three faces—one to the left, one to the right, and the one that can't look at you." But Costello and the other bosses didn't listen, and in 1960, Sam

Giancana, the head of the outfit in Chicago, helped deliver Illinois and the country to the Kennedys by rigging the election.

When Jack Kennedy took over the White House, he unleashed his brother Bobby on the mob and things got much worse. "Giancana never shoulda done that," Frank muttered. "They wanna bother people." Frank ridiculed Bobby Kennedy as "a little girl trying to step on the toes of the big boys. I'd like to tie him up in a chair and cut him. Slow death."

Jack Kennedy was killed when I was in Walpole, and Frank mentioned the assassination once or twice after I got out. "I wish I'd been there," he said quietly. "If I'd been there I would've done it right. No one would have gotten arrested." I think he would have shot both Kennedys himself if he had the chance.

AFTER I GOT back from Florida, me and a couple of other guys pulled off a brilliant armored-truck score that netted more than 740,000 dollars. We knew that a suburban bank would be getting a big cash delivery just before opening time, and we figured the easiest way to get our hands on it was to be inside the bank when the truck arrived. The bank was in a shopping center and we broke in through a small back window late at night. It was easy, the only alarms were in the vault, which we were not going to touch. Then all we had to do was wait until the money came to us.

First we grabbed a bank employee who came to open up, and after him the two guards from the truck. We caught them completely by surprise, and handcuffed them to water pipes in a bathroom. Then we jumped into the armored truck and drove off with all the loot. Johnny Russo had swiped a hat and jacket from one of the guards and was at the wheel. It went off as perfectly as a score can go—until I saw the flashing lights in the rearview. Johnny had been in such a rush he forgot to pull the truck's emergency brake, and black smoke was spewing from underneath. We didn't notice the smoke, but a cop did and wanted us to pull over. I took a close look back. There was just one uniform. The cop was alone. We were way out in the country on an empty road.

"Let me handle this," I said when Johnny stopped. The cop was walking over to us when I jumped out with a Thompson submachine gun in my arms. I motioned him into the woods beside the road.

"Don't kill me," he said over and over as we walked into the trees.

I took his gun and made him lie on the ground.

"Don't kill me," he said again.

"If you keep saying that, I *will* shoot you," I said. "And if you get up I'll shoot you."

That cop was so scared he's probably still there.

When we got back to the North End we decided to relax a little by playing Monopoly—with real money we had stolen in the heist. There were five of us, and we locked ourselves in a club and replaced all the Monopoly money in the bank with real cash. We played by the rules, collected 200 dollars when we passed Go, bought railroads, put up houses and hotels, and paid through the nose when we hit Boardwalk and Park Place. We even went directly to jail. It was a great game.

A new guy, Butch Capone, came with us on that score. Butch I'd been seeing here and there since before I went to Walpole. I liked him because he was smart and always up for anything. He was five years older than me and had a very Italian face, with black hair combed straight back. He ran a lucrative fruit business in the Blackstone Street market on the North End, so he always had a steady supply of easy, straight money. On a good weekend he could make 3000 dollars or more, so I could never figure out why Butch went in for crime. Maybe it was the thrills.

I WISH I could say that all the money I was making and my introduction to Meyer Lansky and the big time kept me out of trouble. But trouble was my middle name. Violence was in me and all around me. I lived in a place where the most trivial argument could easily get out of hand and end up with somebody dying. No one ever forgot anything.

Late one night that August I was cruising through the Combat Zone in downtown Boston with Eddie Greco, Peter Piso, and Joe Bova, a neighborhood kid who had just got out of the service and was no relation to the Bakery Bovas. The bars and lounges along a strip on Washington Street were emptying out. All of a sudden I spotted a big fat guy in a small group of people. Six years earlier, four or five older guys had ganged up on me in the North End. As I was fighting them, the fat guy, who had to weigh at least three hundred and fifty pounds, came up and smashed me in the head with a club. He had moved out of the North End after that and I hadn't run across him since. But as soon as I laid eyes on him that night all the old rage came steaming back. I rolled down the window and started yelling at him. He immediately screamed back, but didn't seem to know who I was. I put the car in gear, jumped out and ran up to him, ready to fight. But the son of a bitch again had a club on him and cracked me over the head before I could lay a hand on him. Bleeding, I ran back to my car and parked around the corner, on Essex Street. There was a big hunting knife in the car. I grabbed it and ran back to find the guy. With my friends right behind me, like animals charging in for the kill, I was breathing fire. When he saw me coming he swung at me again, but I dodged the club and buried the blade in his stomach, and forced it upwards, trying to rip him open.

When the guy went down on the sidewalk we took off and one of his friends ran after us. I stopped quick, holding out the knife and he ran right into it. The blade was seven inches long and two inches wide. Both men survived, how I don't know. About fifty people saw me do it, and the cops desperately tried to get witnesses to testify against me. No one came forward. To his credit, the fat guy stood up and said nothing.

A day or so later Johnny Russo steered me to a score involving a jeweler who was going to be carrying a lot of diamonds from his home to a jewelry company at 6:30 in the morning. Johnny showed me the layout and promised that the score could bring in upwards of 100,000 dollars, and he'd give me at least twenty-four hours' notice.

But the next day the phone woke me at 5:45 A.M. It was Johnny. The jeweler had the diamonds and was leaving his house in forty-five minutes. Some notice! I hated to do rush jobs like that. It's too easy to make a mistake. And I needed a hot car and didn't have one handy. Still, for 100,000 dollars it was worth a shot. I dressed fast, and quickly picked out a '58 Olds that was parked on the street near my house. It belonged to a guy called Biffo and it was well known that any key could turn the ignition. Biffo never locked it, either. It would have to do. I jumped in and roared over to the jeweler's house just in time to catch him coming out. I held him up, and grabbed the black case with the diamonds inside. But the rocks turned out to be worth only 6000 dollars. I gave Johnny Russo hell for steering me to a bum score.

Thanks to that stupid robbery I wound up back in Walpole on a parole violation. I would've gone back much earlier if it hadn't been for my parole officer, a guy named Merullo. He had once been in the seminary and liked me because I had been an altar boy at St. Mary's. I was supposed to have a job when I got paroled in May of 1965, so I said I was working in a neighborhood grocery. The "grocery" was actually a numbers joint owned by a friend of mine. I provided the protection. Anyway, Merullo walked into the place to check on my employment and I happened to be behind the register. He looked around and couldn't believe his eyes. We had two boxes of rigatoni on the shelves and three quarts of milk in the cooler. That's it.

"What kind of grocery store is this?" Merullo said.

"Well, they buy groceries fast over here. We can't keep up."

Merullo came over and looked me in the eye.

"Are you booking?"

"No, no, Mr. Merullo, no. This is a grocery store."

"Well, you better put some more macaroni on the shelves,"

he said and left. Not long after that I got busted for transporting numbers slips. Somebody put the finger on me, because the cops knew I was carrying them. A judge let me off with a 250 dollar fine, but I thought sure Merullo was going to violate me.

Instead, he came up after my court appearance and complimented me on the new mohair suit I was wearing.

"That's one thing I admire about you, you really know how to dress," he said. "At least you're out there making a living, and you bought that suit with hard-earned money. You know what? I'm not going to violate you."

"I knew you wouldn't, Mr. Merullo," I said, real respectful.

Although I finally did get a legitimate job, in the restaurant, I continued to break every rule in the book, and Merullo never bothered me—even when the cops started putting tremendous pressure on him to ship me back to the can. They said I was getting away with everything and he wasn't doing anything about it. Of course, *they* weren't doing anything about it either. They couldn't catch me and wanted the parole officer to do their work for them. After the jewelry holdup Merullo had to do something, although even then he held off until my term was almost over. I'm sure he knew what was going on all along, but as a Catholic he saw the altar boy in me and believed I'd eventually go straight.

CHAPTER TWELVE

PSYCHOS AND BIG SHOTS

IT WAS LIKE a reunion at Walpole, all the old faces were there. Tony Pino embraced me as soon as he saw me, and Jazz Maffie and the other guys were friendly as always. It was almost good to be back, although I probably wouldn't have felt that way if I had any more than a few days on my sentence.

Nicky Femia, who had gotten pinched with Barboza, was doing time on the weapons beef. Nobody had been tighter with Barboza than Nicky. By this time the entire world was aware that Barboza was squealing, and being the best pal of a squealer presents problems. The state was turning the screws: Earlier that summer, the prosecutors made a big show, twice taking Nicky out of Walpole and parading him before a grand jury.

Nicky knew I'd be back on the streets soon and asked if he could have a word. We went to an empty spot on the block. He had a worried look on his face.

"I hope I'm in the clear when I get out." He said this like he was asking a question.

"Why shouldn't you be?" I told him. "Barboza ratted by himself."

Nicky lowered his voice. "He sent word to me that he wants me to corroborate his testimony. He's going to lie about five innocent guys in the Deegan killing. Him and me and Ronnie Cassesso killed Deegan. But he's going to rat on these other guys."

"I'm sure everyone knows you're a stand-up guy," I said.

"I'm not saying nothing," Nicky said.

"I'll tell the right people what you said. No need to worry."

"Thanks for your help," Nicky said. "Some day, I'll return the favor."

Nicky was referring to one of the most heartless and treacherous acts Barboza ever committed: blaming five men for killing a guy he himself had whacked. I said earlier that Barboza had always secretly hated wiseguys, and this was how he got back at them.

It went like this: A petty thief named Teddy Deegan was suspected of killing Anthony Sacramone, a cousin of Rico Sacramone. Rico wanted revenge, and got the rest of the Barboza gang to help him carry it out—Femia, Romeo Martin, Chico Amico, Ronnie Cassesso and, of course, Barboza himself. Romeo Martin knew Deegan a little and won him over by telling him about an easy score at a finance company. When Deegan and Martin drove up to the back door of the place, Barboza, Femia, Amico, and Cassesso were waiting. Barboza ran up and shot Deegan five times.

That was in March 1965. It was known even then who shot Deegan and why, but twenty-six months later Barboza ratted on Ronnie Cassesso and also put the finger on five other men: Henry Tameleo, Peter Limone, Louis Grieco, Roy French, and Joe "the Horse" Salvati. Tameleo was an important man in the family. Along with Limone, Grieco, and Cassesso, he was sentenced to the chair, and spent almost five years on death row before capital punishment was thrown out. Salvati and French drew life sentences. Of all of them, only Cassesso had anything to do with the crime. The others were innocent.

Barboza felt Tameleo didn't protect him enough, which is why he had it in for him. Salvati, who was just a doorman at an after-hours joint, wouldn't swat a mosquito. His big offense was being a good ladies' man and romancing a girl Barboza liked. He was also behind in shylock payments to Barboza, as was Roy French. Barboza hated Limone and claimed he ordered the hit, which is ridiculous. Limone didn't even know about it. Not only that, he liked Deegan. They had grown up together in the West End. Barboza testified that Limone paid him 7500 dollars for the hit. Limone wouldn't have given Barboza 75 cents. Barboza was jealous of Grieco, because he was his own man. I'm not sure why he put the finger on Cassesso, who was supposedly one of his great friends.

The defense lawyers put Wacky Jackie Civetti on the stand, and he told the jury what kind of a maniac the prosecution had for a star witness. I think he even showed his scars. Grieco had witnesses that swore he was in Florida at the time of the murder, and later he even passed a lie detector test. Other juries didn't believe Barboza, though for some reason this one swallowed his story whole. The prosecutor, Jack Zalkind, today is in private practice and I've heard from reliable sources that even he now thinks that some of the men—especially Joe Salvati—might be innocent.

Henry Tameleo died in prison in 1984. He was eighty-three years old. There were stories floating around that he had been one of the hitmen in the St. Valentine's Day Massacre back in 1929. Maybe so, but he had nothing to do with Deegan's murder. In 1991, Cassesso died in prison. For him and Tameleo it was truly a death sentence.

The others are still behind bars for something they didn't do.

NOT LONG AFTER my talk with Nicky, I ran into him again.

"Walter Elliott wants to see you," he said. "He's in Block Four watching television."

"Tell Walter I'll meet him in the yard at noon," I said.

Walter Elliott was a sullen Irish hood from South Boston who had been transferred to Walpole after burning down a bunch of shops at the Concord Reformatory. I met him when I was bouncing between Walpole and Norfolk. Supposedly, he had no love for Italians, though me and him always got along. Jimma Faherty, the Brinks robber, was Walter's uncle, although I don't think there was a lot of blood closeness there, because nobody ever saw them together very much. Walter Elliott's biggest pal was John Robichaud, a huge beefy guy from Rhode Island who had instigated two riots at Walpole. The first was during the famous big blackout of 1965. When the lights went out, Robichaud and some other guys tried to burn the place down. The next year he led the "pill riot," which began when a bunch of guys broke into the hospital to steal drugs. Dozens of guards and inmates were hurt, and I heard that Robichaud was the wildest of the rioters and nearly tore the place apart all by himself.

When I met Robichaud during my first time at Walpole he kept suggesting that we hook up back on the street. I'm always leery of people who want to hook up, but he seemed like a regular guy. In any case, the way he was going he'd never see the street.

Walter Elliott was five minutes late for our meeting and had a strange, cold look in his eyes. Word had gotten around that I was only in for a short time, and Walter said he'd be out himself in three days.

"I want you to do something for me on the street," he said in a way I didn't like.

Like a lot of people, Walter knew of my connections in the North End, and his request was a sit-down with the boss in Providence.

"I want to meet him. I want to do things with him and he better not give me a hard time," Walter said sharply. In other words, if the boss didn't want to play along, too bad for the boss.

Now, I had always suspected that Walter fancied himself a big shot, but from what had just come out of his mouth I knew I was face to face with a madman. The boss would sooner have run this guy and his entire crew through a meat grinder than talk business with him. Walter was out of control, which became all too clear the more I watched him. He was making wild expressions and menacing gestures as if a demon was pulling his strings, and for a few minutes I thought he might attack me right there in the yard. I tried to appease him, and said what a wonderful man the boss was, and that he'd love to say hello to a guy like him.

That calmed Walter a little. Then he went on about what a good man John Robichaud was, and how he could help "our cause"—whatever that meant. I just stood there and listened. Finally, he stuck out his hand and the meeting was over.

"See you in the North End," Walter shouted as he walked away. I'd told him I'd think about his request. Of course, I would do no such thing. This guy was a human volcano. I hoped the matter would drop, but Walter never let anything drop.

Three days after his release I got out, and almost immediately Walter began coming around the North End looking for me. He had a carload of guys from South Boston with him. I laid low, but was ready for anything. Joe Bova one of the brothers who owned Bova's Bakery, kept a spare .38 for me hidden on a shelf.

Walter and his crew intimidated a lot of people, and one night they barged into a social club on Fleet Street that was one of my hangouts. There were six of them, all with pistols. Eddie Greco was there, and hid his face so Walter couldn't see him. It was me they wanted, and Walter made sure everybody was aware that I should meet him if they wanted these visits to stop.

Putting off things like that only makes them harder to deal with, so the next day I hung around on Bova's Corner until Walter and his crew finally rolled by. They stopped and double-parked in front of a drugstore. Three stayed in the car, and two guys jumped out with Walter. He looked even nuttier than at Walpole. The three of them stopped a few feet from me. It felt like the O.K. Corral.

"I've been looking all over for you. Have they told you?" Walter said.

"They have," I said. "I have been here two hours waiting for you to drive by. Seems we keep missing each other."

Beside Walter, a short guy with popping eyes was keeping a stare on me with both hands shoved in his jacket pockets. That meant at least two pistols aimed right at me.

"I need a favor and you're the only guy who can be helpful to me," Walter said.

"How's that, Walter?" I expected him to start where we left off about his desire to meet the boss.

"I'm having a feud with a buddy of yours from Charlestown," Walter said. There was a silence.

"Well, who?" I said.

"Pebbles Doe and I want—"

"Stop!" I shouted. "I know what you're going to say and I don't do that to friends."

I didn't let him come out with a specific request, though I was sure he wanted me to set up Pebbles, either for a beating or a hit, and knowing Walter it had to be the latter. But if his intentions were not put into words, then I couldn't know them. Any beef between Walter and Pebbles was their business. I wanted to stand neutral, and hoped Walter could live with that.

But when he heard my answer his face twitched as if it was going to shatter.

"You're going to tell him! You're going to tell him!" His voice rose to a screech.

"Look, Walter, you're my friend. He's my friend. I have nothing to do with it. I just don't do that to friends and that's final."

I stood there facing three angry glares. Anything could happen, and there was nothing I could do. There were too many of them. When Walter finally spoke, he was so hysterical that he could barely squeeze out the words.

"You made me show my hand and you refused me! I won't forget this!" With that, he turned and went back to the car, his cronies right behind him.

By refusing to go along I had become another of Walter's enemies. Either you're with a guy like that or against him. He doesn't want to hear about neutrality. What his beef with Pebbles was about I never knew. It was probably some stupid thing. If you even looked at Walter the wrong way he'd put your name in a hat.

WALTER GOT INTO trouble with the law soon after that, and had to go on the lam. He had his hands full dodging the cops, yet I couldn't help looking over my shoulder. When bugs like him are on the lam they want to carve as many notches as they can before they get pinched. I was informed by several friends that Walter planned to make the North End his last stop before his luck ran out—meaning that he would be coming after me.

I was ready, willing, and able to take him on, yet I had no idea when or where he might appear. The cops caught Walter before he could get to me, and a lot of guys said I should be relieved. I wished I could have taken care of him myself. A bullet is the only way to get rid of a mad dog.

MEANWHILE, CHARLIE CENTOFANTI, who occupied the cell opposite me at Walpole, put me onto a major bank score in Ashton. While we were setting it up, Charlie got busted on a murder beef. Johnny and I went ahead with it anyway. We hit that bank like lightning. We ran in, grabbed the money, and were gone before anybody knew what happened. The haul was supposed to yield about 100,000 dollars, and we got 20,000 dollars more than that. I sent Charlie's mother the extra twenty grand for expenses and lawyers' fees.

Frank and Henry wanted me to move down to Florida, which made sense because I couldn't stay out of trouble. I was all set to leave town when I got busted on an extortion beef that I had nothing to do with.

It all started when Johnny Russo and another friend of mine wanted the owner of a cigarette-machine business to cut them in for a piece. I told Johnny to forget it. After the score we'd just made he didn't need any more money. But he didn't listen to me and kept harassing the cigarette guy. When the man resisted, Johnny and my other friend gave him a bad beating. They just didn't like him.

In a panic, the guy ran to the police. The cops told him I was behind it, so he put the finger on me. They had me in handcuffs before the ink was dry on his statement. The Florida trip was canceled, and Henry was very disappointed. He had been trying to get me out of town, now he had to try to keep me out of the can. "Once you beat this case, you gotta leave the city," he said. He told Max Glazer to keep postponing the case in municipal court until certain things were taken care of—like getting the cigarette guy to go down to Florida.

Once that was arranged there was another problem. I had made the cigarette guy a little too scarce and the authorities thought he was dead.

Again, my judge was Elijah Adlow, but even he was concerned. He was getting a lot of heat from the DA and the cops.

Glazer got hold of me and said, "Willie, the judge wants to work with you, but he's worried this guy is dead. He wants some assurance the kid is alive. Don't go too far." I couldn't very well bring the cigarette guy back from Florida, so I asked Frank to make a connection with the cops. He had been paying off some of the sergeants and lieutenants for years and knew them well. When he said the guy was alive they knew he was telling the truth. The cops then told Adlow that the witness was unable to testify and he threw out the case.

The cops figured that I'd up back in trouble soon enough so they could get me then.

Luckily, I was able to stay cool until November when I drove down to Florida.

B Y THIS TIME I had already made a few trips to the Bahamas for Meyer Lansky. The first was that previous fall when I was out on bail. The hotels over there in those days were small, but they made a lot of money from gambling. Before I left Miami I was given a suitcase, and Meyer showed me a photo of a guy I was supposed to meet on Grand Bahama. When I got over there I checked into a motel and the guy in the photo would meet me and we would exchange suitcases. The new suitcase had a special compartment containing skim money from the casinos. On those trips I took the plane back to Miami the next day or even the same day, dropped off the money and flew back up to Boston. The customs people never checked the bag, never even gave me a second look, and I had no problems. It was a piece of cake. The trips were very short, and I could be back in Boston before anybody knew I had left. Frank and Henry told me that Meyer was very pleased with me (he was never told about the week at Walpole or the extortion beef) and once I moved down to Miami, there would be plenty of other jobs.

I took an apartment in North Bay Village off the Seventh-ninth Street Causeway. Meyer's people told me to be ready to go any time. So I waited for them to get in touch. And waited. When they did call me it was for more runs over to the Bahamas, but I didn't care about the Bahamas. I was looking forward to the big stuff, the trips to Las Vegas, London, and Paris. Sure, sure, you'll be doing that real soon, Meyer's people assured me. But nothing seemed to happen.

After a few weeks of that I got bored out of my mind and called Frank to ask if I could come home. Frank hated talking on the telephone. "You stay. You'll go to a lot of places. Be patient," he said.

Gradually, I found things to do. Every day was bright and warm, a big improvement over the cold, gray New England winters. I hung out at the beach and went jogging every morning. Except for Frank and Henry, nobody in Boston knew about my dealings with Meyer. I told all my friends I was down in Florida training for a fight, so it made sense to stay in shape. The winter season had just begun and people were pouring into town from all over like snowbirds looking for sun and fast times. It made the nights very exciting, and I never wanted to stay home. A popular joint called Jilly's South wasn't too far from my apartment and I went over there a lot. It was owned by Jilly Rizzo, a close friend of Frank Sinatra, and quite a celebrity hangout. Jimmy Durante came in some nights. Paul Anka was a regular, and so were the actors Dan Blocker, Richard Conte, and B.S. Pully. Blocker, Conte, and Pully were shooting a movie down there called *Lady In Cement*, and the star was Sinatra. Pully had been in *Guys and Dolls* on Broadway and in the movies. He was also an old pal of Henry Noyes. Pully and Conte were nice guys and I saw them frequently. One day Conte called me over as I was walking across the lobby of the Fountainbleau Hotel on my way to meet Pully in the Boom Boom Room.

"Come here, I want you to meet somebody," he said.

A moment later I was face-to-face with Frank Sinatra.

Conte introduced us. "Frank, this is Willie Fopiano, he's a good boy."

Sinatra shook my hand. "How ya doing, Sonny," he said. I liked him right away.

Not long after that I was invited to a party Sinatra threw on a yacht that he kept docked across from the Fountainbleau. We sailed out into the harbor. It was a bright tropical afternoon and the yacht was dripping with beautiful girls. For a young guy like me it was like a few hours in heaven.

You saw beautiful girls everywhere in South Florida. They were as plentiful as the oranges. Soon there was one under my roof. A friend of mine named Jerry brought her over one day. Her name was Joanne, she was from Montreal, and about the most gorgeous human being I had ever come across.

"Hey, Jerry, where'd you find her?" I said.

"At the airport. She said she had no place to stay. She said she likes Italian guys." That was good enough for me. Not long after that Joanne moved in.

All the girls at Jilly's loved Paul Anka the way cats love cream, and he was mobbed by flocks of them as soon as he was in the door. But Anka had eyes for Joanne, and wanted her real bad. Once or twice she went there without me and he made passes at her whenever he saw her, but to no avail.

*   *   *

BACK IN BOSTON, Charlie Centofanti was awaiting trial for murder and one of his partners was trying to get in touch with me. I called Johnny Russo to find out what it was all about. A day or so later Johnny got back to me: A couple big scores were ready to go, back-to-back. I was coming back for Christmas and told Johnny I was in.

It was quite a Christmas: We got away with a few hundred thousand dollars. The money came in handy, because I had plenty places to spread it around. My crew was sort of an extended family and we had to keep up the cash flow to maintain our life-styles. We all liked girls, good clothes, nice vacations, fancy restaurants and fast cars, and all that cost money. There were fifteen of us and seven or eight had families and kids. Only five of us actually did the scores. You have to go down deep inside yourself to get the motivation to go rob a bank or an armored car. The others didn't have that drive, but each man played a role. They were the getaway drivers or the decoy drivers who'd deliberately stall out and block a street if the cops came after us. They handled the smaller robberies, like hijackings, and helped unload and store the stolen loads. They were the enforcers, the muscle that every crew has to have. Every man was good and could be counted on to stand up if he took a pinch. I didn't have to worry about any of them. Still, with that many people on the payroll even a million bucks didn't last long.

My family needed help from time to time and I gave them money before going back to Florida. I also made sure that Joe Semenza was okay, not that he ever asked me for anything. His wife had died very suddenly in 1966. They waited for each other all those years he was in the joint, and now she was gone. Joe was never the same afterwards, yet he never let anybody see his grief. Joe Semenza was a man's man all the way. Back in the thirties he got into trouble for some petty beef and did a year at Deer Island, a minor league joint. When the guard took him to his cell he said: "Shut the door and don't open it till I'm released!" Joe was made of iron, yet now he had to raise a small son on his own. After Angie DeMarco got killed I swore to myself that Joe would never have to risk his freedom or his neck to keep bread on the table. I'd take care of him as long as he lived.

Even with all those expenses I made enough in those years to live like a duke for the rest of my life. Aside from the scores, Meyer was paying me very well. Money should have been the least of my worries, but I had another huge hole burning my pocket: gambling. From those early days playing on the street in Big Mike's crap game, my love of betting had gradually developed into a genuine addiction. I put money on anything and everything—dice, fights, horses, baseball games. A bookie called Stoogie handled all my sports bets—from 2500 to 10,000 dollars a game. Most of those bets were losers, of course, and I warned Stoogie not to let anyone know that I was his best customer. I was throwing away in one pop more than what a lot of people made in a year. If Frank or Henry had ever found out about it I would have been in big trouble. It was insane, I know, and I should have wised up after throwing the fight to get straight with Fiore. Like all sick gamblers, I kept looking forward to tomorrow, because that's when I was sure to hit it big. That's when my luck would turn around. It would be a long time before I learned the lesson that Meyer Lansky and a few others figured out early on: that in gambling the only winners are the guys who run the game.

I WASN'T SORRY to leave Boston after the new year. Miami was a fun spot, and my friends seemed to be going in different directions. Eddie Greco had met a girl and had slowed down a lot. Danny Puopolo had made a big score himself and was staying off the streets. Joe D'Urbano had gotten married and gone straight.

At least those guys were doing good. Others weren't so lucky. Charlie Centofanti beat the murder rap, but got bounced back to Walpole anyway for parole violation. Joe Gorilla was also back in Walpole on yet another beef. He was in and out of that place so much they should've installed a revolving door. Doing time became second nature for him. I know he could've walked on at least one beef and I offered to help him get a good lawyer, but he told me to forget it: "Nah, lawyers just take your money. I'd wanna stay here and do my time." Poor Joe D'Minico was slowly losing his mind. I figured it was because of all the time he was doing. Prisons are terrible places, and when you get out you need time to let your mind and emotions heal before you can go back on the street. It takes awhile to get used to people and places again. But Joe would get out, last just a few days and go right back in. He never had the time to adjust. One time he even told a friend of mine: "My luck is really going good. I did four armed robberies this week and didn't get caught."

After bouncing in and out so much, being behind bars seemed normal, and I think he actually loved being in prison. At Walpole I saw him every morning going to his job with a cup of coffee and a newspaper and a big smile on his face, as if he was an ordinary guy on his way to work. In the yard Joe would look up in the sky and see a bird and get all excited and say, "Hey, I'm going to go to the library and study birds." Or he'd spot a bug. "Look at all those colors. I'm going to the library and read all about insects. That's what I'm going to do."

We made fun of him when he went on like that and he got mad. "You guys can waste your lives, I'm gonna come out of here educated." He was always disappearing into a book, but he couldn't seem to concentrate on one subject. After awhile I realized that his mind was coming apart.

Joe's physical health wasn't much better than his mental state. In the late 1950s he had been shot and badly wounded during a robbery in Texas. A bullet lodged in his liver and couldn't be removed. That gave him a lot of trouble as he got older. Gradually, it got so he couldn't take care of himself, and he didn't seem to be in the real world anymore.

*   *   *

SINCE I WAS flying back down, I asked Johnny Russo and Peter Piso if they wanted to drive my car to Miami Beach—I had a new, custom-made Eldorado—and stay with me awhile. They couldn't wait to hit the road. The night before we left we were hanging around a social club on Endicott Street, and I said we needed somebody to cook for us. None of us knew how. Crazy Carmine D'Minico, Joe's brother, was lying on the couch.

"What about you, Carmine, can you cook?" I said.

He jumped up. "Yeah, yeah, I'm the best cook around. I can cook anything."

"You wanna go to Florida?"

"Yeah, yeah, I'll do all the cooking, leave it to me."

I told him to get packed, and he came back a few minutes later and announced that he was ready. All he had was a bag with a couple pairs of socks, some undershorts, a T-shirt, and some Polygrip for his dentures. I think that's about all he owned.

On the first night we were all together in Florida, I told Carmine to do some shopping and handed him a twenty—which in those days could fill a grocery cart. Me and Joanne and Johnny and Peter were lounging around in front of the TV while he was in the kitchen. "What's on the menu, Carmine?" I yelled.

"*Chimbotha*," he shouted back. "This'll be the best *Chimbotha* in the world. I can cook anything."

"All right, all right, I know that already, just cook."

When we sat down he brought out the *chimbotha*, which is like a stew, something you make when you've got a bunch of this and a bunch of that in the house and throw it all into a big pot. It wasn't bad. Next day, I gave Carmine another twenty dollars, and when I asked him what we were having that night it was like being in the middle of a rerun: "Surprise—*chimbotha*!" He claimed he had some left over from the previous night, and the best thing to do was make more. The only thing different was the dessert. I ate a little, then sneaked out with Joanne and had a filet mignon.

The next night, we had a bunch of people over. They

thought having homemade *chimbotha* was great, and we were happy to let them take it all.

It was the only thing Carmine knew how to cook.

He was a good guy, Carmine, but wacky. My apartment was right next to the Intercoastal Waterway, where a lot of houseboats were docked, and one day I found him by the water running up and down with a long bamboo pole that he had made into a spear. A crowd of people was following him and I asked somebody what was going on. "That guy over there is hunting for barracuda," he said. Carmine didn't listen to me when I told him there was no such animal there. He was so sure of himself that he even made the news on TV that night: the man who discovered barracuda in the Intercoastal.

MY APARTMENT GOT to be like a hotel for pals and pals of pals. Some nights we had seven or eight people sleeping on beds, couches, or on the floor. A classy after-hours joint called the Penthouse was right nearby—everybody went there—and there'd always be somebody knocking on my door in the middle of the night because he was too drunk to drive home. Guys in town for the weekend who didn't feel like springing for a hotel room wound up with me. After a few weeks of getting up to answer the door at all hours, I just left it unlocked.

Girls were constantly in and out of the place, but Joanne was the only one who actually lived there. Carmine couldn't take his eyes off her, and I joked around with him sometimes. "Carmine, don't bother my girl, now," I said.

"No, I'm just looking. I'm looking," he said. But with all the great-looking women coming and going, Carmine couldn't help getting frustrated. The apartment was in the front of the building on the second floor, and you could hear people coming down the concrete walk. One night, there was a *click click click* of high heels. Carmine rushed over to the window and looked out. A beautiful girl was heading for the lobby and he ran downstairs to intercept her.

I called all the guys together and we listened in from the upstairs hallway. We only caught the tail end of the conversation, and it went like this:

"Yeah, this is my place," Carmine said. "I've got friends of mine staying with me." He must have been giving her quite a line, because then the girl says:

"Well, Carmine, since you're a such great lover, do you like to dive?"

He thought she was talking about swimming, and tried to take her over to the pool. The girl said she didn't have a bathing suit.

"That's okay," Carmine said. "You can swim with no clothes on."

"Well, I'd rather not," she said. A couple minutes later Carmine slinks back upstairs with a long face. We tried not to laugh when he was looking.

When Joanne moved in I told her that I disappeared from time to time on business and not to ask me about it. I don't know if the guys wondered what I was supposed to be doing down there, but they also knew enough not to ask any questions. As a precaution, I never installed a phone in the apartment. If there was a phone, that meant calls back to Boston and I didn't want anyone there to start guessing about my comings and goings.

MEYER WAS SLOWLY taking me into his confidence. One of the first things I learned was his schedule. The man was well into his sixties and not in the best of health, so he didn't keep long hours. All business was conducted between 10:00 in the morning—after he walked his dog—and 3:30 in the afternoon, and usually at a restaurant called Wolfie's or at a small hotel on Collins Avenue in Miami Beach called the Singapore. Meyer's brother, Jake, had me come down to the Singapore a couple times, but when I got there I'd just sit around. The second floor had a card room where a few of Meyer's old cronies hung out, and I'd either go there or to one of the rooms and catch a ball game on TV. Meyer was afraid the rooms might be bugged, so our conversations were about everything but what the feds wanted to hear. The Singapore was owned by his old friend Mike Wassell. His real name was Meyer too, but because of the confusion of having two Meyers he was always called Mike. Jake Lansky also hung around the Singapore a lot. He looked like a bigger, heavier version of his older brother, but he was much slimmer in the brains department. Sometimes I didn't know Meyer Lansky had shown up until after he'd been there awhile. He was quiet and very low-key. We'd talk business in the open spaces, in the lobby, or even in cars parked outside. After two or three visits Wassell warned me to stay away because the feds were watching the place. That was fine with me. If I got spotted by the feds it was all over. I took care where I went and who I was seen with. Jake Lansky and the other cronies I saw as little as possible, and never told them what I was doing.

"Where ya been?" Jake used to ask me.

"I was worried about heat," I'd tell him.

"Yeah, yeah, lotta heat," he'd always say, and drop the subject.

This caution even extended to where I socialized.

When money was exchanged I met Meyer at the cabanas behind either the Fountainbleau or the Eden Roc Hotel next door. These were secluded spots, not places the feds or the cops ever thought to look for him. Meyer wasn't into bodyguards or stuff like that at all; the fewer people around the better. He kept someone outside to keep watch when the money changed hands, but usually it would be a guy like Jake. Once while I was there Moe Dalitz, the former Cleveland bootlegger who became a big shot in Las Vegas, showed up with a satchel. He got very nervous when he spotted me, but Meyer said: "Hey, he's with us. It's all right. Just lay it out." Dalitz opened the satchel, which was stuffed with cash.

With Meyer everything had a meaning, and nothing was

done without a reason. I think he had Dalitz open the satchel in front of me to let me know that I was trusted. I also think Dalitz suspected this, because me and him never got along after that.

A COUPLE TIMES Meyer had me drive to New Orleans and deliver packages to Carlos Marcello, the boss of the mob down there. I don't know what was in the cardboard boxes I put in the trunk, but I assumed it was money. It had the weight of money. Even though they could never be seen together, Carlos and Meyer were very close. They each had a piece of a casino in Vegas and talked business on pay phones.

I had a phone number to call when I got to New Orleans. The first time Marcello's people drove up and had me follow them to a motel where I checked in and made the delivery. They wanted to take me out that night. I thanked them but said I had to check out early the next morning. Frank told me to operate like that. I didn't want to be seen with those guys and attract attention. If they were being watched the authorities were going to wonder who the new face was, and might trace me back to Florida. On the next trip I was told to drive to a modest-looking office and made the delivery to Marcello himself, a short, casually dressed fellow who was a bit overweight. He was a funny little guy, and very friendly.

"How's our man?" he asked, meaning Meyer. "Health okay?" I think they were al worried about something happening to Meyer, because he was the one man who was trusted completely. That's why that one drinking bout when he was a young guy had thrown such a scare into the wiseguys.

OCCASIONALLY I BUMPED into Meyer in the public areas of the Fountainbleau when he was with his second wife, Teddy. He was always polite, but it was very brief: Hello, how are ya, see ya later, that kind of thing. Although he had told me we wouldn't socialize, we did have dinner in restaurants one or two times. I liked being with him. He was modest and never tried to over-power me. Business was never discussed when we went out like that. Instead, he asked about me, my family and what it was like growing up in Boston, where he had spent a lot of time. He had made a lot of friends back there who I didn't know, men like Hymie Abrams, who later became very powerful in Las Vegas.

"You'll meet Hymie," he said, and I realized that Hymie was a good man to know.

One time we met at a joint on the Seventy-ninth Street Causeway called A Place For Steak, and were joined by Dino Cellini, a sharp-looking guy who had been with Meyer in Havana and now ran the Colony Sporting Club, a casino in London. Meyer had an interest in the Colony, and since I would be making trips to London I think he wanted me to make contact with Dino.

When I told Dino where I was from he said, "Hey, you oughtta meet Johnny Rosselli. He's from Boston. He comes here all the time." I think it was the next time I was in A Place for Steak that somebody brought me over to a slight, elegant man in an expensive suit. Johnny Rosselli took a liking to me and I gave him my address. When he wanted to see me he'd leave a note on my car. We got together several times, usually at A Place For Steak or in the mornings at a fruit-juice joint in downtown Miami.

In their biography of Rosselli, *All American Mafioso*, Ed Becker and Charlie Rappleye claim he was one of the most pow-erful mobsters in the country from the 1930s to the 1970s. They paint Rosselli as a big-time Mister Fix-it, the mob's liaison with Hollywood and the government, sort of an underworld Henry Kissinger and a major player in the CIA plots against Fidel Cas-tro. All that is probably true—in fact, some of it is well known. But I know what brought Johnny down: he talked too much, way too much. The man had a bionic mouth.

After we went out a few times he started telling me some incredible stuff—and the most incredible part was that he was talking about it at all, and to a young guy he barely knew.

Johnny was real good-looking, well dressed, and always looked perfect. I had heard he was a real ladies' man, though that was one area where he kept his mouth shut. Johnny did say that he had known Marilyn Monroe back in California, and had a good idea why she died: "That girl knew too much. She was with the wrong people. She was going to blow the lid on the Kennedys. They wanted her black book. Jeez, if I only had that black book."

I gathered that the "black book" was a kind of diary that Marilyn kept, and Johnny made it sound like that's what got her killed: "They did it wrong. All they had to do was take the black book. Her memory was gone, she couldn't remember anything. Her head was all messed up from her life-style. But she wrote everything down." Johnny leaned toward me, his arms on the table. Jack and Bobby Kennedy had told her things. "They were talking about the Bay of Pigs, Castro. Can you imagine the Kennedys telling a bitch like that all that stuff?"

Johnny never identified the "they" who supposedly murdered Marilyn. I don't think he really knew himself, but he seemed to believe it was mob guys.

Like Frank Cucchiara, Johnny had a deep, simmering hatred of the Kennedys. Unlike Frank, he spilled it all over. He told me a story, the same story I'd hear in North End social clubs during those years. It went like this: Frank Costello, the New York boss, had connections everywhere, like nobody before or since. His influence stretched as far as the White House itself— everybody said that he knew Franklin Roosevelt. He also became very close to a young businessman, Joseph P. Kennedy, and was responsible for much of Kennedy's financial success. Kennedy was involved in King Solomon's bootlegging operation, and later moved into the immigration racket. Not only did Kennedy get rich off the rackets, the racketeers who ran them treated him like a king at the Cal-Neva Lodge in Lake Tahoe, and during his visits out there supplied him with enough girls to fill a harem. They did the same thing for his son Jack, both in Havana and at the Sands in Las Vegas. Yet as far as the mob was concerned it was a one-way street, because Joe Kennedy seldom did anything for them, and constantly reneged on favors. Still, he must have been pretty smooth, because his relationship with Costello remained solid across the decades. When Joe Kennedy asked for the mob's help in getting Jack elected to the Senate in 1952, Costello extended himself. Of course, once he became a senator, John Kennedy made his name by waging a campaign against organized crime. For Costello that was too much. He felt humiliated and betrayed by Joe Kennedy. At some point in the mid-1950s, Costello or some of the men around him got so angry that they actually discussed putting the hit on old Joe. Word of this got back to Kennedy and he was understandably very nervous—which may have been the real intention all along. He promised Costello that he'd get Jack to turn down the heat. Then he said that Jack had a good chance of becoming president and if the mob helped pull that off, the White House itself would be in their debt.

Once again, the wiseguys played along, despite the warning of Frank Cucchiara, which I mentioned earlier. When the time came, Sam Giancana helped rig the election in Chicago. John Kennedy was sworn in, and again there was no trade-off. "Instead, they turned on them completely," Johnny Rosselli said hotly. "They always turn on you." A big part of the problem was Bobby Kennedy. He was jealous of powerful men, and he attacked Jimmy Hoffa just because he needed somebody to go after.

Hoffa was an easy target, Johnny said. "They knew the unions were corrupt and how to prove it."

After Bobby died in the summer of 1968, Johnny was happy: "He got what he deserved. They [the sons] were just like the father, turncoats. They'd never reciprocate."

Johnny also knocked Santo Trafficante, who he accused of deliberately screwing up a conspiracy to overthrow Castro. "He never followed through," Johnny said. Now, Trafficante was supposedly one of the people who wanted Castro dead, but Rosselli said he faked it and only pretended to go along with Rosselli, Sam Giancana, and the government men.

Over the years others have told me much the same thing. Trafficante feared he'd be a sitting duck if Castro found out about the plots cooked up by the mob and the CIA. After all, he lived closer to Cuba than anyone else. According to one story, Santo resented Rosselli for grandstanding with the CIA and claiming he was trying to win the mob favors from the government by helping to get rid of Castro. Santo suspected Johnny was in the game strictly to feed his own ego. Sometimes older mob guys like Johnny get mixed up in power plays simply to prove that they were still strong.

Other guys told me that Santo was actually fond of Castro and maintained a secret relationship with him for a long time. He hoped Castro would one day reopen the casinos, and the mob could do business there again.

Men like Santo, Frank Cucchiara, and Carlos Marcello considered themselves more Italian than American, and more Sicilian than Italian. I'm sure it never crossed Santo's mind that his dealings with Castro were "un-American." The government had its foreign policy and Santo had his.

JOHNNY HIMSELF WAS very proud of his work for the feds. "The best men are the ones with natural ability and instinct, which makes them clever, cunning and wise," he told me. "No training camp in the world can match that. Our organization has those kinds of men." When he first told me some of these wild stories I was so shocked that I didn't know what to say—so I didn't say anything.

"What's the matter, Willie, don't you talk?" Johnny smiled.

"Johnny, what the hell you telling me for?" I said.

He smiled again. Johnny Rosselli was one of the greatest charmers I've ever known. "Why? Are you going to go against me?" he said. "We're both from Boston, we know the same people. In this business you can't keep everything to yourself. If you can talk to somebody you trust it's a good feeling." To that I didn't say anything, but I had to wonder what made him so sure he could trust me.

Another time I told him, "Johnny, I hope you don't tell this kind of stuff to everybody. What if something got out? Are you going to blame me?"

"I'd never put you in a spot," Johnny said.

"Yeah, but the things you're telling me are not good for me to know."

Johnny made a face as if I was stupid to worry. "Sometimes if you know something you might be helpful, you could put something together for us."

I always got nervous when he used words like "we" and "us," and sometimes I got the impression he was trying to use me in some way, although he never asked me to do anything.

I think one of the reasons Johnny told me so much was because I never asked him anything. If I had, he probably would've been more careful. Even though I became very interested in what he had to say, I pretended to be indifferent, and that made him tell me more. Sometimes he wouldn't say anything when we first sat down and I'd get annoyed. Come on, Johnny, talk, I'd say to myself. Then, something would come up and off he'd go.

Only once did I slip and ask him a question: What became of Marilyn's black book? Who has it? But Johnny just smiled and shook his head.

Meyer knew I was seeing Rosselli and never mentioned it directly, but one time he said, "Be careful who you're with," and I knew instantly who he meant. Back in Boston I told Frank that I had met Johnny. Frank Cucchiara knew him. According to *All American Mafioso*, Johnny had gotten his start in Chicago with Capone. That's probably where he and Frank first met, although Frank also knew Johnny's family, who still lived in Boston (Johnny's real name was Filippo Sacco).

Johnny thought very highly of Frank and called him a "good man," yet I don't think Frank liked him at all, and when I made it clear that my acquaintance with him didn't extend to business, Frank nodded and said: "You know better than that, he's not the right guy." One of the reasons that men like Frank and Meyer survived for so long is that they communicated with as few words as possible. An insinuation like that—"he's not the right guy"— could fill a whole page. They almost always ran something by you fast, never many specifics, and never more than you had to know. You didn't get details or explanations until something was just about to go down. Then and only then would there be a sit-down. Gossips were not to be trusted.

Because of that, and because of his knocking people it wasn't safe to knock—men like Santo Trafficante—I didn't want to be seen with Johnny too much. I think he suspected this. "You're a hard guy to find," he said once. Another time he asked me to go with him to see Sinatra play at the Fountainbleau. Everybody was going to be there. Luckily, I had already had promised to take some pals from Boston.

FLORIDA WAS GOOD for me and things were going well with Meyer, but money-wise the well was running dry. By March 1968 Stoogie had beat me for 50,000 dollars. Since I had plenty of spare time on my hands I decided to put it to good use. With Johnny Russo I drove up to Georgia and checked out a few hick towns. Over the next five weeks we hit five banks. It was unbe-lievable, like taking candy from a baby. Driving to Georgia was like driving through a time warp, because as far as alarms and security went nothing had changed since the days of Ma Barker. Some of the banks didn't even have guards.

WITH MEYER I learned that things were done in stages. You had to be patient. Finally, about a year after that first meeting in North Hollywood, he decided I was ready to be sent to Europe. I couldn't wait.

When the time came he filled me in: "You will be informed by Frank seven days in advance and make all your reservations and purchase a ticket in New York." Meyer held up a Polaroid snapshot of a man. "When you fly to New York, this fellow, Sy, will give you a carry-on bag and one or two pieces of luggage for your trip to Switzerland."

Another snapshot appeared: "When you reach the airport in Switzerland, this fellow, Herb, will make his presence known to you. After you pick up the luggage you will follow Herb at a little distance, always watching his right hand. Once outside the terminal, Herb, with his right hand, will drop a card. It will be a card to a hotel. You will take a taxi to whatever destination the card says. At your destination, Herb will be waiting for you in the lobby. You will follow him at a little distance till you both enter your room. In your room you will exchange identical luggage bags. From there, you will be assigned to Italy or back to the United States."

SY'S FACE WAS already familiar. I had seen him several times in the Bahamas. He really got around. Meyer's network was pretty big, and I lost count of the people I met at various airports and hotels in New York, Zurich, Geneva, London, Paris, Rome, and Palermo over the next few years. They made contact and we exchanged suitcases and bags, which all looked exactly alike and weighed the same. When you opened them you found shorts, T-shirts, shoes and socks. A man's things. Where that stuff came from and who put them there I don't know. I never saw money in the suitcases, but I understood that as much as one million dollars could be hidden in the lining. At first the guys in Florida didn't want me to carry anything of my own or put anything into the bags, even a can of shaving cream. They were terribly concerned that all the bags weigh exactly the same. Shaving was no big deal, I only needed to use a razor once every four or five days. Staying clean was something else.

Before I left Jake Lansky asked me, "Are you going to change clothes when you're over there?"

Yeah, I said. I'd like to put on something else when I shower.

"Well, you're not going to be there that long," Jake said, suggesting I make do with only the clothes on my back. It seemed to me a guy wearing the same thing two or three days in a row can arouse a lot more suspicion than a few extra ounces in a suitcase, but Jake wasn't the brightest guy. Finally, we compromised, and I took along a small carry-on bag.

I used six or seven passports, each with a different name, and tried to make myself look like six or seven different people. Six or seven *boring* people who would melt right into a crowd. I became the kind of man you'd have a hard time describing because there was nothing to describe. In other words, very bland. My hair was short. I wore black glasses, dull-looking suits, and white shirts. I could have been a salesman or a low-level executive.

It usually worked like this: I flew to New York, and was handed a suitcase, then I boarded a flight to Europe. The man I was looking for had a Polaroid snapshot of me, so when I arrived we could pick each other out. He started walking and dropped a card that I picked up. The address of a hotel was scribbled on it. I climbed into a taxi and handed the driver the address. I didn't know where the hell I was going, and when I got there I didn't know where the hell I was. At the hotel the man from the airport or someone else would be in the lobby. I followed him up to a room and where there would be another suitcase just like the one I had brought from New York.

Once the exchange was made I usually stayed a day or two before flying home. The hotel rooms were booked in whatever name I was using, and somebody else checked in for me before I arrived, and checked me out after I left. The front desk never saw me and I almost never left the room. No one told me to do that, and I could have played the tourist, but I thought it was safer not to make any appearances. My contacts had carts of liquor wheeled in, but I never touched it. As time went on the routines changed, and things got a little looser once I got to know some of my contacts. But I never went to too many places. Europe is a place I saw from hotel windows.

*   *   *

AFTER MY FIRST few trips I was told to make a second stop overseas. "You're going to see the old man," one of the contacts said. The "old man" was Phil Buccola, the former boss of the New England family who had retired to Sicily in the 1950s. I was to deliver his "pension."

I flew to Rome, then caught a plane to Palermo, where people met me at the airport. Phil Buccola lived in a village a few miles outside of Palermo. In *The Godfather* movies and other pictures dealing with the Mafia these old dons always have grand villas and big estates. Buccola had a small house and a chicken farm. The whole place stank of chicken shit. I couldn't believe it. Yet he seemed happy where he was, and I don't think he missed the action all.

Unlike your average gangster, Buccola was an educated man. He was born in Palermo, attended the Universita Degli Studi there and another school in Switzerland. He traveled widely, even going to Russia before the revolution, and didn't settle in the United States until 1920, when he was thirty-four years old. I knew who he was when I was growing up, but he didn't come around the North End too much. He lived out in Newton, a wealthy suburb near Boston College. When I met him he was past eighty, and looked and acted more like a retired dentist than an old mobster, let alone a boss. He was really a very modest, conservative guy. He also looked every year of his age: he was pretty frail and what little hair he had was white white. I thought he might die any day, but his mind was sharp and he seemed aware of what was going on in the States. Buccola was "retired," but retirement is always a relative term for a wiseguy.

He was always pleasant and cheerful. "How's everything back home?" he wanted to know, and asked about Frank and Henry. "If you see J.L. send him my love," he said.

I saw him a few times after that, and I began to think that it was probably the dullest mobsters who are the most successful.

Buccola was certainly proof of that: he died peacefully in 1987. He had lived to be one hundred and one, and never spent an hour in the joint.

The Sicilians who drove me to and from his house seemed friendly and once or twice took me to a café in Palermo. But I didn't like Sicily. It was pretty run-down and I couldn't speak the language. Not only that, I was a different kind of Italian— my family came from Genoa and Avellino. To me, Sicily was like a foreign country within another foreign country.

I made trips to London when the Colony Sporting Club was going strong, taking money from there back over to Switzerland. On my first trip Dino Cellini himself came up to the hotel room. In his fancy suit he looked like a duke. There was another guy with him who was going to make the exchange. After shaking hands Dino hung around a couple minutes. Then he said, "Aw, you know what to do," and left.

B Y APRIL 1968 the season was over in Florida. It had been an excellent time, but I was getting homesick. I phoned Frank and he told me to come back. It was good to be home. I had missed my family and friends, and they were all glad to see me, though I couldn't say very much about what I had been doing. Frank and Henry gave me a warm welcome, and Henry said he had heard nothing but good things about my work. Everything was going well, except for the gambling. That sickness was slowly eating me alive. In the first three weeks of baseball season I blew 40,000 dollars betting with Stoogie.

CHAPTER THIRTEEN

SCORES

BEING A COURIER for Meyer Lansky proved very lucrative once I started hitting Europe. Sometimes I got paid when I got back to Kennedy Airport, sometimes in Boston, and sometimes the money came through Frank. Unfortunately, it all went to gambling. It was like being in a hundred-percent tax bracket. By the end of April 1968 I was broke and desperate for a few big scores.

Two guys, who I'll call Charlie G and Mike, told me about a crooked jeweler I'll call Amato who wanted help in setting up a jewelry salesman who would be carrying 100,000 dollars in diamonds. I told them I was in and went over to see Amato. Most of the city's diamond trade is conducted in the Jewelers Building on Washington Street, but Amato's store was in the Dexter Building down the street, which meant fewer witnesses and an easier stickup. That's what I thought until I got off the elevator on the fourth floor and saw a coffee shop right next to Amato's store. Who the hell ever heard of putting a coffee shop in the middle of an office building? They're supposed to be on the street! The food must have been good too, because it was 2:00 and a lot of people were still inside eating.

I got even better news when I found Amato. The score was supposed to go like this: the jewelry salesman had an appointment with Amato. He would come in and lay the diamonds on the counter. I'd walk in behind him and, boom, grab the diamonds and run down the rear-exit stairs. Simple, except that the salesman's appointment was at noon—when the coffee shop would be jam-packed. Anybody coming in or out could look right inside the jewelry store.

Amato shrugged. "All the other people we contacted refused for that reason," he said. I didn't like it. The whole thing had suddenly gotten a lot more complicated, but I needed the money.

THE NEXT DAY just before noon I climbed the four flights of stairs. When I got to the store I slid a mask over my eyes, taking care to keep my face away from the coffee-shop windows. The jewelry salesman was inside talking to Amato, an assortment of diamonds spread out in front of him. I jammed a .45 in the salesman's ribs and told him to stand back. I began scooping the diamonds into a bag when suddenly the salesman jumped on top of me. He knocked me off balance and we both went down. The diamonds went flying all over the place. We rolled around on the floor and the bastard wouldn't let go of me. He was yelling and screaming to attract attention, and out of the corner of my eye I could see people streaming out of the coffee shop. Somebody was probably already on the phone with the cops. I put my left palm under the salesman's chin and hit him with the .45 until he let me go. I got up. A crowd from the coffee shop was standing outside watching us like an audience. I pointed the gun at them and everybody scattered. I left the shop and bolted down the rear stairs, whipping off the mask and sticking the gun in my waistband as I went. At the bottom of the stairs I listened. No one was coming after me—yet. When I came out of the building a big motorcycle cop in dark glasses, boots, and helmet was standing on the sidewalk. I held my breath, walked past him, and kept going. He didn't know about the robbery. If he had tried to grab me I almost certainly would've whacked him on the spot. A rob-

bery like that would have put me back in the joint for a long
time.

THE SCORE WAS a complete fiasco, and I didn't collect a dime,
but Amato was impressed with the way I handled myself.

"If something comes up, you'll be the first to know," he
said.

Something did come up a few days later. Amato called and
we met in a North End coffee shop.

It was something good, he said. "Last week in New York
two guys walked into a jewelry store and robbed a half million
in precious gems. I got word today that a jeweler fence bought
the load and he's coming to Boston, to the Jewelers Building, to
dump it. His name is Cohen (not his real name), and I did business with him before. This guy gets nailed and he can't report it
to the police. He's coming in early Friday or Saturday with the
load. Can you handle it?"

I thought for a minute. "I need to know his routine. How
does he get here from New York?"

Amato smiled a little. He was a frail-looking guy in his
sixties, but talking about money and heists livened him right up.
"He goes to the airport and carries a jeweler's case with a chain
that's locked around his waist."

"Who drives him?" I asked.

"He takes a taxi. When he lands at Logan the first cab he
sees he takes to the Jewelers Building. When he leaves the Jewelers Building he grabs the first cab he sees, jumps into it, and
goes back to the airport."

I told Amato that he could count on me, but I had to know
Cohen's schedule.

"The only thing I'm not sure of is if he'll be ready Friday
or Saturday," he said. "I'll call you tomorrow and let you know."

It was already Monday. I had a plan, but I needed a lot of
experienced help, men who could work criminal miracles, and I
needed them fast. The first guy I looked up was Billy Tomasino,

a professional arsonist. He could set fires that left no trace of a torch job, and he was the man to go see if you needed any kind of chemicals. I asked for something that could knock a man out. Next, I contacted Gerry Presutti, a friend of Butch Capone and an expert at robbing banks and armored cars. He had a big garage in Dorchester that was outfitted with the kind of stuff I required, and people to do the work. Gerry told me to go see his friend, who I'll call Gennaro at the garage. Gennaro met me there with half-a-dozen other guys.

We all shook hands and I laid it out: "I need a car shaped like a taxi, a Checker or yellow cab and the complete paint job to go with it. I need a partition, plastic or glass that separates passenger from driver, and it has to be sealed tight. I want the rear side windows stationary so they can't be opened, and I must have control of the rear locks on both doors with my left hand. I'm going to give you a chemical in a can half the size of a can of Right Guard. I want it placed where the armrest is, and to work so when I put the armrest down, the chemical will shoot into the backseat. Make sure that everything is sealed tight all the way to the floor. I also need license plates for a taxi. I'll bring the chemical tomorrow."

"When do you need it all by?" Gennaro asked when I was finished.

"Any time before eight-thirty Friday morning."

"This is easily a four-day job," Gennaro said. "I don't know if we can have it that soon."

From my pocket I took out a roll of cash and handed it to him.

"Here's ten thousand dollars. Maybe that will speed it up."

"The money will bring the parts a lot faster," Gennaro said. "There's a lot of labor. We'll do our best."

The next day Amato still didn't know what day Cohen was flying in, and I didn't know if my cab would be ready on Friday or Saturday.

On Thursday I dialed the garage and Gennaro answered.

"How's it going?" I said.

"It's just impossible for tomorrow morning," he answered. "We'll definitely have it ready at eight-thirty Saturday morning."

So that was that. There was nothing else I could do but hope Cohen wouldn't show up until Saturday. I called Amato. He wasn't going to learn Cohen's travel plans until the last minute.

On Friday morning at 11:30 Amato called my house. "So far so good," he told me. His contacts in New York hadn't phoned, so that meant Cohen was still there. No news was good news.

At 2:30 Amato called again. "It's getting late and I don't think he's coming. I'll call you later one way or the other." At 4:00 he phoned for the last time. No Cohen. We were both relieved. I told Amato that once I picked up the cab I would transfer it to one of the garages that I had in the North End. I gave Amato the phone number there and said I'd have the cab by 8:50 the next morning.

At 8:20 the next morning Johnny Russo drove me to Dorchester. When I saw the cab I couldn't believe it. They had done a beautiful job. It looked perfect and everything was in place, even the hack plates. I promised Gennaro and the gang that there would be a bonus if it all worked out.

I thanked them and drove away. My only worry at that point was getting hailed by every pedestrian once I hit downtown because the cab was so shiny and new.

Johnny followed me back to my garage and I rolled the cab inside. The garage was gray and flat and set back from the street beside a couple of old houses. From the street it looked abandoned and half buried, the closest to invisible that a building can get. The phone rang at 8:50 on the nose. It was Amato: Cohen was taking the 11:00 A.M. shuttle that got in at 11:35. The plan was to take him after he fenced the jewels. That way we wouldn't have to fence them ourselves. Amato had a friend in the Jewelers Building who would let him know when Cohen was about to leave. We were covered in every direction.

The garage was about two minutes from the Jewelers Building. While I was waiting I got ready, putting on sunglasses, and a cap with fake blond hair sewn on the back. That way, if Cohen did go to the cops they'd be looking for a blond thief.

At 1:20 Amato said Cohen was about to split, and he gave me a description middle aged, dark hair, short, not too heavy, casually dressed, wearing a sport coat. I jumped into the cab and was in front of the Jewelers Building in two minutes flat. My timing couldn't have been better. Just as I pulled up a guy walked up to the curb and put out his hand. He was the description come to life. That's him, has to be, I thought. I rolled up and Cohen hopped in.

"Where to?" I asked.

"Airport. Eastern Airlines," he said.

I took the first right off Washington Street, took hold of the armrest with my right hand and slammed it down. That sprayed the chemical into the backseat. Cohen yelped a few times, but the drug knocked him out in less than ten seconds. I raced back to my garage where Johnny was waiting. We opened the back door and dragged Cohen out. He was out like a light, but the drug would start to wear off in twenty minutes, so we had to work fast. We snapped the chain off his waist and took the jeweler's case. Inside was 175,000 dollars in cash and a lot of diamonds, which we didn't expect. Apparently Cohen had brought along some of his own rocks. That was another 200,000 dollars, a very nice bonus.

Johnny and me hauled Cohen to another car and drove to East Boston. We dumped him on a back street not far from Logan and left him with his wallet and airline ticket.

It was a score to end all scores.

LATER THAT SAME day Gerry Presutti died. He had stopped to see someone at a house in Quincy, and on the way back to his car somebody ambushed him from behind a fence. The first bullet hit him in the head. When he went down on the sidewalk the gunman came over and shot him point-blank in the back of the skull. Why it happened I don't know. The cops told the papers Gerry had been on some kind of "hit list." He was awaiting trial for an armored car beef and out on bail for a house robbery in Rhode Island, but as far as I know he had no enemies.

Naturally, I felt terrible and as soon as I heard I went over to his garage. Gennaro and the rest of the guys were taking it hard. It was one of those awful times. What should have been a big celebration was now a wake. I gave them another 10,000 dollars, yet there wasn't much I could say.

CHAPTER FOURTEEN

PAYBACKS

MY CREW WAS back in action, and a month after the Cohen
score I was casing a bank at a shopping center in the suburbs
that looked like a soft touch. Every Tuesday morning a Brinks
truck came to pick up money, usually around 100,000 dollars.
The cash was in bags and always ready to go before the truck
arrived. It was the easiest money we ever made. With Johnny
Russo sitting in the car, we slipped on masks, went in and told
an employee to open the vault where the Brink's bags were
stored. When he didn't move fast enough we put a bullet through
a wastebasket next to him. That speeded things up, and we
grabbed the bags and ran out. The whole operation took about
thirty seconds and we beat the Brinks truck by minutes. The take
was 109,000 dollars.

Sometime in June Jimmy Sforza drove by Bova's Corner
looking for me. I hadn't seen him since the coin-shop holdup
before I went to Florida. Now, he was hot for a jewelry score. All
we had to do, he said, was get past a thick steel door—no
alarm—and crack two safes—no alarm. It sounded promising,
but Jimmy was pretty small. Smashing through steel required
muscle, and I suggested a neighborhood guy I knew. The three
of us agreed to hit the place that night.

The safes were on the second floor. First we went to work on the steel door. It was a monster, but drills and acid broke it open. Then came the safes, which we attacked with drills and sledgehammers. Waiting for us inside were trays with 500,000 dollars' worth of diamonds, gold rings, watches, bracelets, pendants, and chains.

There's usually a pretty big markdown with stolen jewelry, which we expected when we took the stuff to Amato. He said he couldn't give us more than 80,000 dollars and that was too much. We took the eighty grand and left.

HIJACKING WAS ANOTHER lucrative racket. By 1968, I had several warehouses to store stolen goods, most of them in South Boston near the docks. Me and my crew ripped off truckloads of canned tuna and razor blades. The Gillette factory was right in Boston, and I stole so many blades from them that I don't know how they stayed in business. I also bought loads off other crews, mostly booze and cigarettes from down south. If somebody wanted to unload something he swung by Bova's Corner, where everyone knew to find me. They told me what they had, and if I liked it I paid them on the spot—I always carried at least 10,000 dollars in cash—and gave them a phone number for one of my warehouses. Other guys gave me loads to store on consignment.

Most of this stuff I sold to Arthur Ventola, the biggest fence in New England. He operated out of a small market called Arthur's Farm in Revere. The place was a dump and looked like it would fall down if you coughed, but Arthur took everything I gave him. He was always fair and paid right on delivery. A couple of the Irish crews from South Boston sold their loads through me because Arthur didn't trust them. He had been ripped off by the Irish one time.

A big sports-betting operation was also based at Arthur's Farm, and among the people who hung out there were assorted wiseguys and several members of the Boston Patriots. Putting several rackets under one roof may have been convenient, but it

made Arthur and his pals a little too well known. In 1967, year
of the Impossible Dream, *Life* magazine did a story on Arthur's
Farm. Ironically, there was an article about Meyer Lansky in the
same issue.

Most of the money I made in the scores and rackets wound
up with Stoogie the bookie. I figured out that between 1965 and
1968, he beat me for more than a million dollars. Very little of
that wound up in his pocket. I had warned Stoogie not to give
me up, but years later I learned that a wiseguy called Nicky Giso
was always looking over Stoogie's shoulder when I called in my
bets. I don't know who tipped Giso about me, but Stoogie worked
for the office and Giso was making sure the office got its full
share, especially with the amounts I was dropping. You see,
when a bookie has a big spender who loses a lot and sees waves
of cash washing in, he's tempted to not write down a couple bets
that look like sure losers, and pocket the money. That way the
wiseguys never know about it. It's known in the trade as backing
a bet. A bookie will only pull something like that once or twice
a year, and has to be as certain as the sun coming up tomorrow
that the bet won't win. I remember walking into a social club
once and finding a ball game on television and a man on his
knees pleading with and screaming at the players on the screen.

"What's going on?" I said.

Another guy shook his head. "He backed a bet and the
game's going the wrong way."

A variation on the backed bet is the spot bet. If a bookie
thinks he sees a real long shot that looks like a winner, he'll
make a big bet using a phony name. Since the book doesn't hand
over the wagers until the end of the day, he doesn't put up a
dime. It's a great scam—as long as the long shot comes in, as
another North End bookie called Lubo learned the hard way.
Nineteen sixty-seven was the year of the impossible dream for
the Red Sox. It was the year they'd win the pennant, the year
Carl Yastremski would win the triple crown. On August 20 they

were heavy favorites against the Angels, but Lubo thought California could out-pitch them. So he spotted a 10,000 dollar bet and stood to collect 16,000 dollars from the office. Well, the Sox blew out the Angels 12–2. Lubo skipped town before the game was even over. He couldn't begin to cover the loss and probably figured he'd better get a head start. Lubo hasn't been seen on the North End since.

WITH THE KIND of life I led, violence was never very far from the surface. On the North End you grew up on fights and feuds: you'd be getting back at one guy while another guy was trying to get back at you. When a guy starts something with you, your friends back you up, and he has friends on his side. And you stand with your friends when they've got their own beefs. Pretty soon everybody is in on everybody else's beef. It didn't matter much when we were kids, then it was fists and feet. But we grew up and all of a sudden it was knives, clubs, pistols, carbines, and machine guns. Arguments and street fights could flame up into miniature wars.

That's what happened with Crazy Carlo. After he got out of the can he hung around on Bova's Corner every night. He was a funny bug, sort of like Wacky Jackie Civetti, always joking around. He did some nutty things, but never caused any trouble. I liked him and even palmed him 500 dollars when he was short.

One warm summer night we were cruising around in my new Cadillac convertible when Crazy Carlo spotted two girls on the sidewalk and asked me to stop. That seemed like a good idea, so we threw them in the backseat and went off on a little adventure. Carlo moved fast and before I knew it he was in the back with the better-looking girl. Her friend moved to the front. She wasn't bad-looking, but the chemistry wasn't right. It was a little awkward: We were sort of just sitting there, while behind us Carlo and the other girl were all over each other. The two of them hit it off, and I never saw Carlo on Bova's Corner after that.

The following month I got into an argument with a cop at

an Italian feast. He had been bothering a friend of mine and I told him to lay off. All of a sudden, Crazy Carlo's brother, Joe, who had nothing to do with it, comes over and butts in. I turned around and told him to mind his own business. The cop walked off and Joe told me it was his business. I was already steaming from the beef with the cop and hit Joe as hard as I could. When he went down a bunch of guys who were with me kicked and punched him up and down the street. Bloody from head to toe, Joe staggered into a social club and came flying out a few minutes later with five guys. They all had guns. So did we. One of our guys ran and got a carbine with a banana clip. Within minutes, bullets were flying right in the middle of the feast. People screamed and scattered. Two of the guys with Joe were wounded. They went to two different hospitals and claimed they had been shot in separate incidents nowhere near the North End. But the cops knew about the shoot-out—that social club was riddled with bullets—and put two and two together.

I had to lay low for awhile, and got the word to be on the watch because Crazy Carlo was looking for me. I didn't worry too much because Carlo was no killer. Then in September the phone rang in my house and a voice I had never heard before was on the other end. All he said was this: Carlo has a gun and is looking to kill you for what you did to his brother. He'll be around tonight near your house.

There was no way I would let Carlo come near my family, so Eddie Greco, Johnny Russo, Peter Piso, and me stationed ourselves down the block, using two cars as a shield. The caller knew what he was talking about. About 8:30 I spotted Crazy Carlo coming up the street, towards my house. All three of us jumped up and Carlo took off like a deer. I got off two shots at him, but missed.

Later that night, Carlo showed up at his girlfriend's place and they got into a ferocious argument. It ended when he stabbed her thirty times. Crazy Carlo pled guilty to manslaughter, got twenty years, and wound up at Walpole. He hadn't been there long when he was transferred to Norfolk. One night he tied a rope to a window, wrapped it around his neck, and hung himself.

Of course, the girl he killed was one of the ones we picked up that night in my Cadillac. That night turned out to be a death sentence for both her and Carlo.

EARLY ONE NIGHT in October I was on Bova's Corner with Johnny Russo, Eddie Greco, and Jimmy Sforza when two neighborhood girls came running up crying. Three black guys had been trying to give them drugs and get them to come with them.

"Where are they?" I asked. One of the girls said they had been in front of a bakery at Hanover and Cross Streets.

I told Johnny to put the girls in his car and drive down Hanover Street.

"I'll come from Cross Street on foot. When I get to them, pull right up," I told him. Then I made Eddie give me his gun and go with Johnny. Jimmy Sforza and me ran down Salem Street to Cross Street, then walked toward the corner of Hanover. The three black guys were still there, just hanging out. I moved towards them slowly, as if nothing was wrong, and when I got close I pulled out Eddie's .357 magnum and ordered them not to move.

The car came screeching up beside us. Johnny and Jimmy Sforza grabbed baseball bats and Eddie whipped out a six-inch switchblade. The girls got out. One of them was named Maria and I asked her which guy had tried to give them drugs.

"That one," she said. I stuck the long barrel under the guy's nose and asked him if it was true.

"Yeah, man," he squawked. The sight of them was making me boil, and I asked why they wanted to come into our neighborhood with their cancer.

"I didn't know any better," the man said. Naturally, he was terrified.

I pushed the barrel against his nostrils. "You know why you're saying you don't know any better," I shouted in his face. "Because right now you have no way out. All you want to do is get these white girls high, fuck up their heads and bring them down to your level. Do you know what your level is?"

"No, man."

"Pimps, hookers, and assholes like you are trying to make young people drug addicts. We don't want your cancer here to rob defenseless people, especially the old people. For a two-dollar bill your cancer may cause them to be seriously hurt or killed. Do you understand what I'm saying, black boy?"

"Yeah, man," he said.

"Don't say 'yeah, man' again! It's 'yes, sir.' "

"Yes, sir!"

"Now," I said. "Apologize to these girls and tell them you're very sorry for bringing your cancer down here and you will never come back here again."

The guy did exactly what I told him.

"Now, where's your car?" I said.

"It's under the bridge."

The "bridge" was actually part of the expressway that runs north up to the suburbs, and the parking lot was at the bottom of Hanover Street. We all walked over there. I wanted me and my guys to get a look at the car and the license plate in case they decided to make another visit, but they never did.

We might have had a chance fighting the drug plague if all the dope dealers came from somewhere else, but the enemy was within as well as without. It was like trying to keep back a tidal wave.

LATER THAT MONTH a guy named Woppo hit Eddie Greco's brother, Tony, in the face with a hammer. Eddie wanted revenge and called me. A kid I went to school with called Joe Twist knew the social club where Woppo hung out.

I said to Eddie, "you ought to be laying for the guy instead of going down there and killing him in front of all those people." But he didn't want to wait: "I'll handle it my way," he said. So me and Joe Twist picked him up at his house, and he slid into the backseat with his .357 magnum tucked into his belt. We were getting close to Woppo's social club when all of a sudden there was a loud pop from the backseat. Eddie was so nervous that he forgot the gun was cocked and shot himself when he yanked it from his belt. I slammed on the brakes. Poor Eddie was sprawled across the back bleeding, and I thought he was dead.

"No, he's alive," Joe Twist said. I drove straight to Massachusetts General Hospital, and lifted Eddie into a wheelchair. "Eddie, Eddie, you alive?" I kept saying. He was still breathing. I rolled him into the emergency room. Keeping my face down, I yelled out, "this guy's been shot!" and bolted.

A doctor shouted at me: "Hold on. Wait!" I kept going. We had parked around the corner so nobody could catch my license plate.

Miraculously, the bullet missed every vital spot, and Eddie made a fast recovery. It was a lucky night for Woppo too, because Eddie decided not to go after him again.

All that summer and fall the cops had been bothering me all the time, following me everywhere and accusing me of just about everything. There was one detective who pushed me too far and I snapped. One night in November I hid on a rooftop waiting to ambush the bastard when he came around the North End. When he didn't drive by I got down and went looking for him. I found his car on Commercial Street near the Union Wharf. He'd had a breakdown and gone to get help, and it's lucky he wasn't there because I took out my gun and blasted away, blowing out the windshield and a window on the passenger side.

When Henry and Frank read about it in the newspaper they knew where to look.

"Hi, Henry, is there something wrong?" I asked when he sent for me. One look from him and I knew playing innocent was out. He had me sit down.

"Frank and I care about you," he said. "Right now we're setting up your future. You're twenty-four years old. After awhile the luck runs out. You've done everything. If I lived another sixty-five years, I couldn't catch up to you now. Use all your experience for the future and you'll have a big start. I want you to go down to Florida in February, maybe the last of the month. I'll give you a ten-day notice. The first part of the month make your reservation at the Fountainbleau Hotel for two weeks. Have Joe Twist, and his friend, Mitch (a pseudonym) drive your car down. You take a plane, and make sure they don't know what you're doing." Henry stopped and leaned forward. "Also, stay out of trouble. We're getting closer to bigger and better things." The way he acted and spoke made him seem like a priest trying to talk a bad kid into going straight. He made me feel guilty, and I assured him he had nothing to worry about. We embraced and I left.

I HAD EVERY intention of keeping the promise to Henry, but I had no control over the wild, murderous rages that seized me. They came without warning, and anything could set them off. I nearly blew everything on a frigid night that December. It happened when me and Johnny Russo got stuck in traffic near the Boston Garden because of a Bruins game. The cop directing the traffic looked familiar. As we moved closer I recognized him. It was Blackie, the Irish cop who had tormented me nonstop when I was a kid. He was older, heavier, his dark hair fading to gray. Suddenly, all the beatings and taunts came back in a hot, ugly rush:

"You're always a troublemaker. . . . Go ahead and hit me. Just try it. Hit me . . . You're always a troublemaker."

I could feel his thick hands choking me and hitting me, as if only twelve seconds had gone by instead of twelve years. I was his favorite target, and there had been others after me, other boys. I had seen him chasing them. This big, lousy mick had spent his life picking on Italian boys, and now it was time to settle up. Rising above Blackie in the darkness was the expressway bridge. Johnny was driving my car and I told him to get out of the traffic and head over to a construction site near the expressway. I jumped out and looked for something to throw. A heavy boulder was on the ground and I rolled it over to the car. Ironically, the building going up was the new Division 1 police station. In a way the cops had given me a weapon to kill one of their own. Perfect. Once I had dragged the boulder into the car, I told Johnny to get onto the expressway and stop right over the spot where Blackie was directing traffic. Because of the hockey game, all the cars were going slow. Johnny pulled over and we both got out. We were directly above Blackie now. With all my strength I lifted the boulder over my head, and with Johnny directing me I heaved it over the side. I looked over fast. The boulder looked like it was right on target. I pulled back before it landed and ran back to the car. There was too much noise from all the traffic to hear anything below. Only the next day did I learn the boulder had missed Blackie by inches. He must have moved a step out of the way just in time. I never saw him again.

Word of Blackie's near-miss got back to Frank and, boy, he was mad. "You killa that cop you know what happens to you?" he yelled. "For what? For what?"

Frank and Henry forgave a lot of stuff like that because they trusted me and had confidence in my abilities. Old-timers know that when you're bottled up these things happen, and that in time you'll shape up. Besides, once I began organizing my own family there'd be no time for crazy stuff. The trick was to stay in control till that happened.

My friend Butch Capone had his hands full: after finishing a burglary sentence, he got indicted for a bank robbery in New Hampshire. Luckily, he was found not guilty in October and we all celebrated.

Just before Christmas Pebbles Doe was killed. He was found near the rail yards just off City Square in Charlestown. He had been shot behind the left ear, and the cops said he had been beaten before he died. Pebbles was twenty-five, a year older than me, and I felt bad because we went back a long way. The word was out that Walter Elliott was behind the hit. I hadn't seen

Pebbles since Walter tried to get me to set him up, and I stayed out of whatever beef they were having. I'm sure Pebbles had plenty of warnings, but Walter never gave up when he wanted to kill somebody.

I was lucky to be leaving town. Henry warned me not to tell anybody why I was going down to Miami Beach. That wasn't too hard, because I didn't know myself.

CHAPTER FIFTEEN

THE BIGGEST NIGHTCLUB

ON THE EAST COAST

I FLEW DOWN to Miami at the end of February 1969. B.S. Pully picked me up at the airport and drove me to the Fountainbleau. Boy, did he love Henry Noyes, and that's all he talked about the whole ride.

Henry was about as far removed from the image of a big shot as you can get. He always wore dark glasses and looked like a walking rainbow, wearing all kinds of crazy colors that didn't match. He spent most of his time in North End social clubs and bars, but the more I moved around the country the more I realized that Henry was known in many places. The only expensive item he ever wore was a classy-looking watch. It never left his wrist, until the day I asked him about it. He took it off and showed it to me. On the back was an inscription: TO HENRY, MY GOOD FRIEND—BEST OF LUCK, FRANKIE CARBO. Carbo was a big-time fight promoter and a suspect in the murder of Bugsy Siegel. Henry and Tony Canadian had been out in L.A. a lot in the days of Siegel, Jack Dragna, and Mickey Cohen.

I'd like to think he would have done it anyway, but because of what happened that day in John's Candy Store, Henry took extra good care of me wherever I went, and made sure I connected with all the right people. He said he'd do something good for me, and he was true to his word.

At the Fountainbleau I had reserved two adjoining rooms, one for me and one for Mitch and Joe Twist when they rolled in. On my way back downstairs after checking in I saw Mickey Rooney with his arm around a gorgeous blonde who looked about a foot taller than him. Pully was waiting for me in the Boom Boom Room and we ordered cocktails. I let him take his time to explain what was going on. After we had been sitting there awhile he said: "Something good is going to happen."

"Yeah? How soon?" I said.

"Very soon. David Janssen is in the hotel. He's in charge." Janssen I knew only from "The Fugitive" on television. I asked what he was like.

"A great guy, but he likes his tea, gotta watch that." Pully made a drinking motion with his hand. Then he laughed, so I couldn't tell if he was joking or not.

"Who else is involved?" I asked.

"Dan Blocker, Richard Conte. Conte's here too." Conte I knew from Jilly's the previous year, good people.

"What about Mickey Rooney? I saw him on my floor."

"Everyone's involved, except Mickey Rooney," Pully said.

"Why's that?" I said.

Pully grinned. "I think those eight or nine wives put a dent into his bank account."

"That's too bad," I said. "He looks like an all-right guy."

Pully stopped smiling. "There's something I have to ask you."

"Go right ahead," I said.

"I know Henry thinks the world of you. I just hope you can handle what you're here for."

"I still don't know what I'm here for," I said.

Pully's grin came back. "In a few days we're all going to sit down and discuss it. Can you operate a food and bar business?"

"Of course. The bar I know inside out. Food, I know too, but I prefer to hire a good manager so I can concentrate on the liquor. That's where all the money is."

Pully seemed pleased. "That's terrific. I feel a lot better. Through Henry you were picked by California and New York as most qualified."

"Qualified for what?" My curiosity had finally gotten the better of me.

"A group of celebrities leased a piece of land on Miami Beach with option to buy," Pully said. "They're planning to build the biggest nightclub on the East Coast. You're the guy to run the whole show."

I shrugged. "I'm ready when they are."

"In a few days it will be official."

IT TURNED OUT to be more than a few days. That's the way it always is with those things, but I didn't mind the wait at all. It was great to be back in Miami Beach, and I looked up a lot of old friends.

It took Joe Twist and Mitch a long time to deliver my car because they were stopped by police in every state on the way down. They even had trouble right outside the Fountainbleau. I wasn't there when they got in early in the morning, so they slept in the car outside the hotel. They woke up surrounded by cops who went through the car for the umpteenth time.

"What were they looking for?" I asked.

"They mentioned your name through all the states," Mitch said. "They didn't say what they were looking for. We kept calling your room. We thought something happened to you."

I had been at the Castaways with Josie, a North End girl. Poor Mitch and Joe *looked* like they had been sleeping in a car, and I told them to go up to their room and take it easy.

It's a good thing the cops didn't think to bring along a screwdriver when they searched my Eldorado, because I'd hidden a couple guns behind a panel. Why there was so much heat on me I didn't know. For once in my life I wasn't doing anything illegal. I took the guns out of the car and told Joe and Mitch to hide them in their room.

I had no reason to expect trouble in Miami Beach, but I didn't want to be left defenseless, either. During the winter most of the Boston crew was down there, and I wasn't taking any chances. Feuds can travel, and you always have to keep your eyes open.

When you're out on the streets, like I was, and your life is always in jeopardy, you have to learn people fast. I am able to read a man, size him up, after being with him only a short time, sometimes without even knowing him at all. That's a great gift in any walk of life, and for a criminal it can mean the difference between surviving and getting whacked. For instance, I was a little leery of Johnny Rosselli even before he shot his mouth off. Sometimes I think it's almost a psychic thing, like radar.

You need radar on the streets. You need it in an open city like Miami Beach. And you needed it back then in a place like the Fountainbleau. It was a beautiful hotel in those days, and you could always find wiseguys from all over. The place was like a club for mobsters, and like with any club there were people to know—and people to avoid.

One afternoon I was coming out of the pool and a guy I knew hurried over to me. "Hey, Willie, Vinnie Teresa said he wants to meet you," the guy said. Teresa was from Boston. Back there he was a nobody, but in Miami Beach he carried on like the biggest of the big shots. He had a wife someplace, but the love of his life was a black girl who had become his mistress. He bought her a house and furs and made a huge show of it. I had seen him around once or twice and knew immediately he was a phony.

I started drying off. "He wants me to go over there and say hello?"

"Yeah, that's right," the guy said, and now I could see Teresa sitting across the pool watching us. He was a big fat guy.

I turned back at the messenger. "Well, look, I don't want

to meet him. And don't ever come back to me with his name on your lips." The guy backed away from me and faded.

A few years later Teresa got into some kind of trouble and tried to put the finger on Meyer.

AFTER I HAD been down there a week, Pully finally called. A meeting was scheduled for that afternoon in a conference room of the Fountainbleau. When I got there David Janssen, Richard Conte, and Pully were waiting for me. Janssen sat at the head of the table, but Conte did most of the talking. They asked about my experience, and I told them about the restaurant I had managed in the North End. I had made a million mistakes in that place, but I learned the business. The meeting seemed to go very well and we all hit it off. I looked a little young, they said, but a lot of people had faith in me and recommended me for the job. Everything looked good.

That night I took Josie out for a celebration, and we wound up back in my place at the Fountainbleau. The next morning we were in bed making love when suddenly there was a tremendous crash. The door flew open and several men came charging into the room. I jumped out of bed naked and found myself facing five or six guns. With the guns were badges, Miami police, and Florida state police. I think one of them said "FBI" as they shoved me against the wall. "We got your rap sheet. How many people did you kill in the Barboza war?" one of the cops said. He tossed some clothes at me while the others ransacked the place looking for guns or anything else that could be used to nail me.

I put on my pants and quickly passed two rolls of bills to Josie. It was about 10,000 dollars, but it was in her purse before the cops could get a close look. We both insisted it was her money and there was nothing they could do.

The search turned up nothing—luckily they didn't bother to even look in the room next door. I was arrested anyway—for failing to register as a felon with the local authorities, which was a new one on me. My hands were cuffed, my feet chained, and other chains attached to the cuffs ran down my back and around my waist.

Then they hustled me toward the door. "You're not going to take me through the lobby like this, are you?" I said.

The arresting officer, the one who had seen my rap sheet, laughed at me. He was enjoying every minute of it. "Yeah, you're a bad character and we're going to let everybody know."

So I went down the grand staircase of the Fountainbleau in chains. At the foot of the stairs in the lobby, looking white as a sheet, was David Janssen. He couldn't believe what he was seeing, and that made two of us, because I couldn't, either. The whole thing was right out of a nightmare.

After I was brought in the cops didn't seem to know what to do with me. A big cop came in, looked at me and said: "You don't look so dangerous to me. What are they making all this fuss about?" But they couldn't just let me go after acting like I was John Dillinger, so I got a court date and bail of 100 dollars. That presented another problem: Josie had all my money and I had lost her in all the confusion. I wound up calling Phil Waggenheimer, an old Boston buttonman who had moved south. He found a lawyer and bailed me out.

Two days later a judge slapped me with a 25 dollar fine and a warning: "Next time you come into my county and fail to make criminal registration, you'll be in a chain gang and not staying at the Fountainbleau."

Phil Waggenheimer came up to me afterwards. "I looked into this and somebody dropped a dime on you," he said. The cops had been tipped that I was carrying guns. Me and Joe and Mitch had cleared out of the Fountainbleau that morning, and thrown all our stuff in my car. I told the judge I was leaving the state, but I decided to check in at the Castaways for a few days. We went flying over there from the courthouse, going way over the speed limit, and on the way I spotted a familiar face in my rearview. It was the same cop who had arrested me at the Fountainbleau.

"Do you go to church on Sundays?" he said after pulling me over. "You ought to, with the way you drive."

When I told him I was driving back up north he made me open the trunk, which was stuffed with boxes and suitcases.

"I know they're in there. I know it," he said. This guy had guns on the brain, he wasn't giving up.

"You won't find anything in there," I said.

"I know they're in there," he said again. "You're never without them." He stared into the trunk. Going through every bag would take a long time, and it would be pretty embarrassing if he came up empty again. I think that's why he finally let me go without searching the car. I told him the truth—the guns weren't there. After getting out on bail I handed them over to another friend.

I NEVER FOUND out who set me up or why, but the arrest spooked everybody. The nightclub deal went out the window—nobody in their right mind would hire a guy to run a big nightclub when he's carrying heat like that. The place was never built. I was too stunned to think or feel much of anything over the next few days. Josie was very good to me and eased some of the pain.

Finally, I called Henry and explained what had happened. He told me to come home. Me and Josie flew back up. Joe Twist and Mitch drove my car back, and this time no one stopped them.

I never told Meyer about the arrest, yet I think he knew. Phil Waggenheimer was a friend of his. No one had to tell me to take precautions. On my occasional trips to Miami Beach after that I never again met Meyer in public.

HENRY WAS DISAPPOINTED, but wasn't giving up. He had a new scheme up his sleeve by the time I was back in the North End.

"At the end of May [1969] I want you to take a trip to Hollywood," he said. "I like Mitch, let him drive you out there."

"Whatever you say, Henry," I said.

By the time I was ready to go, Henry had a long list of people to look up in California, including his old pal George Raft.

CHAPTER SIXTEEN

CALIFORNIA

I THINK HENRY and Frank had a few motives for sending me out to L.A. For one thing, they wanted to keep me out of trouble, so I could still move money for Meyer. Then, as I have said, the plan was for me to eventually establish my own family somewhere away from Boston. My crew was the best around. Butch Capone, Eddie Greco, Danny Puopolo, Jimmy Sforza, Peter Piso, Johnny Russo, Charlie Centofanti. All of them knock-around good guys. You couldn't find better men anywhere.

"Something has got to come of this," Frank said. "It's too good a thing to waste." Frank's idea was that we set up in open territory: South Florida, Southern California, or Nevada, with me as the boss and him as the *consigliere*, the position he had held when the Boston mob was founded. Florida was his first choice, but because of the mess at the Fountainbleau, Florida was out and L.A. was in.

Meanwhile, Henry seemed to think I had the looks to make it in television or the movies. Before I left he told me: "While you're doing your business [the courier trips] maybe you can get yourself something out there. You can make more money on the screen than what you've been doing." Acting didn't turn me on at all, and compared to what I'd been doing, it was pretty tame.

But Henry insisted that I stay in Los Angeles through the summer, so I drove out there with Mitch at the end of May and got an apartment on Moorpark Street in North Hollywood.

Frank and Henry kept me out of trouble, but they forgot that I get bored easily. Hollywood was dull, show business was dull, and people in show business, most of the ones I met, anyway, weren't worth knowing. Southern California was beautiful and sunny, but there was no big exciting scene like in Miami Beach. Before long I was looking for a bank to rob just to have something to do. Mitch got stir-crazy after a few weeks and beat it back east. I didn't blame him. In fact, I envied him.

Henry wanted me to touch base with wiseguys and movie people, and he picked somebody who was familiar with both worlds to take me around: George Raft. I called him up about a week after I got out there and we met at a lounge on Sunset Boulevard called the Body Shop.

There's a great moment in Robert Lacey's *The Little Man* when a Cuban mob charges into a Havana casino a few days after the revolution, looking to smash up the place. They are met by George Raft, who had a piece of the casino. Like a gangster who has just stepped down from a movie screen, he orders them to clear out of his joint, and that's just what they do. Lacey also tells us that real gangsters wanted to look like George Raft, instead of the other way around, and even asked for the name of his tailor.

George was still a sharp dresser when I met him, but he was getting old and having a lot of problems. A few years earlier the wiseguys who ran the Colony Sporting Club in London brought him in as the host—the sort of thing he had done back in Havana—and gave him perks fit for a sheik: a Rolls-Royce with a chauffeur, a fancy apartment, a young girlfriend, and a blank check for an expense account. It was a great deal, until January 1967 when the British suddenly barred him from the country because of his underworld connections. Poor George was in California at the time and was the last to know. A reporter called him up and told him. He couldn't believe it, but it was on front pages all over the world. He was being called a crook—a real-life crook—and now everybody wanted to know about associations and friendships he'd had all his life. Back in this country the IRS came after him for back taxes and eventually stripped him of everything he had. If he was still young maybe he could have started over, but George was past seventy. His career was on the late show.

GEORGE WAS REAL nice to me, a perfect gentleman and a regular guy. He liked the fights and we hit the Forum to see the welterweight Indian Red Lopez, his favorite, and Mando Ramos, the lightweight champ. When we went out to dinner it was usually to the Villa Capri. The owner was from Boston and his wife baked apple pies just for George. He never talked about his troubles too much, but you could tell they were eating at him. His mansion in Beverly Hills had been lost to the feds and he was living in a small apartment in Coldwater Canyon. I never saw it. I think he was ashamed to take me there. Aside from the money problems, the ban from Britain had been devastating. George had a lot of pride and I don't think he ever got over it.

"My life has flip-flopped," he said. "I was riding high and now I'm at the lowest ever." In the good days he had never refused anybody a dollar—and there had been plenty of sponges. Now he was the one who needed help.

He told me that Frank Sinatra was the only one who took care of him when things got bad. "I got a call from Frank and the first words he said were, 'How much ya need?' He sent me a blank check."

The wiseguys who ran the Colony Sporting Club, the men who were supposed to be his friends, hadn't lifted a finger for him. I think Sinatra's generosity embarrassed them, because by the end of 1969 I was given envelopes on my trips overseas to take back to George Raft.

George had known gangsters and wiseguys since he was a

kid back in New York's Hell's Kitchen. He had a lot of affection for Henry Noyes, but he told me that Bugsy Siegel scared him.

JOHNNY ROSSELLI HAD been a big shot in Hollywood back in Bugsy Siegel's time and remained one long after Bugsy screwed up. If Bugsy was organized crime the way it had been, loud, violent and unpredictable, Johnny was what it was trying to become, smart and polished with just the right touch of menace. Johnny was the perfect Los Angeles gangster, and Los Angeles was his town. He had friends and influence everywhere like you wouldn't believe. Unfortunately, none of that helped him with the feds. They'd been after him a long time, and in the year since I'd seen him he'd finally been stung. In the spring of 1968 he was found guilty of failing to register as an alien—he had been born in Italy and lied about it. That was no big deal, it only meant a small risk of deportation. Then, just a few months after that trial, a federal jury convicted him of being part of a card-cheating scandal at the Friars Club. He was appealing that when I got out there, but it looked like he was going to do time. Johnny was in his sixties, and the joint is very hard on a man that age. He was carrying a lot of heat, and that was reason enough to avoid him. Still, I figured it wouldn't hurt to see him once or twice. After all, I liked the guy.

Johnny sounded glad to hear my voice and immediately suggested taking me to the Brown Derby or some other very public spot. I said I couldn't do that—I couldn't afford to have any feds watching me—and we wound up meeting at the Villa Capri, which at least wasn't as well known. He had just come from his mother's funeral back in Boston, and was feeling pretty low. Her death was the hardest blow of all. He said he wished he could have spent more time with his family, especially his mother.

Johnny was still handsome and perfectly groomed, like a Hollywood prince, but you could tell the bad year had taken its toll. The legal troubles made him very bitter. When the CIA asked him for help, he provided it. When he was in trouble they let him hang, and I think that made him feel very alone. Maybe that's why he spilled his guts to me the way he did. I'll never forget it.

I always made sure we got together in out-of-the-way places, drugstore fountains, drive-ins, and the submarine joints off Sunset Boulevard, the kinds of places you always found hippies hanging out.

One day we were on our way to get a submarine and Johnny seemed even more depressed than usual. He looked worn-out.

"Johnny, you'd better get a hold of yourself," I told him. He didn't answer and kept his head down.

"It disturbs me," he said suddenly. "I was there for them and they're not there for me. They want you to help them, then when things go the other way . . . "

He touched my hand. "Who do you think got Kennedy?—the French." I turned to him and he nodded. Over the next hour or so he laid out an incredible story—a combination history lesson and conspiracy. It went like this: While the mob and the CIA were trying to get rid of Fidel Castro, the Kennedy brothers never let up on the mob for a moment. Sam Giancana had FBI men on his tail everywhere he went, and Bobby Kennedy and the Justice Department were looking to put him away for the rest of his life. That was his thanks for delivering the election to the Kennedys on a silver platter, and doing all he could to help the government take back Cuba. Santo Trafficante too, was feeling the heat, as were many others. Again, the Kennedys had turned their backs on the mobsters who had handed them fortune and power. Here they were trying to do a good act for them, and it still wouldn't stop. The Kennedys never delivered. But as far as Trafficante was concerned this was the final betrayal. Now the very survival of the mob was at stake. Johnny Rosselli said Giancana and Santo Trafficante met in 1963 and decided to reverse the plot. Instead of Castro, John Kennedy was to be the target. Giancana and Johnny Rosselli didn't know it then, but Trafficante had secretly been trying to undermine the conspiracy against Castro from the very beginning. Johnny said that Trafficante even tipped off the Cubans about the scheme. Castro did his own investigation and found out it was true. Then, he figured that two could play at the same game, and soon Castro and Trafficante were discussing a course of action.

Giancana, meanwhile, felt disgusted and betrayed. After the first few attempts on Castro had failed, Giancana's "partners" in the government urged him to send in a crew of his own buttonmen and do it the way they did in the twenties—open up on Castro with machine guns. It didn't seem to matter that no one could possibly survive a stunt like that. "They think we're a bunch of donkeys," Giancana told Johnny. "They don't care about us." For Giancana that was the last straw.

Once Trafficante and Giancana agreed to switch the focus of their conspiracy, Trafficante made contact with a wiseguy in Dallas who enlisted the help of a small-time hoodlum and nightclub owner there: Jack Ruby. Ruby was told to hook up with a man who had been supplied by Castro, Lee Harvey Oswald.

"Castro knew Lee Harvey Oswald, they met in Cuba," Johnny told me. "And Jack Ruby knew and associated with Lee Harvey Oswald."

A few months before the assassination Ruby went to New Orleans, supposedly to enlist strippers for his nightclub. Actually, he had several meetings with Oswald, who was told of the conspiracy, but led to believe that the Russians and the Cubans were behind it. At some point, Ruby was also approached by two Sicilians. They gave him the probable route of the president's motorcade when he came to Dallas in November. These men also told him about the Texas School Book Depository overlooking Dealy Plaza. Oswald would be working there; it was a perfect setup. It was all arranged. It was also understood that Oswald would not be around very long after Kennedy was killed.

According to Johnny, the Sicilians were imported and had been brought into the picture by Santo Trafficante and Frank Cucchiara. They were used to take any heat off the people in America. I knew that Frank had a lot of contacts back in Sicily, and if one Sicilian was involved, they all were. In those years, mob bosses who needed some good imported help usually went to Phil Buccola in Sicily. He was a master at putting people together, but Johnny never mentioned his name.

Frank and Trafficante had their associates in Sicily contact professional killers in France, men the Sicilians knew from the heroin trade. Three assassins left France in October 1963 and entered Mexico with Italian passports. In November they crossed over to Texas with a party of Sicilians, then made their way to Dallas, where they were put up in a house not far from Dealy Plaza. According to Johnny, one of the gunmen had the same height and same build as Oswald, and combed his hair the same way. This man went to the Book Depository on November 22, 1963, and was taken upstairs by Oswald, who handed him a rifle.

As Kennedy's limousine glided across Dealy Plaza, one rifleman shot at the president from the book depository and at least one other assassin opened fire from somewhere in the front. Johnny didn't say exactly where the other killers were stationed. In those days the term "grassy knoll" was unknown. Oswald, Johnny, said, "didn't kill anybody."

ONCE KENNEDY WAS dead, Ruby took Oswald out of the picture. "Did you ever give a thought to the guy shooting him in the stomach?" Johnny asked, and I knew what he meant: If you want to kill somebody, you go for the head or the heart, shoot him in the stomach he's likely to survive. But Johnny said he had heard that the bullets Ruby fired were coated with some kind of chemical, a poison that would cause heart failure.

Again and again, Johnny mentioned that a government agency was involved somehow. He shook his head. "It's amazing, everybody around the assassination dying like that."

Although the whole thing came together in New Orleans, Johnny said Carlos Marcello had nothing to do with it. He had already attracted heat for making threats against the Kennedys, so the other wiseguys shut him out.

The whole story sounds pretty bizarre, I know. I've told it the way it was told to me more than twenty years ago. Johnny spilled it just that once, and in the few times I saw him after that he never brought it up again. And I never asked him about it. Just like with all the other stuff he told me, the less I knew the better. Johnny never said how he knew about this conspiracy, or if he was involved in it himself. I do know that Johnny wasn't the type of guy to invent stuff; besides, he was agitated and depressed when he told me, like he had to get it off his chest. I also know that he was very close to Sam Giancana. Maybe that's where his information came from.

Believe it or not, I never gave it much thought at the time. I really didn't care about politics or who killed the Kennedy brothers. My interests lay elsewhere. So how true any of it is I can't say. But when I think about it now my mind swings back to the Florentine Café and Frank Cucchiara muttering about the assassination: *I wish I'd been there. If I'd been there I would've done it right. No one would have gotten arrested."*

JOHNNY ROSSELLI STRUCK out with all the appeals courts, and in 1971 went to prison. He was out by 1973, and a year or two later I ran into him in Las Vegas. We were both on our way somewhere else and just said hello. Later I mentioned this to a guy from Chicago, and this time there was a specific warning: "Never get involved with this guy," the man said. "He talks. He spilled his guts to his lawyer. He talked to some committee in Washington."

It sounded like Johnny's lawyer had taken over my role. Apparently he got so he couldn't exist without a pair of ears. What the Chicago man said about talking to a committee was true. In 1975 Johnny testified before the Senate committee investigating the CIA and the FBI. According to one source, Johnny laid out what he knew about the plots against Castro, and didn't rat about business. But sometimes the mob isn't big on distinctions. Sam Giancana was supposed to testify before the same committee, but never got the chance. Somebody whacked him a week before he was supposed to go to Washington.

GIANCANA MAY HAVE died because of what he knew, but I suspect he was killed for what *Johnny Rosselli* knew. Johnny was talking too much, and the wiseguys may have guessed that Giancana had been doing some blabbing of his own. I never saw Johnny again. The word was out, and it wasn't safe to be around him. I liked him. He was an interesting character with everything going for him. He just slipped too many times. The thing with the CIA was his big power play. If it had worked, if they had whacked Castro, taken back Cuba, and gotten the Kennedys off everyone's back he would have been way above everybody. But it didn't work, and when you take a chance like that and fail—especially with the government—the game is over. Of course, Johnny tried to keep playing, and that only made things worse. When a guy that big starts saying and doing the wrong things, it sticks out. So it wasn't much of a surprise when I read in August 1976 that Johnny Rosselli's body had been found in a steel drum floating on the Intercoastal near Miami.

His mouth got him killed.

I WANTED TO go home at the end of the summer, but Henry told me to hang on, something big was sure to happen. George took me around to meet a lot of people, and as soon as they heard I was with Henry Noyes, they were jumping out of their chairs to make me feel at home. Wiseguys, entertainment types, restaurant owners, it didn't matter, they all knew Henry. He was top shelf with them, and that made me top shelf too. I got to meet a lot of producers, actors, writers, directors, and stuntmen, although nothing ever came of it. To pass the time I went to a gym and did a lot of jogging. I also hung around with boxers, and got friendly with Joey Giambra, who had been a middleweight contender from the late 1940s to the mid-1960s. Joey had battled all the old warhorses. He was the only man to knock the great Tiger Jones off his feet, and that was after Tiger had given Sugar Ray Robinson a bad beating. In the 1950s he beat Joey Giardello twice before Giardello went on to win the championship. Joey Giambra should have been champion himself. He was intelligent and very strong, but always seemed to have a run of bad luck just when it came time to go for it. Yet he never complained when things didn't work out. I think the fighters of that generation were a classier bunch than the people who came up later. Rocky Marciano is a classic example. Marciano was from Brockton, Massachusetts, and when I was a kid he used to visit a family that lived just around the corner from me in the North End. Every time I heard he was around, I'd dash over there to shake his hand—me and half the kids in the neighborhood. Marciano was mobbed like that wherever he went, yet he always took the time to say hello to everybody and sign all the autographs. It was like he was this good, humble guy who just happened to be the heavyweight champion of the world.

Through Joey Giambra I met Robert Conrad, who at the time was starring in "The Wild, Wild West" on television. Although nearly thirty-five, Conrad was looking to get a professional boxing license. Joey showed him all the moves, and he did have some talent, but then he got a bad concussion while doing a stunt on his show, and that was the end of his boxing career.

In October George called sounding very upbeat. A meeting had been arranged with a big shot at one of the major studios, somebody who supposedly could do great things for me. Both George and Henry had high hopes. I still didn't think much of the whole idea, but since they had gone to all the trouble, I'd at least go see this executive. He was a tall, distinguished-looking guy in his fifties with dark hair that was gray on the sides. His office was enormous, and his desk so huge that I couldn't touch him when we went to shake hands. He had to come around. For about an hour the two of us sat there just shooting the breeze. He asked me about who I knew, where I was from, and I asked him about the movie industry. Small talk. Then he stepped out from behind the desk, walked over and put an arm around my shoulder. His whole manner, even his voice, had suddenly changed. He said there were people I should meet, Rock Hudson and another popular movie star. "It's not who you know, it's who you blow," he said softly. "They're the queen bees, they'll be here next week, and we're going to have a big party. I would like you to be there."

I couldn't believe what I was hearing, and I was too shocked to say or do anything, except throw the guy's arm off my shoulder and walk out. "Hey, you've got nothing to say?" he said before I slammed the door. I couldn't believe what had happened. Don't forget, even in the late 1960s nobody talked about homosexuality. And the idea that a famous actor like Rock Hudson could be gay seemed incredible. I knew people who'd been out there for years and even they didn't believe it.

Hollywood was just too weird for my blood. After leaving the executive's office, I drove back to my apartment, packed up, threw my stuff in the car and left a message for Henry: "I'm leaving L.A. Will be home soon."

Six days later I went over to Henry's house and told him the whole story. He immediately reached for the phone and called George Raft in Hollywood. Henry was furious, and I felt bad because I didn't mean to blame George. But a minute later Henry was screaming into the phone and poor George on the other end was trying to calm him down.

"Henry, Henry, I swear I never knew this guy was a fag," he said.

I leaned over. "C'mon, Henry, George has been great with me. I'm telling you he didn't know."

"He's a closet fag and they let themselves loose at rare times," George pleaded. "Henry, for God's sake, would I do something like that?"

"All right," Henry said. "Maybe you didn't know, but you should have known. All that young stuff is making your brains soft."

George laughed. Henry laughed. The storm had blown over. It was always that way with Henry, he never stayed mad. When he got off the phone I asked if he had any other destinations for me.

He looked up at me. "Yes, Las Vegas."

CHAPTER SEVENTEEN

A LOT OF GOOD-BYES

WHEN YOU'RE OUT robbing and hijacking like I was in those years, you had to have at least two stashes of money. One you kept well hidden in case you took a fall, so if you did ten or fifteen years you'd have something to fall back on instead of coming out broke and desperate. After doing fifteen straight you can't go back to what you were doing, because if you get busted again, that's another twenty or twenty-five years, and that will destroy you. Everybody understands that. But you also can't hit the streets appearing weak, like you're down to your last dollar, because that will ruin whatever credibility you built up by doing your time like a man. As Frank Cucchiara always said: "You can do a thousand good things, and one bad one wipes out the thousand."

In that life, money is everything, the bottom line, and the big stash is like your insurance or your pension. You hide it where no one will find it. You don't touch it and you don't tell anybody about it, except maybe your family. I had more than one million dollars in cash buried under three inches of concrete in a basement. It was wrapped in nylon and cloth and covered with plastic bags.

The other stash is loose money for bail and lawyers. And payoffs to cops and judges. I always made sure to keep at least 200,000 dollars on hand. You never knew when you might need half that just for a reduction in sentence. You'll pay that much—you'll pay just about anything to knock off a few years—because when you're talking hard time, those few years make all the difference in the world.

I had to dip into the loose stash in November 1969 right after I got back from L.A. A nasty motorcycle cop was tagging cars right and left every day and had a real attitude. There were a lot of complaints about him in the neighborhood. Me and my crew hauled an old refrigerator up to a rooftop and planned to drop it down on him or one of the other cops who was always bothering us. The street below was narrow and clear. A couple nights we actually waited for the cop to drive by. It would be like crushing a cockroach. Of course, something like that was certain to bring enormous heat down on everybody, and get us into trouble with the cops *and* the wiseguys, so we settled on a less drastic form of revenge. One night we were driving around and spotted the cop's bike parked on a sidewalk at Hanover and Cross Streets. I jumped out and flattened his tires with a switchblade.

The next night, after his tires were fixed, the cop came roaring over to Bova's Corner where a bunch of us were lounging around, and told us to scatter. Nobody moved.

"Get off the sidewalk," he barked.

"No," I said. "We live here. Why should we get off the sidewalk?"

"You're blocking the sidewalk. Move!" he shouted. When we didn't, he radioed for reinforcements. More cops arrived. They shoved us. We shoved back, and all hell broke loose. It turned into a small riot. Hundreds of people came pouring out of the shops and tenements to see what was going on. Two of the cops took a bad beating and went to the hospital. Me and three other guys were hauled back to the police station, charged with assaulting a police officer.

*   *   *

A COUPLE HOURS later I was out on bail, back at Bova's Corner
and ready for more action. I found it right away when this huge
policeman came swaggering up, his face a big sneer. He towered
over everybody and had enough arrogance in him to fill ten normal cops. "You guys still hanging around?" he said, and swung
his heavy arms for us to beat it.

"What are you going to do, arrest us for hanging around?"
I said. "You're just looking for trouble. You just want to instigate
a riot."

The cop made some crack, so I went right up him. "You
got no balls," I said. "Why don't you take off that badge and let's
you and me go in the playground and see who walks out."

The cop lunged and got me by the arm. When he did that
a bunch of people who had been watching yelled for him to let
me go and tried to get between us. Then Georgie Bova, who
owned Bova's Bakery, rushed out and grabbed the cop so I could
get away. Georgie's father, who was in his seventies, jumped right
in with him. I got away, and Georgie got busted for assault and
battery.

O UR FRIEND JUDGE Adlow in municipal court was handling the
case, but the cops were pushing to have me bound over to su-
perior court for felony charges, where I risked getting three-to-
five in a state prison. Henry Noyes called Max Glazer, who said
I could beat a felony rap, but I'd have to do some jail time.

"Look, Willie," Max told me, "The judge has gotta sentence
you to ninety days. Those two cops are in the hospital and he's
getting a lot of static."

I was more concerned about Georgie Bova. He had been
arrested on account of me. Max assured me he'd take care of
Georgie. Then I thought of something else.

"Max, I can't do ninety days. I'm opening an after-hours
joint and I want to have it open on New Year's Eve."

Max threw up his hands. "For God's sake, do the ninety days and open in February! You've gotta get the judge off the hook."

"All right," I said. "Tell him to sentence me to ninety days, and I'll go for an appeal."

Adlow's court was a zoo that day, and packed with people from the North End.

A cop pointed at me. "Your honor, we've had a lot of trouble with Mr. Fopiano in the past. His record is atrocious."

Adlow glared at him. "I know all about his record," he said, but the cop insisted that it be read into the record and the judge had to go along.

So the cop boomed out my entire criminal record, every arrest, even the ones I beat. It took seven minutes.

When he was finally finished, the big cop who had arrested Georgie Bova stood up. He was there for that case, but now he was staring at me.

"Your honor," he said. "This is the same character who started the second incident. I knew a William Fopiano was coming to the courtroom today, but I didn't know that was the man who tried to pick a fight with me. He was bailed out and went right back to the corner to start more trouble."

Then he told Adlow how I challenged him to a fight in the playground—quoting me word for word—and that Georgie Bova helped me escape by punching him in the face.

Adlow looked over at Georgie and asked him to step out of the prisoner's box and come over to where the cop was standing.

"Mr. Bova, how tall are you?" Adlow said.

"Five foot three."

The cop was at least a foot taller, and Adlow asked: "You mean to tell me he hit you on the chin?"

"Yes, your honor," the cop said quickly.

"Well," Adlow said. "If he hit you he must have done it from a stepladder or had extensions on his hands. I'm not going to buy that." The last six words were nearly drowned out by the laughter from the North End crowd. They loved it, but Adlow wasn't through.

"Do you own that bakery, Mr. Bova?"

"Yes, your honor."

"And do you object to these bullies being on your property?"

"No, these people are my friends."

So Adlow turned back to the big cop. "What right do you have to make them get off his property?" he said, and let Georgie go.

Then, it was the motorcycle cop's turn and he plowed right into his story. He hadn't gotten too far when Adlow had a question. Why did he come all the way over to Bova's Corner, at Prince and Salem Streets, if his tires were flattened at Hanover and Cross, on the other side of the North End.

"Did you see who did it?" Adlow said.

"No, your honor."

"Well, that's a heck of a thing. Why did you go down to Prince and Salem?"

"Well, we've had a lot of trouble with people on that corner. It's a troubled corner."

"A troubled corner," Adlow raised his eyebrows. "Looks like I know where the trouble's coming from."

The cop didn't know what to say, obviously, Adlow was new to him. "Your honor, I'm not on trial," he said.

"Well, I'm putting you on trial," Adlow said, and turned to me and the three guys who got pinched with me. "Look at these guys," he said. The cop kept staring straight ahead. "You're not looking at them. Look at them." The cop looked at us. "Look, they're hoodlums," Adlow said. "You're never going to rehabilitate them. They don't squeal on anybody. They're my kind of kids. I wish you'd stop bothering them."

After that Max Glazer got up and made this big speech about how I had gone back to Bova's Corner that night "to make peace." He made the same argument for the first fight. Me and the other kids were just nice neighborhood boys who got pushed around by the cops.

When Adlow had heard enough he sentenced us to three months at the Deer Island House of Correction, but we didn't serve a day. The fix had come pretty cheap, only about 3000 dollars. I would have gladly laid out a couple thousand more.

An appeals judge threw out the ninety days and gave me a year's probation instead. He also made a nice speech. "Mr. Fopiano apologizes to you," he told the cops, who just sat there stony-faced. "From now on he's going to be a respectable citizen. These neighborhood things do happen, and it wasn't done with malice. I'm going to give him a chance. He assures you and the Boston police department that this will never happen again."

I always had a good time when I went to court. In those days nobody really cared that much about going to jail. Everybody just sat back and enjoyed themselves. We certainly would've seen the inside of many more jail cells if it wasn't for judges like Adlow, who was a real character and genuinely liked us. He loved the restaurants in the North End, and once he came by Bova's Corner when a bunch of us were around. "Hey, Judge," somebody yelled.

"You look familiar," Adlow said. "Have you been in my court?" The guy said he had.

The judge laughed. "Well, try to stay out of trouble."

EVEN THOUGH I had gotten off easy again, Frank and Henry were upset.

"You ain't back three weeks and you get arrested for assaulting some stupid cop," Henry said.

"They provoke me," I told him. "What do you want me to do?"

"Walk away! You can't keep living this way."

He stopped talking and Frank shot me an icy glare. "This has to stop, one pinch and you're gone," he said. "Twenty-five years. We'd never see you. By the time you get out, we're dead.

Look at Eddie, he's doing so good in the Canteen." Eddie had taken a steady job in a restaurant and was looking to go legit.

"I can't settle down," I said. "I don't know what's the matter with me."

It was Henry's turn again: "This place is no good for you. As soon as we make the arrangements you're going to Vegas. That tavern on Prince Street, Savino's, is for sale. Buy it. It will keep you busy until we set things up in Vegas. Put it in your brother-in-law's name."

BY THE TIME I bought the tavern my after-hours joint on Salem Street was going full blast. We opened right on schedule, on New Year's Eve, 1969, and it was a big success. It seemed like every wiseguy in New England was there that first night. I loved having them, but it's smart to be a little wary when you're surrounded by armed men slapping down drinks. I made payoffs, of course, but the cops still tried to make trouble and shut the place down. I was ready for them whenever they showed up. On the wall was a charter that allowed me to run a private club. Everybody there had a membership card and all the bottles had somebody's name on it. There was nothing they could do.

Savino's Tavern only cost me 7000 dollars, plus a few thousand more to fix it up a little.

EARLY IN 1970 I ran into a woman named Joanne White, who had just moved back from Las Vegas. I first met Joanne in the summer of 1965 at a club in downtown Boston called El Morocco where she was a waitress. I had gone to the place with some of Frank Cucchiara's old pals, but wound up giving Joanne most of my attention. She was beautiful. After that I found myself going back to the place just to see her. That kind of surprised me, because our conversations were always brief, and I was not a settle-down kind of guy. But the next thing I knew Joanne was out in Vegas, the head cocktail waitress at a big new casino:

Caesars Palace. She became friendly with Frank Sinatra out there and started going out with his pal Jilly Rizzo. After a few years she got tired of the life out there, left Jilly, and headed back east. When I saw her again she was working in a bar called the Jib Lounge. This time we hit it off and began seeing each other. The relationship was sort of on-again, off-again. My hectic schedule and my mood still wouldn't allow me to settle down. Joanne didn't appreciate that too much, but tolerated it rather well.

IN MARCH, HENRY Noyes told me to call a guy who ran junkets to Las Vegas and reserve a seat on his next flight. I flew out there with a friend and we stayed at the Stardust Hotel. Henry had given me a long list of people to look up. That way, once I moved out there I'd be known by all the important people. I had told Meyer Lansky that I was heading out to Vegas, and he also made sure I was welcomed in the right places. With the good word of Henry and Meyer, I got the red-carpet treatment everywhere I went. Among the people I met were Jay Sarno, who had built Caesars Palace and later was one of the movers behind Circus Circus, and Hymie Abrams, a big shot at the Sands. Hymie was from Boston and known to both Frank and Meyer. They were great and couldn't do enough for me. It was a different story with Moe Dalitz. He tried to act like he was overjoyed to see me when I looked him up, but he didn't want me around at all. Whenever he ran into me he'd give my hand a quick shake and say, "Nice to see you, nice to see you"—and be backing away while he said it! He got nervous just being in the same room with me. After all, Moe Dalitz was supposed to be a legitimate businessman and philanthropist, the owner of casinos and lavish resorts and a big pal of politicians like Paul Laxalt and celebrities like Bob Hope. I knew too much about him. I knew about the satchels full of cash in the cabanas behind the Fountainbleau. I think I was an unpleasant reminder of where he came from. Guys like that are very selective about their memories.

Dalitz was such a bastard that I toyed with the idea of shaking him down after I moved out there. I'd demand a hundred grand a month, and settle for fifty. He might have been a tough guy back in the days of the Purple Gang, but the years had made him soft. Frank vetoed that plan immediately: "Noooo! Don't bother him! He's with other people." He got so excited I thought he was going to have a heart attack. I told Frank not to get nervous, I never would've done anything like that without his okay.

Another guy I didn't get along with was Carl Cohen, an old associate of Meyer, who was an executive at the Sands. Cohen had publically insulted Frank Sinatra there a few years earlier. Now, I had only met Sinatra that one time in Miami Beach, but he showed a lot of class. He had saved George Raft and a lot of other people from the poorhouse or worse. He was my kind of guy. I didn't think much of the way Cohen had treated him, and didn't mind sharing that opinion. On my second trip to Vegas that year I ran into Cohen at Caesars Palace. Out of respect for Meyer more than anything else, I went over and said hello.

"And how are you doing!" Cohen said in a tone I didn't like.

I stepped a foot closer. "What's your problem?"

"You've been talking about me!" he snapped, shoving his finger in my face. I grabbed the finger and bent it back. Cohen winced.

"Look," I said. "I don't like the way you acted with Frank Sinatra in the Sands. And if you put your finger in my face again, you won't have a finger."

Cohen was a big guy, but put his finger to his chest like a little kid.

"Do you understand?" I said.

"Yes," Cohen said quietly.

"Good, now get lost."

Later that year, a business associate of Cohen, Sandy Waterman, pulled a gun on Sinatra during an argument at Caesars Palace. Sinatra refused to press charges.

*   *   *

IN SPITE OF Cohen and Dalitz, I liked Vegas the best of all the places Henry sent me. It was bright, fancy, and glamorous, and there was always something exciting going on. The desert air was clean and clear, and just breathing it in made me feel more alive.

Of course, the biggest thrill was the gambling. I loved it and loved the casinos. I spent all my time at the tables—literally. At the Stardust I once played craps for twenty-three hours straight. I didn't eat. I didn't drink. I didn't even go to the bathroom. I stood in the same spot, and because I was in such good shape it didn't bother me. I had the stamina. The limit in those days was 500 dollars a shot and I never bet anything less. Cocktail waitresses kept coming over with free drinks, and I shooed them away. I was winning and nothing mattered but the game. Finally, I realized that three shifts had gone by since I first got to the table. The dealers and waitresses were amazed, and they were saying to each other what's with this guy, he hasn't moved for an entire day. I figured maybe it was time to pack it in, so I headed upstairs and went to bed. But an hour later I was back up, feeling as though I'd slept through the night. I felt good enough to go right back to the casino. I went home with about 5000 dollars.

I made the second trip out there in April, and again had a good time—except for dropping 40,000 dollars at the baccarat tables. By 1970, my gambling losses for the previous five years ran upwards of 2 million dollars. Everybody knew I was a heavy bettor, but had no idea how heavy. I spent 500 dollars a day on numbers and between 2000 dollars and 5000 dollars a day on horses and sports.

Even with all the cash that was coming in, losses like that were a strain, so Charlie Centofanti, Butch Capone, and me stuck up two banks, one in June, the other in July. Our net from both scores was a little less than 100,000 dollars.

Butch and Charlie were my best customers in the tavern and were there every day. Butch was having some problems, that was easy enough to see. He was drinking too much and gambled away every cent he made from the bank scores, close to 32,000 dollars. But whatever was gnawing at him he didn't talk about. Butch wasn't the kind of guy to be open about personal stuff. He was thirty-one. Maybe he knew that we were all getting too old for robberies and heists, and that made him feel empty. The party was coming to an end.

I offered to give him back what he had lost gambling, but he told me he didn't take handouts.

One night that August he came into the tavern and asked me and Charlie if we wanted to do a score with him and his kid brother, Joe. They wanted to hijack a truckload of lobsters. I asked how much was involved and he said the load was worth between 30,000 and 40,000 dollars.

Stealing lobsters is a real hassle. You've got to make sure they stay alive till you can get rid of them, and if some of them die the whole load stinks, and nobody wants to buy it. So I said I wasn't interested.

Charlie turned around and growled: "I only steal cash." He also didn't trust Butch's brother, yet didn't want to say so.

But there was something else going on. I couldn't put my finger on it, the whole thing just felt wrong. As he was about to leave, I looked into Butch's eyes and knew something bad was going to happen. If he went out on that score he wasn't coming back. I was as sure of that as the sun coming up the next day.

"Try to stop him," I told Charlie when Butch stepped away. He was a lot older than we were and Butch had a lot of respect for him.

"I did try. He won't listen," Charlie said.

I grabbed Butch when he was on his way out the door and tried to talk him out of it. Better scores would come along, lobsters weren't worth it. But Butch Capone never walked away from a score.

*   *   *

THE LOBSTER TRUCK with three men in the cab was coming down from New Brunswick, and the Capone brothers grabbed it at a red light in East Boston. They drove the three men to Topsfield, Massachusetts, tied them up, and left them in a cornfield. Several hours later two cops in a patrol car saw the truck in the North End near the water and decided to check it out. When they pulled up, Butch and Joe jumped out of the cab and started running. The patrol car went after them and Butch fired three shots at it. The cop who was driving ducked, and the car jumped the sidewalk where Butch was standing and crushed him to death. Joe Capone was found hiding in a building by a police dog.

The next day there was a photo of the cops carrying Butch away on a stretcher. He was face down, his arms dangling. They seemed so short. I used to kid him about his stubby arms. You could spot him a mile off from those arms, they were his giveaway. He had been like a brother to me. It was so senseless.

JUST DAYS AFTER the funeral Henry Noyes got very sick. He had been falling apart for a long time. Everything inside was giving out on him. Henry had no use for doctors. When they told him no salt, he paid no attention. He threw salt on just about everything that went into his mouth. At the Florentine he even salted his beer!

He was in bed when I went to his house. One look and I knew he was done. He knew it too.

"I think my time has come," he said. "I heard about your friend Butch."

"He was a stand-up guy," I said.

Henry smiled a little. "What made him go after lobsters?"

I shrugged. "I don't know. He had problems and never shared them with anybody. He was too proud. I didn't know how to help him."

Henry reached for my hand. "Remember the promise you

made to Tony Canadian?" he said. "Frank is almost seventy-five. He hasn't got many years. When we're gone, who's going to be left? Those other people are no good. They're only for themselves. Promise me you do good in Vegas and don't get involved with those other people here."

"That's a promise that's very easy to keep," I said. "You got my word on that."

"You've only been to Vegas twice. Try to touch base with all those people you reached out to there. Keep the contacts alive."

"I will, Henry," I said. We had been talking only a few minutes, but he was already starting to tire. I kissed him and thanked him for everything. Then I told him I loved him.

Henry hung on for two more weeks, until August 27, 1970.

THE CREW WAS coming apart. Maybe Joe Gorilla was the handwriting on the wall. He came out of Walpole a heroin addict, a junkie. I tried to get him to stop and told him he was destroying himself, but it was no good. There's no reasoning with junkies. We couldn't afford to associate with him any more. Something like that happens to a friend, and you think twice about going out on the next score. When you're twenty you don't care about going to the joint, the risk means nothing because time itself means nothing. But when you're cruising into your late twenties, you begin to wonder if you could still handle fifteen or twenty years. You like to think of yourself as a stand-up guy who can take anything that comes along. Yet they don't make them tougher than Joe Gorilla, and all that time finally got to him. It ruined him, he might as well be dead.

Eddie Greco called it quits first. He had come to enjoy the restaurant business and decided to buy a place of his own. I didn't blame him and wished him well. I also wished I could be as dedicated to going straight as him. In the meantime, gambling had left me short on cash, so I went back to bank scores. Over the last five months of 1970, me, Charlie, and Johnny Russo hit seven banks in New England. Johnny saved most of his share and told me he was packing it in too. About the same time Peter Piso said he'd had enough. I respected their decisions.

Charlie was fifty-two and way too old to change his ways. He was as rough as they came, and unlike most of us, *looked* like a hoodlum. Holdups were his life, and he was going to stay in it till the bitter end, which came a lot quicker than I expected. On January 13, 1971, a bulletin came over the radio: the cops had killed a bank robber in Medford. I knew right away it was Charlie. The score had gone bad from the start. A cop happened to be in the bank when Charlie and his partner went in. Charlie jumped into a car and tried to get away, but it was too late: the police had sealed off the whole area. There was a shoot-out and he got it in the neck. That's probably the way he wanted to go out.

Charlie died on a blood-freezing, below-zero day, and my mind shot back to the summer and Butch's wake. Charlie just sat there staring at Butch in the coffin, not saying a word. Now, he was occupying a box of his own. Charlie was a paranoid-schizo, but everybody liked him. He was always up for anything and never left the house without a gun. He lived with his mother in East Boston. The old lady was as hard as he was. Whenever I see the old Jimmy Cagney movie *White Heat*, I think of Mrs. Centofanti and Charlie. She visited him faithfully every week all the years he was in the can. She backed him up all the way and even hid him from the cops. Charlie was all she had, and when he died she wanted revenge. She went to a wiseguy and asked him to put the hit on the cop who killed her son. The wiseguy couldn't believe it; this woman was in her seventies. He told her to forget it, so she decided to do the job herself. Luckily for the cop, Mrs. Centofanti didn't drive and didn't really know where to look for him. But she did take the bus to Medford with a gun in her purse. And if she'd ever found out where that cop lived she would've been right on his doorstep.

*   *   *

IT WAS A time of good-byes. Not long after the cops killed Charlie, Jimmy Sforza got busted for two bank robberies. He was going up for a long time. I had to shut down the tavern—it was like working in a haunted house. Too many memories. I didn't bother trying to sell the place, I just locked the door and never went back.

After all that I needed to get out of town for awhile, so I went down to Florida for a week with a friend named Anthony. He had bought and renovated two of the houses torched by the firebug in 1967, and I had taken an apartment in the basement of one of them. There were several burned-out shells around the neighborhood, but nothing was done to them for a few years. Nobody wanted outsiders buying them and moving in, so they stayed empty until local guys like Anthony could afford to do something with them.

But all this time too many insiders were spreading the drug cancer. It was getting very close to home—as Anthony and me found out when we got back from vacation and found our place burglarized. I couldn't believe it—stuff was scattered all over the floor, clothes thrown everywhere. It looked like a cyclone had hit the place. We both knew right away that it was junkies. Nobody else hit homes like that. I ran out into the street looking for somebody who could give me information, and I spotted Joe Bova hanging out on the corner. Joe was a nice North End kid who had been with me that night in 1967 when I stabbed the fat man in the combat zone. Back then Joe was just out of the service and looked terrific. Then he got mixed up with drugs. Why I don't know. He had a lot going for him. I couldn't believe it when I heard he was hanging around with junkies. Then the next few times I saw him he looked more and more like a junkie himself. But Joe was never a bad junkie, he never robbed anybody, so I didn't bother him.

In a way, we were still friends. I went over to him. "Joe, do you know who robbed my friend's building?"

"There were kids running all through the building today," he said. The junkies must've heard we were away, but they messed up—hitting the place the day we came back.

"Where can I find them, Joe?"

He nodded at a tenement across from us. "They're on the last floor on that side. They're in there now."

I went over to the building and raced up the stairs. At the top I found the apartment I was looking for and kicked in the door. A kid was standing in the middle of the floor with a .45 in his hand. It was at his side, pointed at the floor. Before he could react and level it at me, I rushed him, grabbed the gun away and pushed him down. Stuff that belonged to me and Anthony was strewn all over the place. I moved further into the apartment and heard footsteps behind me in the hall. Somehow, the junkies had gotten out another door. I ran down the stairs after them, firing the .45 whenever I saw their hands on the bannisters. Down in the street I took a few more shots at them, but they were flying like deer. When they were gone, I went back up, collected our property and took it home.

MEANWHILE, MEYER LANSKY'S money-running operation was folding up for good. My final trip was in January 1971, but Frank had warned me far in advance: "They ain't gonna be calling you too many more times. Meyer's had a lot of problems."

That was putting it mildly—the FBI and the federal prosecutors were circling him like vultures. They were determined to see the old man die in prison. Of course, Meyer was used to investigations, to the FBI watching every step he took in public, but the feds kept turning up the heat and his health was failing. The strain must have been enormous. Still, he was too much of a gentleman to complain about anything, and only once did I see him lose his composure. Somebody had mentioned all the surveillance on the Singapore hotel. "These bastards are following me around!" Meyer exploded, looking like he was going to whack somebody. But the next minute he was calm as a catacomb and went right back to discussing business like nothing had happened. By the summer of 1970 the heat finally got to be too much for him and he flew to Israel, hoping to find refuge there. He applied to become a citizen. Now, the way Israel was set up, that should not have been a problem. Under the Law of Return, any Jew from anywhere is supposed to have the right to settle in Israel. But the U.S. Justice Department wanted Meyer real bad, and the Nixon administration put a lot of pressure on Israel to give him up. So the Israeli government decided to make an exception in Meyer's case, and started a huge legal battle to kick him out. The case wound up before the Israeli Supreme Court, and that's where Meyer probably made a mistake—by going for a fix. He tried to pay off one of the judges and other government officials. I was told the offer went as high as 10 million dollars. But before any money could change hands the government found out about it and that killed the deal. Worse, it made the Israelis look upon Meyer as a threat. If he had stayed cool I honestly think they eventually would have let him stay. The Supreme Court ruled against him and Meyer left the country in November 1972, hoping to get another country to take him in. But it was no good. This was one time his money and his connections worked against him. So Meyer wound up back in Miami, where the feds had indictments waiting for him. Not long after getting back to this country he made a trip to Las Vegas to visit a friend from the old days. I was out there at the time and wanted to say hello to him. Now, you can't just walk up to a guy like that, especially with the kind of problems he was having. You have to go through channels, and I decided to reach out to Meyer through Jay Sarno, who had become my friend. Sarno told me to forget it. "Meyer's got fifty agents watching him. If you're seen with him nobody out here can be seen with you for the next six months."

Meyer Lansky had always seemed to lead a charmed life where the law was concerned, one of those guys who could run between the raindrops and not get wet. But in 1973 he was convicted of contempt of court for not coming back from Israel fast enough to suit the feds. And when he went on trial for tax evasion the same year, it looked like he was washed up. The man was tired and sick, and I'm surprised he survived the ordeal. But the feds made a fatal mistake in the tax trial—their chief witness was none other than Fat Vinnie Teresa, a pathological liar and the world's biggest phony. Teresa testified that he collected gambling debts from losers at the Colony Sporting Club and handed them over to Meyer and Dino Cellini. Believe me, those guys wouldn't have trusted Teresa with a dime, and Meyer wouldn't get within a mile of somebody like that. The jury didn't believe a word of it and chucked the case back in the sewer where it belonged. The following year Meyer's contempt conviction was thrown out by an appeals court. So in the end, he beat the feds at their own game and was able to enjoy his remaining years a free man. According to most accounts, Meyer spent that time in retirement. I have no reason to believe that isn't the case, but my coauthor has heard an interesting story: In the late 1970s, a great deal of money disappeared mysteriously from a South Florida bank. The company that owned the bank called in three auditors from out of town to find out where the money went. It was all very hush-hush. Each auditor came from a different part of the country and didn't know about the other auditors or even what was going on till he got to Miami. After a lengthy investigation, the auditors came to the conclusion that the money had been stolen in an elaborate scam and that Meyer Lansky was behind it. But any trail back to him had vanished along with the cash. I don't know, maybe retirement bored him.

Meyer Lansky died peacefully in 1983 at the age of eighty-one. I always liked him.

VINNIE TERESA'S STATUS as a professional squealer made him something of a celebrity and he later wrote a book that must have set some kind of record for more lies per square inch than anything ever put on paper. Teresa claimed to be the number-two man in the New England mob—and he wasn't even a made guy.

The book did pretty well too, though I don't know how any sane person could have believed it. Teresa was all brag and blubber.

I'M GETTING AHEAD of my story. In the fall of 1970 my association with Meyer went into low gear, and I knew there wouldn't be many more trips. I wasn't crazy about losing the income, yet it was just as well my career as a bagman ended when it did. It meant one less risk. The deaths of Butch Capone and Charlie Centofanti had forced me for the first time to take a hard look at my life. Rather than wind up like them, I decided to go the route of Johnny Russo, Peter Piso, and Eddie Cisco and call it quits. The old dream of running my own family seemed hollow, the intrigue had faded. What good was a family if the men you loved and trusted the most were gone? The thrill of a score had vanished too. I'd had enough. I'd pulled my last armed robbery and it was time to put away the masks and guns and start a new life. Frank still wanted me to establish myself out in Las Vegas, but I began to think about a place very different: Vietnam.

After leaving Walpole in 1965 I had been classified 4-F because of my record. That was fine with me then, but five years later the army didn't seem like such a bad deal, so I wrote in, telling them I wanted to enlist. It wasn't a snap decision. I needed a fresh start, and to make one I had to pull away from the old places and the old people. Sure, joining the army was a very big switch, but deep down I knew that only a big switch could save me. Now, I hadn't paid too much attention to the war and wasn't sure what it was all about, but I couldn't stand the antiwar protesters. Hordes of them were out marching at Harvard and other colleges around Boston. There they were, some of the most privileged people in America, pissing on the country that made them. They had lots of fun, waving their banners and shoving their faces into the TV cameras, because they knew it was all a big joke—people like them don't fight wars. No, it's people in places like the North End who wind up on the battlefield. And for the kids in my neighborhood, patriotism was like breathing, and I was no different. In spite of all the bad things I'd done I loved my country. I was twenty-six years old and it was the last year I could enlist. The war was still raging and they needed bodies, so I figured my criminal record might not be a problem. I passed the physical and all the tests and filled out all the papers. A sergeant asked me how I'd like to participate.

"Combat," I said.

My papers were approved and they told me to come back in two weeks to take the oath. I was happy about it and felt this was the change I had been looking for. I just hoped I'd come back in one piece. Back in the North End I told everybody I'd been drafted. Frank was very surprised and I don't think he believed me. My mother and father were proud, but worried.

When I went back to the Custom House to get sworn in the sergeant had some bad news. There had been some kind of "oversight" in my file, he said, and I couldn't be accepted for the armed forces. He wouldn't tell me what the "oversight" was.

I left the Custom House feeling terrible. It was one of the biggest letdowns of my life. When I called Frank he was very happy.

IN SPITE OF that disappointment there was a lot of promise: I made more visits to Las Vegas and was becoming known out there. By now I had 2 million dollars stashed away and money was coming in from the after-hours joint. There would have been a lot more if I had been able to resist the betting windows and crap tables. But even with all my gambling losses, things were going pretty good. The McLean-McLaughlin War was a bad memory. Joe Barboza was long gone. Another enemy, Walter Elliott, had been convicted of murdering a couple in South Boston and was doing two life terms at Norfolk. Even my feud with the Boston cops seemed to be cooling off.

My troubles appeared to be over—or so I thought, until I got word that John Robichaud, Walter Elliott's partner, wanted to see me about something.

CHAPTER EIGHTEEN

ROBICHAUD

I HAD NO idea what Robichaud wanted, and didn't care to know. We had gotten along okay in the joint, but he was a friend of Walter Elliott and anybody who liked that maniac had to be pretty crazy himself. I didn't think about him too much. Moving to Las Vegas was the biggest thing on my mind, and I couldn't wait to get out there.

In September 1971 I was playing softball in the North End park. When the game was over I noticed two men who looked like football players. As I moved closer to the exit I made one of them: John Robichaud. Robichaud was six-two or six-three and massive, and the guy next to him was even larger. They came over, Robichaud with a smirky grin, his friend anxiously puffing a cigarette. I figured they hadn't been hanging around to watch the game.

"Hey, Willie, long time no see," Robichaud pumped my hand. "Say hello to Jack Smith (not his real name)."

I shook hands with Smith and asked Robichaud how he was doing. He wondered if we could go somewhere to talk, so I suggested the Florentine. That seemed safe enough.

"My car is double-parked," John said. "Let's all ride down there together." There was no way I was going to get into the same car as those guys, so I made some excuse and told John to follow me to the Florentine.

When we walked in I felt like a midget beside the two of them. Not wanting to get caught sitting between them, I tossed some money on the bar, told them to order what they wanted and went to the men's room. When I came out, they were sitting beside each other and I took a stool on John's right. He said he had lined up a 100,000 dollar armored-car score and needed some help. Nicky Femia had told him I had given up the occupation, but he wanted to make sure I wasn't interested. I said I was retired, and Robichaud finally got around to the real reason he had come around. He wanted me to set up a meeting with a high-ranking wiseguy who I will call Harry. I said Harry was about to go to trial and it might not be the best time to discuss business.

John changed the subject. "Oh, by the way, I thought I would let you know I stood neutral between you and Walter Elliott," he said. "Walter was wrong. He shouldn't have asked you for that kind of favor. You were right not giving your friend up. I would've done the same thing."

I shrugged. "Thank you for saying that. I often wondered how you felt, knowing you and Walter were so close."

John took a sip of his drink. "Back in Walpole, Walter asked if he could meet with the boss. The boss is in Providence. Harry's right here in the North End."

It was my turn to sip my drink. "Look," I said. "I will try to contact Harry tomorrow and tell him what you said. How can I reach you. Do you have a phone?"

Robichaud's smirk of a smile came back. "I'll be here tomorrow night at nine o'clock."

"All right," I said. "I'll see you then, but no promises."

At that, all three of us got up and shook hands. Smith hadn't said a word since we sat down. He still looked nervous. I had no intention of saying one word to Harry. He had serious problems of his own, and I wasn't going to bother him. Besides that, Robichaud was bad news. I wanted nothing to do with him. But from long experience I knew I couldn't not show up, because then he'd come looking for me and it'd be kill or be killed. At least this way there was a chance of avoiding something serious. When he turned up, I'd say that Harry couldn't see him until his legal problems were resolved and hoped that would be that. I didn't think Robichaud would dare try anything right in the Florentine, but I had a few friends around just in case. We were all carrying pistols, and I told them if Robichaud or Smith pulled a gun on me to let them have it right away. If the cops found out about it I'd just have to plead self-defense and hope for the best.

AT THAT POINT in my life I thought I had seen everything, but what happened next horrified even me. I got to the Florentine the following night at 7:45. When 8:15 rolled around I wondered what kind of game Robichaud was playing. I waited another fifteen minutes and left. At 9:00 John called the bar. That I found out later from Jerry Vara, the owner.

"He sounded mad and upset and said he wanted to talk to you," Jerry said. "I told him you left about half an hour ago."

Robichaud must have gotten tied up someplace, and that made him very late for our appointment. Realizing that an hour had passed since we were supposed to get together, he pulled over at a motel phone booth. An elderly man was about to make a call. There was an argument and Robichaud threw him out of the booth. While he was making his call the man got up and started screaming. Robichaud slammed down the phone, took a baseball bat out of his car and nearly beat him to death. The man's wife saw what was happening. She was petrified, but managed to jot down Robichaud's license number when he drove off. According to the newspaper, this happened right at 9:00.

Robichaud was arrested and charged with attempted murder. The case looked airtight, and since Robichaud was already on parole I figured I wouldn't have to worry about him again until about 1995. But Robichaud had no intention of going back to prison. He made bail and went to work. The man he had beaten,

William Woodhead, was an executive for the Ford Motor Company and lived in Detroit. After Woodhead recovered he received death threats warning him not to testify. He flew back to Boston anyway and was scheduled to take the stand on February 23. In Detroit that morning his wife, May, went outside to start the family car after she came back from church. This time she was the victim. A bomb was wired to the ignition and blew her through the roof. She lost both legs in the blast and died a few days later. Woodhead went back to Detroit under guard, and the attempted murder trial never happened.

RIGHT AROUND THE time of the car bombing Robichaud was arrested for knifing a guy in an East Cambridge café and again indicted for attempted murder. But the victim apparently learned through the grapevine what could happen to witnesses against Robichaud and clammed up. I was concerned about these events because the grapevine was also saying this: that Robichaud and Walter Elliott were blaming me for everything that had gone wrong.

Walter was a first-class bug, but he had plenty of company in South Boston, where he was from. The area is known for producing politicians—like Tip O'Neill—and cops. The other side of that coin are the madmen who become hoodlums. Because the docks are right there some became skilled hijackers. You could at least do business with those guys. The rest were completely reckless, and couldn't be levelheaded about planning a score or weighing the risks. They'd do anything and kill anyone just to get a dollar. And if they weren't out looking to kill guys from other neighborhoods they'd be killing each other. Even though Walter Elliott was a hardened criminal, he never really got to know the streets and had no sense of how to keep things in balance. And that made him more dangerous than any of his pals. In his mind, he was another Al Capone, and his grip on reality was so weak that nothing made him think otherwise. The man had no brakes.

John Robichaud had none, either. I don't know much about his early life, except that he was from Rhode Island somewhere and that he beat a murder beef there before moving to Boston. We had a mutual friend, Gerry O'Brien, who I knew from Walpole. He is probably the only man alive who was close to Robichaud and Walter Elliott. Gerry advised me to stay away from Walter early on. He was on the same block with Robichaud at Walpole, and was with him when he led the riots there.

Gerry told me years later that Robichaud wasn't a bad guy to begin with, but in the joint he hooked up with Elliott, who was already well on his way to becoming a lunatic. The two of them popped all kinds of uppers and downers to chase away the blues, and when pills weren't handy they went for plastic tubes of Vicks—they'd crack them open and swallow what was inside. A thirty-five cent tube could go for as much as eight bucks in the joint. I was told the high was tremendous—but coming down was like falling into a grave. I think stuff like that blew what little sanity they had right out of their heads, and they became savages.

After the car bombing a friend from Walpole told me that Robichaud and his buddy Jack Smith had been hanging around with Walter Elliott's gang in South Boston, and that I should be careful. Elliott had convinced Robichaud that I betrayed them both—that I had never spoken to any of the mobsters I was supposed to put them in contact with. My friend also said that Robichaud was making the South Boston guys nervous. Murdering an innocent housewife with a car bomb was too much even for them. Only a nut does things like that, and no one trusts a nut, not even in South Boston. I went to Frank for advice, and he urged me to reach out to Jimmy Troy (not his real name) who ran one of the saner South Boston gangs. Maybe they could take care of my problem.

As I suspected, Troy was just as eager as I was to get rid of Robichaud. I suggested that he speak to Smith, who needed to stay on good terms with the South Boston people. Maybe we could turn him against Robichaud.

"Take Smith into your confidence," I told Troy. "Tell him John's committing suicide going against the North End. Also, tell him that I like him very much and John is blaming me for something that had nothing to do with me."

Troy thought for a minute. "All right," he said. "I'll talk to him tonight and call you when I'm through. I know what to say."

That night I heard from Jimmy. He had told Jack Smith it was bad business to be conspiring with Robichaud against me. "I told him there'll be a price on your head by every wop in the city. It's a losing proposition."

When Smith said something about Walter Elliott, Jimmy cut him off: "Walter's finished. He's got double life and doing it bad. The next thing he'll do is tell John to kill you."

That last part made Smith paranoid, and later that night him and Robichaud had a big argument. The strategy seemed to be working.

A day later Smith made up with Robichaud and helped him plan a hit on me in the North End that night. Smith drove and Robichaud was on the passenger side. A couple South Boston guys were riding in the back.

When they got close to the North End, Smith pulled over, took out a .32 automatic and said:. "I'll do the shooting. He'll least expect it from me."

"Okay," Robichaud said. At that moment, Smith leveled the .32 at Robichaud's face and fired three times, then he threw open the passenger door and shoved Robichaud onto the pavement. As he was about to put the car in gear, Robichaud got up and leaped back into the front seat, shouting, "Ha, ha, I'm still alive! Shoot me again!"

Smith whipped out the gun and put another bullet in Robichaud. "Ha, ha, I'm still alive," Robichaud laughed and taunted him. "Shoot me again? Shoot me again?"

Smith aimed for the heart and emptied the magazine. Robichaud lurched backwards, his body half out of the car. Smith and the South Boston boys jumped out and ran.

Somebody heard the gunfire and called the cops, who found

Robichaud. He had been shot five times and was still breathing. They got him to Memorial Hospital in time and he survived.

WHILE HAVING THE trouble with Robichaud, I hooked up with three guys who had a brilliant scheme for ripping off a bank, and the best part of it was nobody had to pull a gun. It was Dickie Nutile who came to me first. He knew I was familiar with banks down in Georgia, and asked me to help him find one that suited his plan.

"First, what's in it for me?" I asked.

"Full partner," Dickie said.

"Who else is involved?"

"Morrissey, Poliskey, myself, and a Jewish guy from Brighton." Mickey Morrissey and Chester Poliskey I knew pretty well. The Jewish guy I'd never heard of before.

"I'll do business with you three, and no one else," I said.

Dickie stuck out his hand. "It's a deal," he said.

In the mid-1960s, Dickie and Poliskey operated a sophisticated check-cashing scam in the Back Bay. Eventually they got busted, and the cops found all kinds of fake credit cards—a novelty in those days—fake driver's licenses and checks from banks all over the country. As far as smooth, big-time frauds went, these guys were the masters. They could easily have done the bank scam without me, but they also wanted a bit of protection. Because of my reputation and my connections, no one would try to muscle in.

After I suggested a fairly small suburban bank near Atlanta, Morrissey and Poliskey flew down there in September and passed themselves off as executives of a large New England construction company. They told the bank president their firm was planning big projects in the area and they wanted to transfer 1.2 million dollars to his bank. They gave him checks that had been stolen from the construction company. Of course, all their documents and papers were forgeries, but looked real. So when the bank president called a phone number on one of the papers to verify everything, he was really talking to one of Dickie's men back in Boston. A few days later most of the money in the Georgia account was transferred to a Boston bank, and Dickie's people withdrew it, again using phony identification. By the time the Georgia bank and the construction company caught on, everybody was in the wind. My end was 281,000 dollars, and I didn't have to do a thing. It was the easiest money I ever made.

Unfortunately for Morrissey and Poliskey, it was their last scam. In December 1971 they were both murdered.

IN JANUARY 1972, exactly a year after my final delivery for Meyer Lansky, Frank gave me a message. Some of Meyer's contacts in Europe wanted to meet me in Paris. Usually I had at least a week's notice before making a trip, and I'd use a false passport. These guys wanted to see me in three days and told me to travel on my own passport. I asked Frank what it was all about, and he said he didn't know. The whole thing gave me a bad feeling. Meyer was in Israel, the money-running game had been shut down for a year. There was no reason for me to go to Europe. It didn't make any sense—unless somebody wanted to shut me down too. Over the next couple days that possibility grew in me like a tumor. Maybe they thought I knew too much. Just before I was supposed to leave I did something I'd never done before—went back to Frank and asked him if I would be all right.

"Why do you ask me that?" he said, looking very insulted. "Don't ask me that. You don't gotta worry. Just go." So, out of allegiance to him I went.

The flight across to Paris was one of the most miserable experiences of my life. It felt like my last ride. I stared down at the Atlantic and wanted to jump in. Frank just wouldn't do this to me, I kept telling myself over and over. Frank wouldn't do it. But what if these guys didn't tell Frank?

It got worse when I landed and saw four well-dressed men waiting for me in the airport—three of them were guys I knew from Sicily. The fourth man was French. We all shook hands and walked over to a hotel across from the terminal. The men said they had a room there. Two of them were in front of me and one on each side. This is it, I thought. I'm going to get whacked in that hotel room and no one will find me.

When we got up to the room one of the Sicilians told me to sit down and went over to the wet bar. The three other guys just stood there. They were speaking French to each other, as if they were afraid I might know Italian, which I didn't. Did I want a drink, maybe some espresso, the Sicilian at the bar asked. Espresso's fine, I said. The guy turned his back and I tried to keep an eye on what he was doing. For a few seconds I couldn't see his hands, and I thought he must be putting poison in the cup. After a couple minutes he handed me the espresso and the other guys shut up. Then the Sicilian began to speak to me, slowly and seriously.

I took a sip of the espresso. It tasted all right.

Meyer Lansky's money-running business might be finished, the Sicilian said, but my talents had not gone unnoticed in Europe. I was a good man, and good men were hard to come by.

"You're with Meyer. He makes millions," the Sicilian waved his hand. "That's nothing compared with what we do. Over here, we make billions, not millions. Billions. You understand what I say? You know what we're getting at? You don't bring money out of the country any more. You bring heroin into the country. It'll bring a lot of opportunities, for you and for your family. Money is power. When you have power, it is good for family. You grow on power."

My ears were ringing and I felt like my finger had gotten wedged in a light socket. A minute earlier I thought they were putting the hit on me. Instead, they offer me a piece of a heroin racket. A bunch of things occurred all at once, and it was something the Sicilian said—"*your* family"—that put the puzzle together. Frank had set up the whole thing; it was his idea. His iron determination had brought me here. I'd have my own family, and it would be built with drug money. Almost all the key guys in my crew were dead, in the can, or retired. But money could replace them. With a deal like the one these guys were offering I could easily handpick a new crew, an entire family. If you've got a racket where everybody eats, you can choose who eats with you.

So there it was, my dream there for the taking, like fruit on a tree. It wouldn't just be a family, it'd be an empire. I'd be cruising on an ocean of cash. No one could stop me. Yet, as the shock wore off, all I could see were the faces of the junkies back in the North End. The faces flooded my brain. They were the kids I'd grown up with, gone to school with, guys who'd been my friends, like Nano, Joey Bova, and poor Joe Gorilla. They'd ruined themselves and the neighborhood. I'm no saint, but there was no way I could be a dope pusher, for any price. There was no hesitation. I knew what the answer had to be.

When the Sicilian was through talking, I asked if I might stand up and say something. You have to be delicate when you refuse guys like that.

"Look," I said. "I respect everybody here, and I have no animosity or personal feelings against anybody. I'm honored that you picked me. It's just that I don't get involved in drugs. I don't knock people who do, that's fine. It's just not my line of work."

The four faces looking at me turned cold and hard. People like that are not used to hearing the word *no*, and I began to wonder if they were going to whack me after all because of all the stuff I now knew. When they finally spoke, it was to each other, in French again. Then they all headed for the door.

"You can check out tomorrow," the Sicilian said on the way out, and they were gone.

Although he didn't say so, Frank was disappointed that I didn't go for it. But you can never force a guy into something like that.

"It's all right," he said. "You donna wanna do it, you donna wanna do it. Big deal."

The Sicilian was right, in a racket like that you do grow on power. You grow until you destroy yourself, because a racket like that always gets too big to control. The money is unbeliev-

able, more than you could spend even if you lived a couple
hundred years. But usually you don't last very long, because all
that cash makes you blind and crazy. And greedy—no matter
how much comes in, you find yourself wanting more. Then, somebody's always looking to grab a piece of it, and after a while that
makes you paranoid. You're so afraid of getting killed that you
lose touch. I'd seen the same thing happen to guys who were
involved in much smaller operations. And with drugs there's
another factor that most guys didn't think about twenty years ago:
the federal government.

If I had said yes, I'd probably be a big shot in the mob
today. I'd probably also be writing my memoirs from prison. The
Sicilians in that hotel room were part of the notorious Pizza Connection heroin ring that got busted in the early 1980s.

AFTER GETTING OUT of the hospital, John Robichaud went back
to Rhode Island to recuperate. On May 23, 1972, he was arrested
in Pawtucket, Rhode Island, for an armored-car holdup the year
before. This time the charges stuck, and he got seven years.
Although they were now both behind bars in different prisons,
Robichaud and Walter Elliott sent messages back and forth.
Robichaud's misfortunes sent Walter into a frenzy. He passed
the word that he considered me responsible for everything that
had gone wrong. If I had introduced him to the boss in Providence that time back in 1967 everything would be wonderful.
Since I was the one responsible for their downfall, Walter urged
Robichaud to take action, to break out and hunt me down.

None of that bothered me much because I was planning to
head out to Las Vegas any day. All of my contacts out there were
in place. I went to Frank and he gave his blessing. He said Elliott
and Robichaud and all the guys like them were nothing but scum
and it was time to move on to bigger things.

But thanks to my one-man antidrug campaign, I wound up
spending another six months in Boston, a time when I might as
well have been wearing a target on my back. Sometime in May

three schoolgirls came running over to Bova's Corner, all excited and out of breath.

They all went to St. Anthony's and pointed back in the direction of the school. "Willie, hurry to the playground," one of them said. "There's a bunch of junkies giving drugs to kids." I didn't need to hear any more and went charging over to St. Anthony's as fast as I could. The junkies—there were four of them—saw me coming and froze in their tracks. Something about them was familiar. Then it hit me—they were the same scumbags who had ripped off my place the year before. I smashed into them at top speed and they went down like bowling pins. The dope had made them weak. In a matter of seconds I had knocked out all four of them, but when I smashed the last guy a bone in my right hand snapped. Other kids came running up and started beating on the junkies, but I was out of it. By the time I got back to Bova's Corner my hand was throbbing, and I couldn't ignore the pain. The doctors at Massachusetts General put on a cast and told me to come back in six weeks. When I did, I expected to get the cast off and finally head to Vegas. Instead, the doctors said the bone wasn't healing properly. They'd have to do an operation and put in a pin. The pin wouldn't come out until November first. That was just great; now I'd have to stay around the North End until the fall with only one hand.

WHEN I GOT out of the hospital in mid-July I went back to hanging out on Bova's Corner. One day I was there by myself when a car with two men inside pulled up beside the drugstore across the street. I recognized one of them instantly. It was the pop-eyed character who came around with Walter Elliott in 1967. Then he was pointing two guns at me. This time he raised his hands getting out of the car to show he was unarmed. He walked over to me while his pal stayed in the car. Pop-eyes looked down at my arm, and I showed him it was just a cast. He had South Boston written all over him.

"What do you want?" I said.

"I have a message from Walter Elliott."

"What's the message?"

"He told me to bring to your attention the way you've been living out here. With all these fights, it's only a matter of time before you're back in Norfolk or Walpole. And when you are, Walter says he's going to kill you on sight."

"Why don't you kill me?" I said to Pop-eyes.

"Walter says he didn't like your remarks about him letting other people do his dirty work. He says he wants the pleasure himself."

"Can you get a message back to Walter?"

"There's no problem with that."

I didn't have to think a second about what I wanted to say: "Tell Walter that when I see him I'm going to fuck him in the ass and I'm going to let his wife watch."

The man's eyes swelled up like little balloons and I thought they'd float right out of his head. "You're just kidding!" He said it like a question.

"You tell Walter that you questioned me that I was kidding. Then tell him when I see him I'm going to fuck him in the ass twice and his wife is going to watch twice." The tone of my voice stayed low, but Pop-eyes got loud.

"Yeah! Yeah! Walter will hear about this!"

"Good. Now that you got the message, get lost."

Pop-eyes backed up to the car, not taking his eyes off me. I thought he might reach for a gun in the car. Instead, he got in and the two of them roared off. I wished I could have seen the look on Walter's face when he got my message.

ON THE MORNING of July 31, 1972, Walter Elliott's wife, Katherine, went to see him in the visitors' room at Norfolk. Despite the hot weather she was wearing a long granny dress, the kind that was popular then. Norfolk didn't have metal detectors in those days, and no one bothered to frisk her at the gate. The dress concealed two pistols and ammunition that were strapped to her legs. In the visitors' room she quietly loaded the guns and passed them to her husband. Walter stood up with a gun in each hand and ordered everybody—inmates, visitors, and the three guards to get down on the floor. Katherine Elliott was standing right behind him. One of the guards, James Souza, apparently didn't move fast enough and Walter shot him in the arm. Then, Walter and his wife ran into a hallway, apparently heading for the front gate. But something happened and a minute later they came back. Walter walked over to Souza, who was still on the floor, and put a bullet in his head, killing him. One of the visitors, a woman, told a newspaper that she thought Walter was going to kill everybody there. Instead, he went to the middle of the room and announced that he was sorry. His voice was shaking, the woman said. The Elliotts left the visitors' room again and headed for the rear gate through the prison yard. In the yard Walter killed a shop instructor, Alfred Baranowski. Another guard, David Mackay, was running towards the visitors' room to help the other guards. He ran into the Elliotts near the chapel and was shot in the jaw and neck. He survived.

For some reason, the Elliotts ducked into a three-story dormitory seventy yards short of the gate and barricaded themselves on the top floor with mattresses. More than a hundred state troopers rushed in and sealed off the prison. Walter wasn't going anywhere.

Sharpshooters covered every window and other troopers fired more than a hundred tear-gas shells into the building. After nearly two hours of that, a dozen troopers in bulletproof vests and armed to the teeth forced their way inside and made a room-to-room search. They found Walter Elliott dead with a bullet through the heart. Katherine Elliott was lying close by. She had been shot in the head and died the following day. All the papers said she was very devoted to her husband.

FOR WEEKS BEFORE that there had been rumors of a bust-out by Walter Elliott and several other inmates, so it could be that he was already plotting to escape when Pop-eyes gave him my message. Maybe he just got impatient waiting for Robichaud to escape and decided to do it himself.

But back in Rhode Island, Robichaud was blaming me for provoking Walter into his insane act. He knew all about my message and was certain it had pushed his friend over the edge. Jack Smith, meanwhile, had cleared out and was in the wind, and that put me at the top of Robichaud's list.

On September 23, 1972, less than two months after Elliott's attempted escape, Robichaud and three other guys escaped from the Adult Correctional Institutions in Cranston, Rhode Island. They picked some locks and broke out through a chapel.

People told me that he was heading for Boston and that I should watch myself. Coming back to Boston was stupid, of course. He had already gotten on the wrong side of a lot of guys there and now he was also a fugitive. Even the psychos wouldn't dare to have anything to do with him. But Robichaud apparently had his own priorities. He probably figured it was only a question of time before he got pinched, and he might as well whack as many guys as he could. I was enemy number one. Once again, the thin, twisting streets of the North End felt like a big shooting gallery. Once again my friends stayed with me at all hours. Johnny Russo and Joe Semenza were always watching out, and Eddie Greco and his .357 magnum didn't leave my side.

We were ready for anything. If Robichaud showed up with an army, we could've chopped them all to bits. But Robichaud didn't appear, and nothing is worse in a situation like that than the wait. It was Walter Elliott all over again. It was Barboza all over again. Everywhere I went I had to be prepared to meet a killer. Eyes, ears, nose, nerves, all the cells in my brain became antennas tuned to detect the first hint of an ambush. He was close, I could feel him. I just couldn't see him.

It was late one night and some of us were in a club near Bova's Corner. All of a sudden a guy named Peter Plagenza ran in and said Robichaud was circling the neighborhood in a black car. We all had pistols but I wanted some heavier artillery. Robichaud didn't know Joe Semenza, so I sent him back to my place to pick up a carbine. The carbine had a banana clip that could hold fifty rounds. Joe left and came back a few minutes later with the carbine hidden under his trenchcoat. He told us a black car was parked right outside Bova's.

I told Joe and Eddie and Peter that me and Johnny Russo would handle it from there. There was no sense in having all those guys involved. I put on Joe's trenchcoat and stuck the carbine underneath. Me and Johnny put on stocking caps that could be slid over our faces before going into action.

We walked out of the club just in time to see Robichaud's car making a right on Prince Street. We ran toward Bova's hoping to head him off, but Robichaud was already far up the street. At Hanover Street he took another right. We figured he must be going around the block and waited for him in a little side street called Noyes Place, right off Salem. But Robichaud never came back.

The next morning some workmen found a body in a field off McGrath Highway in Somerville. The dead man had been shot six times with two guns and dumped there. It was John Robichaud. Whoever did it made sure he was dead this time. I never heard where he died or who killed him. "He was bad news," a district attorney said. "There were a hundred guys ready to knock him off."

I SEEMED TO find all the nuts, or they found me. I couldn't get away from them. First it was Joe Barboza. Then, when he went out of the picture, it was Walter Elliott, and after he destroyed himself, I had to deal with John Robichaud. I don't know who was worse. If they ever ran a derby for maniacs, I suppose Barboza might win by a head. Because of the war, guys who should have known better relied on him. He also knew how to play the game, so it took a lot longer for him to screw up. That made him the most dangerous of the three. But if you held a contest for savages, Robichaud would win hands down.

CHAPTER NINETEEN

VEGAS

THE PIN WAS removed from my hand on November 1, 1972, and the next day I was heading west in my new Eldorado with 600,000 dollars in cash. Vegas was supposed to be a fresh start, only it came too late. Frank and Henry wanted me to move my crew out there and establish the new family, but by the time I finally got to Vegas the crew was wiped out and I was too disgusted to care much about anything. My life was empty, and over the next two years gambling swallowed me up and spit me out, taking everything I had. It's a miracle that the addiction didn't ruin my health too, but luckily I still did care about staying in shape.

Las Vegas isn't a party town—the town *is* a party: Champagne and shows and girls and fancy restaurants and craps and blackjack, all the time, nights bouncing into days. You toss sleep right out of your life, no one does it. Too much is going on, the lights are too dazzling. Thanks to all the contacts I had made on my earlier trips, I had the red carpet like you wouldn't believe: limos, free shows, huge dinners, comps for friends, anything I wanted. All these fast times were indoors, and I got so caught up in them that I'd lose track of the sun for days on end. I'd catch it going up or coming down, never in between, and sometimes I'd wake up in the dark, look at the clock and not know if it said A.M. or P.M. Then I'd count the minutes and hours till I could get back to the tables or place a sports bet. Whenever the cash ran low, I could always reach into a 20,000-dollar line of credit, and that was in the days when the normal credit line was only 2500 dollars. Sometimes I came out ahead. I had good days and even good weeks, but you never really win in gambling, you just hold it awhile and give it back.

M Y FIRST APARTMENT was in the Paradise Spa on Las Vegas Boulevard South. I liked the place because it had a gym that was open twenty-four hours. I put up my own punching bag and went in there at 4:00 in the morning when no one else was around. That's about the only time I was ever home. For the first six months I went out every night.

Friends came out from Boston and we did the town. Joe Semenza couldn't get enough of Vegas and he especially loved going to see Louis Prima, the bandleader. Back in Charlestown, the inmates listened to the radio on earphones that were hooked up to a big set on the block. In the forties, the radio played Prima's music all the time. He was Joe's favorite. As soon as he got off the plane, he'd ask, "Is Louis playing tonight?", and when I said Prima was at the Hilton, Joe would smile and go "I'll be there." If Joe came in at night we sometimes went straight from the airport.

Friends like Joe kept me out even more. Luckily, I had found some good, levelheaded friends out there and getting together with them helped me to chill out from the cards and dice—even if only for a few hours. One couple, I'll call them Jill and Steve Cohen, had a beautiful house with a pool overlooking a golf course and I saw them fairly often. A girl who lived next door, Christine Maheu, seemed to be there a lot, and after awhile I noticed that she popped over whenever I showed up.

I asked Jill Cohen about it. "Oh, She's crazy about you," Jill said, as if I should have figured it out for myself. Christine was slender and pretty and had a sweet, bubbly personality. She was only eighteen. I had ten years on her. She wasn't the kind of girl you fooled around with, she was the kind you married, and for me that was impossible. Her old man was Robert Maheu, a top aide to Howard Hughes and a former FBI man.

Still, Christine was fun to be with. We hung out by the pool or played Ping-Pong. We also had an interesting adventure. It started when Jill asked me to do her a favor. The Boston fur designer Ray Le Nobel was throwing a big celebrity party for the opening of his new boutique across from the Dunes. Le Nobel needed a male model to show off his furs, and Jill suggested me. Sure, I said. Jill had already enlisted Christine to model the womens' coats. The party was quite an event, Joe DiMaggio came, and so did Alan King.

Christine was very nervous before we went out. "What do you do, how do you move?" she wanted to know.

"It's easy," I answered. "You just dip and turn like this." And I pranced around in the fur, pretending I knew what I was doing.

Christine was impressed. "Is this what you do?" Jill had told her nothing about what I did for a living.

"Yeah, I model," I said, and went out before the crowd. It was a piece of cake. Afterwards, Christine introduced me to her father, who was one of the guests.

I first heard the name Robert Maheu from Johnny Rosselli back in Miami Beach. Johnny asked if I knew him. I didn't, and Johnny paused and said: "Well, he's tight with Howard Hughes, and changed the subject. But in L.A. Johnny told me that Maheu had been one of his partners in the plot to knock off Castro, and one of the guys who later let him down when the feds put the heat on him. "That bastard Maheu, he'll sell you out," Johnny kept saying. Now, the couple times I met Maheu he seemed pleasant enough, but there was no way I was going to get serious with the daughter of a guy like that.

A few weeks after the party Christine came over to the

Cohens with a sour expression on her face. "You're no model," she said, doing her best to act mad.

I laughed. "Whattya mean?"

"I know what you do." Christine was half-smiling now.

"What, what do I do?"

"You said you were a model."

"Well, I was a model—that night. I told you that's what I was doing. I just didn't say for how long."

By that time we were both laughing and she never brought up what I did again. I don't know if she really knew or not.

As my gambling losses piled up and my stash shrank to nothing, I eventually stopped coming around to the Cohens. Jill said Christine used to ask for me, and I think she thought I was avoiding her. That wasn't the case: I was so burnt out and ashamed by that point that I avoided everybody.

SOME OF THE cops out there in those days were bad news— nasty, dumb, and crooked. They were rejects from other states and had no business carrying guns and badges. They were always bothering people. I first saw them in action at the Tropicana when they arrested a guy named Shorty at a blackjack table and took him out in handcuffs.

I asked somebody what was going on.

"He's a felon and he failed to register at the police department," the guy said.

I had an instant flashback to the disaster at the Fountainbleau. Shorty was back at the Trop in a few hours.

"Someone dropped a dime on me," he said, and he asked if I had registered.

"No, I didn't know you had to," I said.

The next day I drove down to the courthouse, registered as a felon and gave them my address. It seemed very routine, but the following week two Las Vegas detectives stopped by for a visit. They had a photograph of a man on the FBI's ten most wanted list and claimed I knew him.

The man was one of two men accused of maiming Joe Barboza's attorney, John Fitzgerald, in January 1968. Somebody put
a bomb in his car and it went off when he switched on the ignition. Fitzgerald lost his right leg in the explosion. The newspapers, the politicians and the other professional do-gooders
screamed about it for months, although they hadn't batted an
eyelash over the piles of bodies in the McLean-McLaughlin War.

I told the detectives I didn't know the guy wanted in the
bombing, which wasn't true. They let me know that I was being
uncooperative. After that the cops were constantly busting my
balls.

One night I got pulled over on the freeway with a friend
named Sal Zarba. The cops towed my car and said we were both
under arrest. The charge: loitering!

Another time me and Sal were sitting in a coffee shop at
the Frontier and a detective named Dave Hansen spotted us. He
asked Sal for his ID, then said he was arresting him for being
with me.

"What's the charge," Sal asked. "Lunch with Fopiano?"

Arrests like that came to nothing, of course, yet they happened all the time. Hansen was the worst. He came from a suburb
of Boston and tried to make points with his bosses by going after
me. The harassment went on for months. One afternoon I went
to visit a friend at Caesars and bumped into Hansen. He went
over to the dice pit and pointed me out to some of the employees.

I'd had enough and yelled at him from across the floor.
"Dave, you're nothing but a coward! You think you got balls, that
badge gives you balls. The difference between you and me is I
don't need a badge, you fucking asshole!" Nobody moved, even
the dealers stopped dealing. Hansen put his head down and
walked out.

I bought a nice house trailer in a mobile-home park on
South Decatur. It was a great place, with three bedrooms and a
sunken bathtub. After registering my new address, the detectives
became fixtures in the front office and told anybody who'd listen
what a bad guy I was. A girl who worked in the office kind of

liked me and told me every time they showed up, which was often.

By this time it was late summer of 1973, time for a change of scenery, I thought, so I flew back to Boston for a visit.

TONY PINO FINALLY got out of the can in July 1971. As part of his parole he got a job in a liquor store on Massachusetts Avenue in the South End, and whenever I was around, Joe Semenza took me over to see him. He was the same old Pino, always kidding around and laughing. I think he'd stashed away plenty of money before he went to Walpole, because he never seemed to be hurting for cash. Pino seemed determined to enjoy the time he had left. He took life as it came, and only when the name Specs O'Keefe came up did he stop smiling. Whenever that happened, a black look would come across his face and he'd lose his composure.

Me and Joe went to visit him a day after I got back to Boston. Tony had just gotten out of the hospital, and he seemed to have gotten a lot older and grayer since I had moved to Vegas. "They pumped I don't know how many gallons of fluid out of me," he said. "I'm built up with fluid."

We got to talking about the old days at Walpole and Tony shook his head. Specs was haunting him again: "That son of a bitch ruined my life! If I had him here right now, I'd kill him."

Tony stopped and stared at me. "He's out there in California, near you, Willie. I know he's out there."

I nodded. "I'll find him for you, Tony," I said. "I'll go out there and do that for you." Still gazing into my eyes, Tony slowly nodded, then went back into his rage: "I'd put my hands on his neck and strangle him. I'd do another life sentence and be happy. He destroyed my life. . . . "

Tony didn't want me to just find Specs, he wanted to put the hit on him. It was a lot to ask, but I couldn't refuse, not after the way he took care of me at Walpole. I could never forget that.

I think he asked me to do it because he realized his days were numbered. Tony wanted revenge before he died.

Specs O'Keefe had been given a new identity by the government after he got out of prison. The FBI had tried to keep his whereabouts a secret, but the word was out that he was living somewhere in the Beverly Hills area. As soon as I got back to Vegas, I took a plane to L.A. and made some inquiries. The people there told me to go back to Vegas and wait for a call. Several weeks passed and in October I got in touch with the guys in L.A. again. They told me to be patient, the kind of information I wanted was hard to get. Then I called Tony and let him know I hadn't forgotten about him.

"That's fine," he said.

A few days after that Joe Semenza called. Tony Pino was dead. I hung up without saying another word to Joe. I felt terrible. This was Tony Pino, the mastermind of the Brinks robbery, a bigger hero to the kids in the North End than Paul Revere. He had watched out for me in the joint and made my life there bearable. It was like a big piece had fallen out of the world. My next call was to Los Angeles. I told the people out there to forget the inquiries and thanked them. With Tony dead, revenge seemed pointless.

As it turned out, Specs was working as a chauffeur for Cary Grant. He died in 1976.

THAT CHRISTMAS I was back in Boston, and for something far more important than the holidays: I needed a refill. In just a year I had gone through the entire 600,000 dollars that I took out to Vegas. I went straight to the basement where I kept my big stash, smashed open the concrete, grabbed 500 grand and buried the remaining 500 somewhere else. Once the money was in hand I felt better. A few hundred thousand dollars always makes you feel strong, and I believed all the promises I made to myself that I wouldn't throw away any more money. I had a nice Christmas with my family, and hit the casinos again almost as soon as my plane touched down at McCarren Airport.

By April the bookies and the crap dealers had taken nearly every cent. I borrowed 50,000 dollars from Jay Sarno to tide me over and went back to Boston for one day to fetch the last half million. Somewhere, I knew that a disease had me in its grip and that it was wrecking my life. All I did was gamble. I knew I had to stop, and I also knew I couldn't. It was like watching myself sprinting at top speed towards the edge of a cliff. I thought of Tony Canadian, Henry Noyes, and Frank Cucchiara, and all they had done for me. They had put so much effort into planning my future. My future! Now, I was thirty years old and living that future, pissing away thousands of dollars every day, squandering everything I had.

Every day I woke up and fell asleep in shame, but shame didn't keep me away from the tables. By September I was broke.

CHAPTER TWENTY

DREAMS AND NIGHTMARES

SO THERE I was, with a gambling habit the size of Nevada and barely enough cash to scrape me through the next couple months—maybe a little longer if I ate at Burger King every day. The bottom had dropped out of my life and I had no idea what to do next. I kept thinking that I had to take some action, to do something, so I moved in with Joanne White. She had gone back to Vegas about the same time I arrived. I had two friends bring her furniture out by truck and she moved back into the nine-room house that Jilly Rizzo bought for her. She expected me to live there too, but I just couldn't do it. That was something I couldn't do with any woman. Still, the romance survived. Through Sandy Waterman I helped her get a job as a cocktail waitress at the Tropicana. Waterman hired her right away, in spite of my feud with his buddy Carl Cohen.

But after all my problems with gambling, I thought maybe living with someone might straighten me out, especially a good woman like Joanne. I sold my house trailer and that improved the money situation a little. But after moving in together all we did was fight. After a few weeks of that I took off for Boston. I was too embarrassed to tell Frank that I was cleaned out, although I think he knew. The old man didn't miss much, and the amount of gambling I did was hard to keep a secret.

After I moved to Vegas Stoogie the bookmaker made a very bad move. It had been very frustrating taking all my big bets and having to turn almost every cent over to Nicky Giso. But after I left town Nicky didn't hang around him as much and Stoogie saw a golden opportunity to pocket some of the proceeds. Some guys came to him and put down a sports bet for sixty grand that looked like a guaranteed loser. Stoogie backed the bet and kept the money—but the bet won. Now, you don't fool around with people who can afford to throw down 60,000 dollars a pop. When they win you pay them, and Stoogie couldn't pay. So he went to Nicky and confessed. Giso laid out the 60,000 dollars and paid off the bettors. That took the heat off Stoogie, but it made him Giso's slave for the rest of his life. I'm not exaggerating when I use that word— Giso owned him. Although Stoogie worked for the office he had always kept his own hours and did what he pleased. He had a wife and kids and a girl on the side. Now his life revolved around Nicky Giso, who made him do numbers every morning and take sports bets all afternoon—when he wasn't booking he was Nicky's chauffeur and errand boy.

Everybody knew what was going on and that made the humiliation worse. Stoogie began to drink a lot and when I saw him in the Coliseum after I got back from Vegas he looked half-dead.

"Stoogie," I said. "Why don't you just lam it? Grab a chunk of money, rob it, and get out."

He looked over his shoulder. "Willie, Nicky's a vicious guy. Don't let him hear you talking like that."

Never mind him, I said, and told him again to skip town.

Stoogie shook his head. "What am I going to do? I got my family here. No, I'm going to stick it out." He eventually drank himself to death.

A decent wiseguy would have told Stoogie he couldn't book anymore and to pay back the money when he made a score. But Nicky Giso was anything but a decent wiseguy, and loved turning people into puppets. I've met the best and I've met the worst and he was right at the bottom of the barrel, rotten and evil. If he didn't like you he'd start rumors about you and make sure they got back to other wiseguys. He could make the most innocent situations in the world look like treason. When he destroyed somebody he did it quiet and smooth, the way a snake does. A lot of guys lost favor thanks to him, and some even got whacked. In those circles, a liar is worse than a stool pigeon. In his personal life Giso had no control at all, especially when it came to sex. He went for anything, female or male, and he had a girlfriend who was only thirteen years old. His headquarters was the Coliseum restaurant and you'd see the girl hanging out there all the time, right in the open.

RICO SACRAMONE, WHO had been tight with Buddy McLean and Barboza, got killed about that time. Rico had always been a stand-up guy, but then his mind started going. He was found wandering on a highway one time, all bloody, his clothes torn, babbling to himself. No one knew how he got there, and he couldn't tell them. He was incoherent. After that Rico went around acting weird all the time, and, worse, started shooting his mouth off. Because of all he knew that made some people very nervous. He had friends, but you can never save a guy who talks. Whoever whacked Rico tortured him first. Me and him always got along, even though he was with Barboza, and I felt bad. The streets had cracked him, and that was one more reason to stay off them. But I didn't need any more reasons. Bank scores were out, heists were out, scams were out. The party was over, yet I had to find some way to survive, and fast.

One of the surviving members of my crew, Sparky Martignetti, knew about my problems and thought he might have the solution. Sparky was an ex-boxer and a pretty sharp guy in spite of all the punches he'd taken. He said the next time I came back east I should take a look at a neighborhood kid he was training, Patsy Marcello.

"I seen him in street fights. He always wins and he's got some good moves," Sparky said.

Patsy was twenty, and I had known him since he was in grammar school. He worked construction and was a pretty rowdy kid, but a nice kid. He wasn't into crime at all.

Me and Sparky took Patsy up to the Harbor House in Lynn, and I could tell right off that he was a winner. His ability was unbelievable. He knocked out all the other fighters in the first round and barely broke a sweat. We took him back to Harbor House, and it was always the same story: knockout after knockout. Patsy was strong, quick, and didn't have an ounce of fat on him. He was even good-looking—he had everything going for him. None of the other fighters could lay a glove on him. Sparky swore that Patsy could be the welterweight champ, without rushing him, in two years—with the right kind of training, and him and Patsy had me in mind as the trainer. Their plan was for me to take him back to Vegas. The Silver Slipper had fights every Wednesday night, and we could launch Patsy's career there.

The more I thought about it, the better and better that idea looked. My two goals in life were to get out of Boston and to make as straight a living as I could. And here all of a sudden was probably the best chance I'd ever see. Patsy wasn't a sure thing, but he was a good bet. And opportunity coming in the form of a fighter felt like fate. Ever since I threw that fight for Fiore DeChristoforo, I'd been looking to get back into boxing. It was my first love, and even after all the years I still carried that shame with me. I was too old to step into the ring myself and make things right, but here was a chance to make a champion who could. I'd work with him, I'd teach him everything I knew. And I'd do it right this time. I'd wipe the slate clean and truly make a fresh start.

Patsy was into it, and very excited about going to Las Vegas—even after I warned him he'd have to live like a priest for the next two years.

The one catch was money. I figured me and Patsy needed at least 60,000 or 70,000 dollars to last a couple years. Then, I saw a way to clean up with the Muhammad Ali-George Foreman fight in Zaire at the end of October. Everybody had Foreman down as a sure thing. After all, he was the champion. Ali had already been beaten by Joe Frazier and looked like he was on his way out. But I knew that Foreman couldn't beat a boxer with height and reach. Twice he had fought Gigorio Peralta, a light heavyweight from Argentina. In the first match Foreman won by decision. In the second, he KO'd Peralta in the ninth round. If it took the man nineteen rounds to knock out a light heavyweight, there was no way he'd beat Ali.

The books in Vegas had Foreman a 12-5 favorite. If you bet Ali most bookies gave you 8-5. But I had a bookmaker I'll call Al who was so certain Foreman would win that he was willing to give me 12-5 on Ali. I borrowed 30,000 dollars from Johnny Russo. If I won, I'd get back 102,000 dollars, minus the thirty grand I owed Johnny. Even after all my losses, I knew in my bones that this was the safest bet I'd ever make. I swore to myself that it would also be the last.

After Johnny gave me the money, I booked a junket to the Frontier in Vegas. I got all kinds of comps and a big credit line for staying there. After the fight, I'd fly back east and collect Patsy. Before I left Boston I told him: "Al thinks it's impossible for Foreman to lose. What a surprise he's in for."

"Are you betting much?" Patsy asked.

"I'll bet enough to cover us for two years. After that I'll quit gambling."

Ali won with an easy knockout. The junket only lasted four days, but I decided to stay in Vegas for an extra week. I shipped the 30,000 dollars back to Johnny Russo. Then I hit the tables, and, boy, did they hit me. I just couldn't resist. Within days the 72,000 dollars plus 3000 dollars I had for expenses had been vacuumed right out of my pocket. I called Patsy and told him Al had backed out. I didn't have the heart to tell him the truth. I told him to stay in Boston through the holidays and I'd bring him out to Vegas after the new year. Patsy was a little disappointed, but still very enthusiastic about working with me. After getting off the phone with him I called Johnny Russo and asked him to send me 5000 dollars.

I didn't dare stay in Vegas, or else the five grand would've disappeared in a blink. Joanne White and me split up and I decided to head to California, to Encino. There was a girl there, a cocktail waitress, who I'd been pretty hot with in Vegas. Her name was Rita, and she was about the sweetest thing that walked. She was the girl who got the box that Albert DeSalvo made. I moved into an apartment around the corner from her at Burbank and Balboa. Most of my time was spent working out and figuring how what to do next. As it happened, Robert Conrad lived in the same complex and one afternoon I ran into him at the pool. He didn't remember me at first, until I mentioned our mutual friend, the boxer Joey Giambra. He said he'd been meaning to get in touch with Joey and I gave him Joey's number. Conrad went right over to his apartment and called Joey. When Conrad came back it was obvious that the two of them talked about me.

"You look in good shape. Do you work out?" he asked.

"I always exercise no matter where I am."

"I'm going to Europe to do a movie. I'll be back in three months. When I come back we'll do something." Henry Noyes's old idea about acting didn't seem so bad anymore—especially now that I needed the money. I'd even take stunt work. Conrad was a good guy, but couldn't help me for several months. I was still determined to train Patsy, and that had to get underway soon. The big question was how to get the money to do it.

December 15 was a Sunday. The phone rang early that morning, and from the sound of Joe Semenza's voice, I knew he had bad news.

"Patsy got killed last night," Joe said.

The air in the room formed into a giant fist and punched me in the solar plexus.

"How?" I said.

"He got shot near Bova's Corner."

"Was anyone arrested?"

"No," Joe said.

"Is the word around who did it?"

"Yeah."

That's as far as either of us would go with a subject like that on the phone.

"All right," I said, "I'm coming home next week and we'll talk about it."

JOE AND SPARKY met me at the airport when I got in on the twentieth. They both looked as upset as I was.

"We'll talk about it at your apartment," I said to Joe. We got in the car and didn't say a word until we got to Joe's place.

"Now, tell me what happened," I said.

Joe laid it out for me: "Patsy was having an argument with Joey DiFronzo. Patsy wanted to fight, and Joey told Patsy the shoes he had on were too slippery and he'd go home and put on jogging shoes. Well, Patsy waited—and Joey came back with his brother Jackie and Joey shot Patsy five times."

I shook my head. Patsy was a tough kid and a good street fighter, but he didn't use his head. The DiFronzos were both dope addicts and also pushed the stuff. They were bad, everybody knew that. And when a bad kid like Joey DiFronzo tells you he's going home to put on sneakers, you should know that he's really going to get a gun. You either get a gun yourself, or you run. The last thing you do is hang around and wait for him. But if I hadn't blown the 72 grand, Patsy would be out in Vegas and still alive. The DiFronzos never would've touched him. He looked up to me and I let him down. It was my fault. Only one thing mattered to me now, and that was getting the DiFronzos.

The following night I picked up Johnny Russo and we went to a lounge and restaurant on Fleet Street that was one of the DiFronzo hangouts. We waited an hour before Joey DiFronzo walked in. As soon as he saw me he walked over and put out his hand. I grabbed the hand and crushed it. He screamed from shock and pain. Then, I twisted his arm behind his back, spun him around, and lifted a .38 out of his waistband. Now he was harmless. The place was pretty crowded. A lot of the people were his friends, but nobody made a move.

I was seething. "What did you kill Patsy for?"

"He wanted to fight me," Joey whined.

"And why didn't you fight him, you no-ball bastard?"

Joey didn't say anything.

"Answer me, you motherfucker!"

All he could do was shriek and moan. By this time about fifty people were watching us. I couldn't kill him with that many witnesess, so I finally let him go and he scooted over to his friends. "Now, run and tell your asshole brother," I said.

As I went out the door, Joey yelled: "Yeah, my brother will hear about this!"

I turned around and came after him again, but he bolted out another door.

Joey and Jackie DiFronzo were both good-looking—they looked a little like John Travolta—but they had always been bullies and were very jealous of anybody who had something they wanted. One time Jackie DiFronzo saw another kid with a new leather coat. He wanted to know where the kid got it and asked if he could try it on. He put it on and never gave it back.

Joey picked on a neighborhood kid who worked in a furniture store. Sometimes he waited for the kid to cash his check, then robbed him of his whole week's pay. Nobody wanted to fight them, because if they did they'd probably get killed: Jackie and Joey had several notches between them when they were only in their teens. And unlike a lot of junkies, the DiFronzo brothers were smart, especially Jackie, and I couldn't afford to ignore them.

I first heard how they operated a few years earlier. Two junkie friends of theirs, Peter Asenza and Guy De Prizio, had gone on a house score, which turned out to be a very bad move because the house belonged to the mother of a wiseguy, Paulie Intiso. Whenever Intiso had a problem he went to another wiseguy—Nicky Giso.

Naturally, De Prizio and Asenza jumped out of their skins when they found out Giso was after them and they ducked. But Jackie DiFronzo saw the situation as a way to gain favor with the wiseguys. He took De Prizio to see Giso, and De Prizio copped a plea—except he said Asenza had put him up to it. Bad as he was, Giso wasn't a stupid guy, and asked De Prizio how he knew that Intiso's mother owned the house. De Prizio explained that Jackie DiFronzo had told him, and that it was Jackie who made him come forward, because Giso was a fair man. Of course, Jackie was just grandstanding, and Giso was too vain to see through it. The only loser was Peter Asenza. He was from Italy and a decent kid. Surprisingly, he stayed decent even after he got hooked on dope. Asenza was the best of a very bad lot, he never ratted on anybody, and when he went to the can he went alone. I didn't bother him, he was just one of those guys who couldn't help the way he was.

Anyway, after the meeting with Giso, Jackie DiFronzo told Asenza to come out of hiding and he'd fix things up for him too. They arranged to meet on the Parado, which is between Old North Church and Paul Revere's statue. When Asenza showed up Jackie told him to walk with him. He let Asenza get a step ahead and shot him in the head.

I WAS A threat to the DiFronzos. Sooner or later one of us had to go, and they were looking to get me first. They didn't dare confront me, that was too dangerous. Instead, they used their junkies.

Right after I humiliated Joey DiFronzo, Sparky warned me to watch out for a Somerville guy named Paul Raymond. He had been making all kinds of threats when he was drunk and doped up. One of the things he kept saying was that he was going to come to the North End and shoot me. Raymond was the boxer at the top of the card the night I threw the fight in 1960. At one time he had been the New England heavyweight champion. He had been friendly with Buddy McLean during the war, and Sparky said Raymond held a grudge against me because I refused to hook up with Buddy. Everything had gone downhill for Raymond after Buddy died, and for some reason he was blaming me. As beefs go, this one had to be the stupidest ever heard of. I didn't know the guy and hadn't even seen him in years. But Raymond's brains had been scrambled by booze and drugs, and a guy like that is easily swayed. He bought his dope from the DiFronzo brothers and they poisoned his mind. Maybe they said they'd give him a little on the house if he came after me.

Just before Christmas I met Joe Semenza and Sparky at Bova's Corner and we drove over to My Place Lounge on Commercial Street, an old hangout. We stuck around about an hour, saw some old faces, and left. Not long after that Paul Raymond walked in, went over to the owner, Anthony Gioia, at the bar and demanded to know if I had been there that night. Gioia didn't say anything. Raymond asked him again, and Gioia just stared at him and turned away. Raymond started drinking at the bar and arguing with Gioia and his younger brother, Angelo. Finally, they kicked Raymond out. He went to his car and came back with a gun. The door was locked and he started banging on it. Angelo Gioia told his brother to leave Raymond outside, but Tony said he'd fix that bastard once and for all. Not seeing the gun, he threw open the door and took a bullet in the heart. As Angelo rushed over to where Tony lay, Raymond blazed away, hitting him in the hip. Raymond walked towards Angelo to finish the job, and Angelo reached into his pocket. He had a gun on him and fired right through the pocket. He hit Raymond five times, killing him. Luckily for Angelo, somebody got rid of the gun before the cops came and all the witnesses kept their mouths shut.

FOR THE NEXT year I bounced between the coasts, drifting—to where, I didn't know. After the holidays I returned to Encino, and in March I flew back to Boston. A kid who lived next door to my family was receiving confirmation, and his parents asked me to stand up for him. Joe Semenza and Johnny Russo said the DiFronzos were lying low. In a situation like that you always want to know where your enemy is and what he's looking to do. It's no good if you can't see him.

I stayed around after the confirmation. In April, Charlie Palazolla, a neighborhood guy, asked if he could speak to me. It seemed that Frank Vesuvio, a local pizza man, was having a lot of trouble with a junkie named Vinny Perez.

"What's the problem," I asked.

"Vesuvio just closed the store because Perez tried to stab him," Charlie said. "The DiFronzos know you like Vesuvio and they're sending Perez in there every night to antagonize him. I like Vesuvio myself. He's just come from Italy and trying to earn a living. You're the only one who gets results from these junkies."

I promised that I'd go see Vesuvio immediately.

"Willie," Charlie said, "Don't let anyone know we talked—I don't want to get involved."

VESUVIO HAD HIS pizza parlor on Hanover Street, and the junkies hung around on the sidewalk outside. They were always giving him trouble, and he came to me for help. I roughed up some of the junkies, including Vinny Perez, but because I wasn't in town that much there wasn't a lot I could do. The junkies had never been violent, so when Charlie told me that Perez had pulled a knife on Vesuvio, I smelled the DiFronzos. They must have put him up to it.

The pizza place was shut down when I got there. No one was inside. All of a sudden, Vinny Perez appeared, coming toward me down the street. He was higher than a kite and didn't see me. No one else was around, and I waited for him to get closer, so I could eliminate Vesuvio's problem right away. When he was still a few doors away a carload of junkies pulled up and

Perez got in. I finally found Frank Vesuvio on Bova's Corner, looking pretty scared.

"Willie, that junkie Vinny Perez, he come into my store and bother me every night. Tonight he pull a knife."

I had an idea. "Frank, do you have a license to have a gun in the store?"

"Yes."

"All right, now listen to me closely. You know I wouldn't do anything to hurt you. Do you believe that's right?"

"Yes, Willie."

"Then, go to Hanover Street right now and open your place of business. Let Vinny Perez see you're open, put all the lights on. He'll think you're defying him. Chances are he'll pull that knife again. When he does, shoot him in the head. I'm with you one hundred percent, Frank. Do as I say and I'll handle the rest."

Frank nodded, his fear fading. "I'll do as you say, Willie."

"Good. After you shoot him, don't touch him or the knife. The police will come and you tell them exactly what happened. Except don't say you planned it. You did it from fear. Understand?"

Frank nodded again. He went back to his store and opened up, and I drove around the neighborhood looking for the DiFronzos. Perez went back to Vesuvio's sooner than I expected— about half an hour after the place reopened. When he showed up, Frank Vesuvio was behind the counter making dough. Sure enough, Perez pulled his knife and in a second Frank shot him in the face. Unfortunately, he didn't aim high enough—the bullet went through the junkie's mouth and lodged in his neck. When the ambulance took him away it was pretty clear that he'd pull through. In the meantime, people I knew said that Joey DiFronzo had driven past Vesuvio's after he reopened and coaxed Vinny Perez into picking up where he left off. I think Joey hoped I would be in Vesuvio's and that Perez would kill me too—or that I'd get arrested for killing him.

If that was the idea, it backfired. Frank stuck to his story and the cops didn't file any charges. I sent Joe Semenza down to the police station to tell Frank in Italian not to press charges against Perez and that I'd take care of the problem. We didn't need the police. Perez probably guessed that, because he disappeared as soon as he got out of the hospital.

Nicky Giso had something to do with Vesuvio's troubles. He had been looking to buy the pizzeria and turn it into a fancy restaurant. I'm not saying he encouraged the junkies, but he didn't do anything to stop them either. The first obligation of a wiseguy is to protect his people, but all Nicky cared about was the property. Poor Vesuvio didn't want to sell, but the shooting really spooked him.

"People don't want me here," he told me. "They want my store."

He decided to sell and Giso offered him 2500 dollars, which was an insult. Vesuvio had built the business up from nothing and the equipment alone was worth a lot more than that. Because of Giso's interest in the place, no one else made an offer.

I tried to help Vesuvio and went to see Giso myself.

"What do you want to do, rob this guy?" I said. "A guy from Italy comes here, the junkies bother him and he doesn't get any help."

None of that fazed Nicky: "Look, my offer is twenty-five hundred dollars. Nobody else is going to buy this place."

It was no use. Finally, I told him Vesuvio would accept his price and he handed me 2500 dollars. On the way back to the pizzeria I took another 3500 dollars from my pocket and slipped it into the roll of bills. I told Vesuvio that Giso had agreed to pay 6000 dollars and he was very happy.

Vesuvio might have stuck it out if it hadn't been for the DiFronzos. Again, they got one of their junkie customers to make trouble for me, and this time a good working man had gotten hurt.

It was now May, and Robert Conrad was back from Europe, but I had no intention of returning to California until I had settled with the DiFronzos. They stayed well hidden.

Sparky Martignetti died of cancer in August. He had had a lung removed a few years earlier, but the cancer spread. He was only forty-seven, and one of the nicest, most loyal guys you'd ever want to meet. Sparky was a great fighter, yet he never picked a fight in his life. I was close to the family and was godfather to one of his children.

After he died his wife had me come over to their house in Somerville. Sparky had left me something. When I got there she handed me a heavy sack. Inside were thirty pistols—an arsenal. "He wanted to leave you these because you're going to need them," she said.

Sparky was dead right about that.

SUMMER ROLLED INTO fall. The Red Sox played Cincinnati in the World Series and lost in the seventh game, a heartbreaker some people never got over. I went to every home game and sat right behind the Red Sox dugout. In spite of the way it went for Boston, it was the best series I had ever seen. I borrowed money from Johnny Russo to open a restaurant on Prince Street, which is on the Freedom Trail. The restaurant was supposed to be my ticket out of Boston. I'd cash in on the Bicentennial, sell the place and move to California or Vegas. But then I began having an eerie dream that felt as real as life: Somebody shoots me point-blank on the street at night. Over and over it came back, like an instant replay that wouldn't shut off. I tried to shake it away, but along with the dream came a black, sticky feeling that told me something bad was about to happen. It was the same kind of feeling I had before Butch Capone died. Only this time it was me. It was like I was doomed, and had no power to do anything about it. I tried to put the thought out of my mind, but it kept shoving its way back in.

Meanwhile, Joey and Jackie DiFronzo cooked up a new scheme, and again they got an addict to do what they were afraid to try themselves. This time the junkie hitman was their old pal Guy De Prizio. I had beat him up several times in the past for selling drugs and breaking into houses. For a while in the early seventies he went straight and tried to get on my good side. I never liked him, but decided to give him the benefit of the doubt—until I heard that he was back on drugs again. I didn't go back to beating him up after that, I just ignored him and acted like he didn't exist. In early November I had given one of De Prizio's junkie friends a bad beating, and the DiFronzos had pumped it into his head that he was next, only this time I was going to whack him. The only way De Prizio could save himself was by killing me first, they said. When Paul Raymond came after me, I had plenty of warning. And Vinny Perez was never a threat. With De Prizio, I was completely in the dark—until the night he aimed a .38 loaded with dumdum bullets at my head and pulled the trigger. . . .

THE COPS PICKED me up out of the gutter, threw me in a police van, and took me to Massachusetts General Hospital. I passed out as a priest began the Last Rites, woke up on the last two words, and passed out again. When I came to again two days later I was breathing through a tube at the base of my throat and my broken jaw had been wired shut. My mouth and throat were paralyzed and my tongue couldn't move at all. I couldn't swallow and kept choking on my saliva until a suction tube was put in my mouth. For three weeks they fed me through an intravenous tube. When my veins gave out another tube was inserted in my stomach, and I had to eat that way for months afterwards. The dumdum bullets had exploded on impact and tore my insides apart. The doctors took one slug out of my neck and kept finding fragments everywhere. One lodged in my throat, another went through my mouth and down to my lungs. Others damaged the main nerve that controls facial movements and nicked a carotid artery, which supplies blood to the brain. A fraction of an inch more, and it would've been a waste of time to take me to the hospital.

Joe Semenza told me that the same day I was shot Frank

Cucchiara got some bad news. The doctors found cancer in his jaw, and it was spreading up to his brain. Frank had had cancer before, but it was supposed to be in remission. It didn't sound good, but I figured he'd be tough enough to fight it. Frank himself came to see me not long after that. He looked depressed and worn-out. But when he saw me some of the old fire came back.

"That sonoma bitch, I'm gonna get him!" He meant De Prizio. He had men looking for him. I couldn't speak but scribbled on a pad that I'd take care of it.

"This is schoolyard stuff compared to what we've been up against," I wrote. Frank smiled a little. I didn't want him to do anything. He was seventy-nine, and way too old for that kind of stuff.

On December 19, after five weeks in the hospital, I went home, but the recuperation was just beginning. I was a long way from being well. Towards the end of January, Joe told me he had seen Frank. He was sick and depressed and didn't look good at all. He had given Joe a message: "Tell Willie he's a good boy. I miss him and to take care of himself. And, good-bye."

Given that message and some other things he had said, maybe what happened the following day shouldn't have been too much of a surprise. Still, there's no way you can expect a thing like that. Early in the morning Frank went up to his wife, Santa, while she was sleeping and shot her in the head. Then he put the gun in his mouth and killed himself. Santa Cucchiara was a wonderful woman. I liked her very much. Other wiseguys cheat every chance they get; Frank was faithful as a rock. The two of them were very close.

"When I go my wife comes with me," he said one time, and that's what happened.

THE BULLETS DIDN'T change me. After waking up in the hospital I got up and tried to check out. I wanted to go after De Prizio and the DiFronzos immediately, but a doctor persuaded me to stay. Yeah, let me heal, I thought. Let me heal so I'll be back in shape when I come face to face with those bastards. Revenge could wait, though not for long. Nothing had changed, it was still them or me. I really had no desire to hit the streets again, but I had no choice. They were looking to finish the job, and I couldn't let them live. Then a few days later something happened, something that turned me away from all that. Something that, finally, did change me. It was an experience I can't explain to this day. You might say that I had a vision. I was sleeping one day and all of a sudden I woke up. Someone had come into the room and I noticed a man standing by the bed. He was wearing a white suit, a regular suit; he wasn't a doctor. He was good-looking and seemed to be about my age. Because of the wires I couldn't say anything to him. I had never seen him before, but he acted like he knew me.

"God let you live not to go out and kill people," he said. Then he turned around and walked out. I don't know who or what he was and I never saw him again.

For a long time after he left I lay there and thought about what he said. At first I didn't know what to make of it, then gradually a few things became clear. I had been trying to get off the streets and it hadn't worked out. Now, I saw why: I tried to do it on my own, never realizing that I needed help. God's help. I had always relied on my instincts and strengths, yet I had lost control of my life. I needed to put my trust in Him. Only He could save me. Even though I'd had nothing to do with religion in years, I never stopped believing in God. But I had been taking a broad, winding road, and it was time to take a different route. The man in the white suit was right. Still, my old self warned me that I was crazy to listen to his message. I wanted to believe it. I didn't want to be violent anymore, but De Prizio and the Di-Fronzos, they were going to come after me again and I had to protect myself. Then some words entered my mind, calming my anxiety. It was like a voice was speaking through my thoughts. "They will self-destruct," the voice said. "They will self-destruct. . . . "

CHAPTER TWENTY ONE

EPILOGUES

IN JULY 1976, the body of Guy De Prizio was found floating in Boston Harbor. He had been beaten to death.

On December 11, 1977, firemen found a body while putting out a fire in an apartment building on Endicott Street in the North End. It was Jackie DiFronzo. At first it was thought the fire had killed him, until somebody discovered a bullet hole in his head.

On November 4, 1978, several men shot and killed Joey DiFronzo outside the Florentine Café. Ironically, he died in the same spot where I got shot almost exactly three years earlier.

THEY SELF-DESTRUCTED, AND without any help from me. The stories of other guys I knew ended the same way. Some stories ended peacefully, and some are still going on. . . .

AFTER JOINING THE federal witness protection program, Joseph Barboza Baron went out to California, supposedly to start a new life. He got a free ride for his testimony and never did a day for all the murders he committed in the McLean-McLaughlin War. The government gave him a new identity, but another name didn't make him any less of a maniac. He was still Barboza, and incapable of living with normal people. He couldn't have gone straight if he tried, which he didn't. In California he got involved with stolen securities, and killed one his partners in that racket during an argument. After doing four years for murder, he got out in the fall of 1975 and moved to San Francisco. On February 12, 1976, he was walking to his car near his apartment on La Playa Street in the Sunset district when a white van rolled by. Somebody inside fired a shotgun, and Barboza was killed instantly. The cops found a gun on him, but this time he was the one caught off guard. Barboza was forty-four when he died.

BARBOZA'S PAL PATSY Fabiano, who had to be put in jail to save him from getting whacked in 1966, was murdered in 1976.

Nicky Femia was one of the few guys Barboza never ratted on. After getting out of Walpole on the weapons beef, Nicky hit the streets again and never gave them up. In 1978, five men were murdered in the Blackfriars disco on Summer Street in Boston. Each had been shot point-blank with a shotgun. The Boston cops had never seen a body count like that, and the case became known as the Blackfriar's Massacre. The whole thing was a beef over cocaine, and the word on the street was that Nicky Femia was one of the triggermen. He became a prime suspect. But before the authorities could get him on that, somebody got him in 1983.

HENRY HUNT, WHO tried to turn every white kid into a punk at Walpole, died there in January 1969. He got the pin for a young inmate and wouldn't let up. One day when Hunt was at a water fountain, the kid came up from behind and cut him open. Hunt was forty. He committed a murder at sixteen, and except for a brief time on parole spent the rest of his life in prisons.

*   *   *

VINNY PEREZ AND Crazy Nano both died of drug overdoses in the 1970s.

In the spring of 1992 Joe (Gorilla) Maioli was found dead with a needle in his arm. Joe was only in his late forties, and had spent nearly twenty-five years of his life behind bars.

LOUIS ARQUILLA, THE guy who nearly pulled off the escape of the century, was murdered in Boston in January 1976.

IN THE MIDDLE of the 1970s, I ran into George Raft at the Galleria in Caesars Palace. He was sitting at a big table with Frank Sinatra, Leo Durocher, Jilly Rizzo and a few others. I called the security man over and asked him to tell George there was somebody to see him. When George looked over and saw me he threw up his hands and rolled his eyes. Then he came over and we talked for several minutes. George was in his early eighties and in pretty bad shape. He had a long list of illnesses. Still, even then you could see a trace of the old movie tough guy.

He looked back at Sinatra. "If it wasn't for the chairman I don't know what I'd do," he said. "Without him I'd be in a lotta trouble."

George Raft died in 1980.

FRANK VESUVIO, THE pizza man, died in a fire in the summer of 1983.

JOHNNY RUSSO DIED of an infection in 1986. It was very sudden.

WACKY JACKIE CIVETTI died of a brain tumor in 1992. He was only in his mid-forties.

*   *   *

Towards the end of his life, Joe Semenza had a small part in the movie *The Brinks Job*. You can see him in a diner scene with Peter Falk, who plays his old friend Tony Pino. Joe Semenza died of a heart attack in 1981.

In 1984 JOE D'Minico tied his mother to a chair and stabbed her in the heart. He has been in the Bridgewater State Mental Hospital ever since. Luckily, his brother Carmine was no longer around when that happened. Carmine D'Minico died from complications of diabetes a few years earlier.

In the old days, when Frank and Henry and Joe Lombardo were still running things, Nicky Giso never would've gotten away with having a thirteen-year-old girlfriend. He went around with her openly and nothing ever happened to him. It was unbelievable. Nicky seemed to lead a charmed life, until diabetes got him. It was slow and painful: The doctors had to amputate a foot, and towards the end his mind went. Nicky Giso died in 1990. He was sixty-seven.

Danny Puopolo did all right for a long time and put together a collection of antique cars. Then, a few years ago he got into trouble again. He's now doing time in a federal prison.

Gerry O'Brien, my friend from Walpole, got a legitimate job after getting out of the joint and worked for many years. He is now semiretired, lives in a suburb of Boston, and does charity work.

*   *   *

Joe Guarino and Joe D'Urbano are also living in Boston and staying straight.

Joe Bono, who helped out that day Henry Noyes and me got into trouble in John's candy store, is an actor and living in New York City.

Eddie Greco settled down and today is the part-owner of the Villa Francesca restaurant in the North End.

Back to me: In a way, the shooting was the best thing that could've happened, because it forced me to change my life and to finally get out of Boston for good. In the old days I was all fire and rage, and thought I'd live forever. Getting shot in the head makes you think twice about that.

My recovery was very slow. Luckily, my system had a high tolerance for pain. I had to eat through my stomach for such a long time that I got weak and the canned liquid stuff I "ate" gave me tremendous heartburn. Real food I could only look at and smell. But through it all I remained in good spirits, and that came naturally. More important, it rubbed off on my family. No one was ever down, and that made it easier for all of us.

My friends were great. There'd be nine or ten guys over at my house every night and my mother cooked for everybody. It was like a party, and parties always put me in a good mood.

The wires finally came out of my jaw, and gradually the insides of my mouth started coming back to life. Half my tongue and part of my throat remained paralyzed and I had to learn how to chew and swallow all over again.

The doctors told me I should move to a warmer place, otherwise arthritis might set into the bones that had been broken. I knew they were right; the New England dampness literally gave me headaches. So I went back to Las Vegas in 1976 and wound up getting back together with Joanne White. We got married on St. Valentine's Day 1977, and later that year our daughter was born.

Even a vision couldn't make me change all at once. After all, I thought everybody lived the life I did, or if they didn't they'd be willing if they had the chance. My belief, my faith grew strong over time. Quietly. It chased the worries away and helped me to settle down. After a couple of years I was a different man. Faith helped me to kick my gambling habit. Of course, being dead broke helped too, but after awhile I just lost the desire, and even when I had money gambling didn't hold any thrill. Living in the casino capital of the universe might seem crazy for somebody like me—like a recovering alcoholic moving next door to a distillery—but I couldn't stand at a crap table for five minutes now even if you paid me to do it.

My faith protected me, and no matter how rough things got, the wild old ways were cut off for good. I had plenty of opportunities to go back—like the time in the mid-1980s when Johnny Russo tried to get our old crew back together. He had moved to New York, but came up to Boston when he heard I was flying in. We met in a social club on the North End. He wanted to do one final score. Danny Puopolo was also in town at the time, and all for it. That left me and Eddie Greco.

One final score: "Come on, we'll do one more and we'll quit," Johnny told me. "We'll invest it this time."

"Times have changed, it's tougher now," I said. "Besides, Eddie's very happy with what he's doing."

"If we plan it right we can do it," Johnny said.

"John, I'm out," I said.

I was out. I had to start all over again, and this time there was nothing to fall back on. Frank Cucchiara, Henry Noyes, and all the rest were gone.

How I survived would take up another book. Briefly, here's how it went: A few deals came up, real estate and other things, and that generated some income. I was always able to hustle a buck here and there, but now it was a legitimate buck. Now and then I made a little by playing the middle in sports bets. Basically, you bet both sides and either break even or win. In the lean periods my family has helped me out. Thanks to God, I've gotten by.

So . . . Willie Fopiano is living in Las Vegas, keeping out of trouble, and not doing too bad at all.